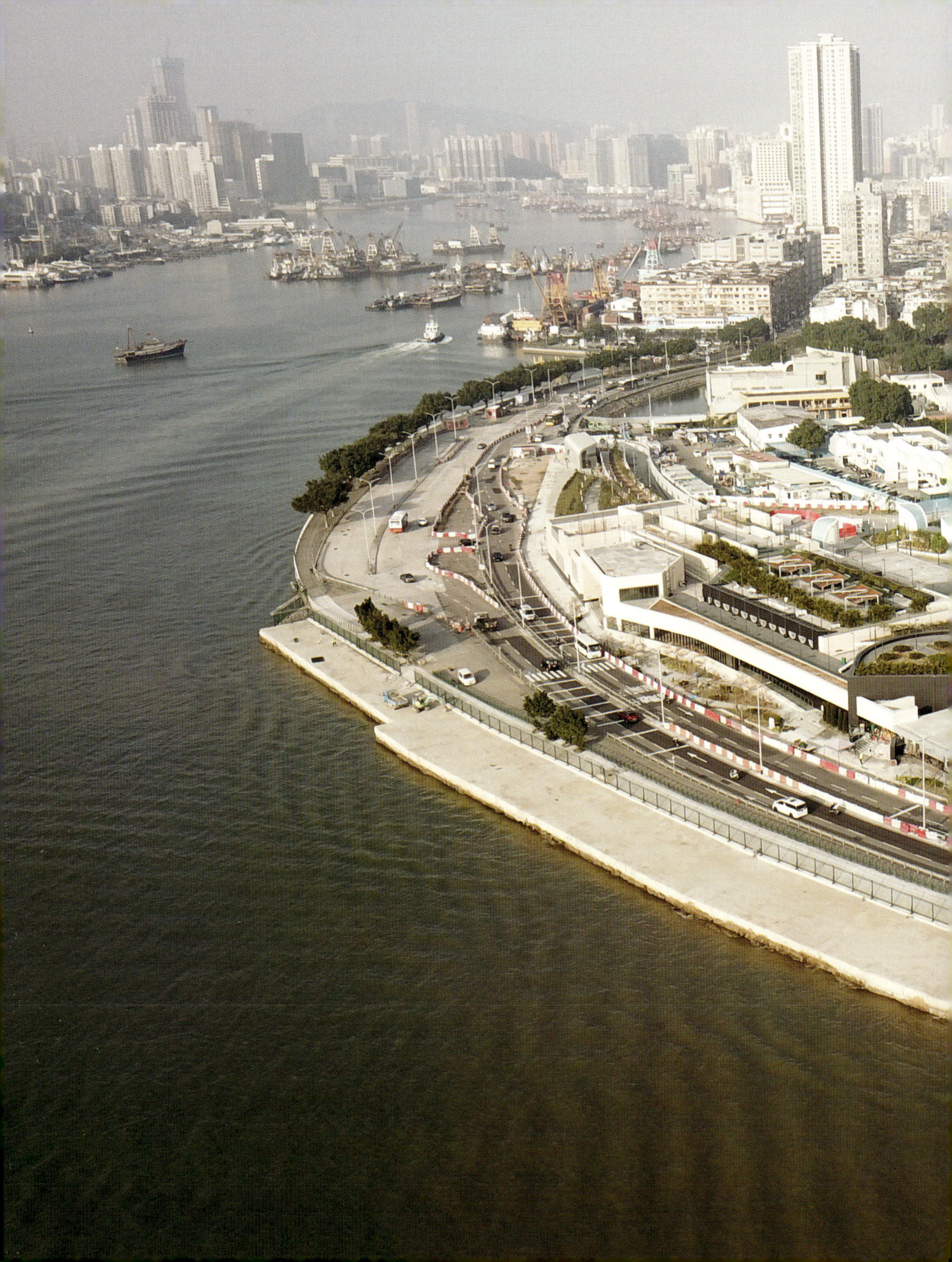

STOP

电话 18923334546

CATERPILLAR

頂
大
吉
60
SOCIEDADE DE TRANSPORTES COLECTIVOS DE MACAU, S.A.
澳門公共汽車股份

LAYERING THE CITY
疊構城市

LBA
MACAU

LAYERING THE CITY

F. CARLOTTA BRUNI
RUI LEÃO
LBA MACAU

RE-PROGRAMMING INFRASTRUCTURES FOR PUBLIC SPACE
OPPORTUNISTIC PLANNING AS URBAN STRATEGY FOR MACAU
RUI LEÃO

SHAPING MACAU'S UN-PURPOSED SPACE
DESIGN IN CONTEXT
FRANCESCA CARLOTTA BRUNI

PUBLISHED BY
Actar Publishers, New York, Barcelona
www.actar.com

TRANSLATORS
António Conduto Oliveira
(LBA: Caressing Entropy. Macau, 1999-2049; Post-casino Macau in the perspective of China's historical process and strategic planning)
Tomás Lai In Lam
(Post-casino Macau in the perspective of China's historical process and strategic planning)

GRAPHIC DESIGN
Olga Pipnik

PRINTING AND BINDING
Arlequin & Pierrot

DISTRIBUTION
Actar D, Inc. New York, Barcelona

New York
440 Park Avenue South, 17th Floor
New York, NY 10016, USA
T +1 2129 662 207
salesnewyork@actar-d.com

Barcelona
Roca i Batlle 2-4
08023 Barcelona, Spain
T +34 933 282 183
eurosales@actar-d.com

INDEXING
ISBN 978-1-63840-063-9
LCCN 2022945038

Printed in Europe
Publication date: 2024

Cover image: © LBA MACAU

The *Lucciola* of Macau

By Nicholas Boyarsky

Nicholas Boyarsky is an architect and teacher. He studied at the AA School of Architecture and completed his practice-based PhD at RMIT in 2016. He is a partner of the London-based studio Boyarsky Murphy Architects. Nicholas is a Professor of Architecture at RMIT, where he supervises practice research PhD candidates in Europe and Asia.

LBA, the practice of Rui Leão and Carlotta Bruni, has developed in response to the context of Macau; its Portuguese colonial history; and, since 1999, its status as a Special Administrative Region (SAR) of the People's Republic of China. Their responses are highly specific to the grain and fabric of Macau and they are deeply immersed in a particular heritage of late 20th century postmodernism exemplified by their mentor, Manuel Vicente. Their practice is brought to life by a form of pragmatism that embraces the complexities of daily life in the city of Macau. It is motivated by an ethical stance of resistance to global neo-liberal practices of architecture and urban design. This has led them to craft an ideology of "urban activism", which operates locally and above and beyond the narrow confines of professional practice. What distinguishes this ideology is a self-awareness of their own individual identities as architects, their long-term commitment to Macau, which is the unique site of their work, an innate appreciation of collage as tool of spatial engagement, and a form of opportunism that seeks out and invents possibilities for improving the life of the city. This attitude extends across different scales of operation, whether arguing for an extra half meter to transform circulation space in a housing project into an open-ended site for un-purposed space or transforming large infrastructural projects to create new opportunities for public benefit.

I first met Rui and Carlotta at "Urban Flashes" events in 2002. Instigated by Ti Nan Chi, Urban Flashes comprised a loose collective of architects, writers, artists, and thinkers who met in Asia and Europe to discuss and debate the realities of the Asian city and to thrash out creative approaches to urban density and the informalism that close readings of these cities revealed. Urban Flashes marked a turning point in discourses around urban density, gathering together work that was ethnographically focused and forensic in its mapping and detailing of the ephemera of daily life by protagonists such as Yoshiharu Tsukamoto of Atelier Bow Wow; Laurent Gutierrez and Valérie Portefaix of Map Office; Sand Helsel, Lorenzo Romito, and Peter Lang of the Stalker Group; the writer and curator Manray Hsu; and the filmmaker Karl-Heinz Klopf.

During these "Flashes", we debated the notion of "dirty cities" and how, influenced by the anthropologist Mary Douglas, tensions between a set of ordered relations and a contravention of that order formed the dynamics of the city. For Douglas, dirt, by which we understood the ephemeral and the informal, was "matter out of place," [1] whilst disorder offered unlimited opportunities for recombination and variety. We explored the phenomena of urban plasm where, in Chi's words, "countless ongoing exchanges and clashes take place... indicating the primal state of living that has long been ignored and misinterpreted in architecture and city planning."[2] From these dialogues the notion of micro-urbanism emerged with certain references to the Situationist concept of *detournement*, the writings of Paul Virilio, and Sun Tzu's *Art of War* of 500BC. Simply put, micro-urbanism reframed discourse away from the top-down practices of urban development and city planning towards a bottom-up focus on the actual conditions of the city and its inhabitants and their tactics for survival. This new focus on ephemeral occupation, flexibility, temporality, and the densities of lived experience effectively challenged the conventions of surgical and tabula rasa architectural and urban interventions that had defined Western-influenced Asian urbanism.

Strands of influence from Urban Flashes can be found in Bruni's practice of promoting un-purposed space as a tactic by the designer to build in possibilities for porosity and expanded thresholds which "allow for a non-prescriptive use that relates the project to the urban experience of its surrounding context."[3] Bruni also acknowledges the influence of Giancarlo De Carlo's ideas for participation in architecture, which are reframed in the context of the particular Asian city of Macau. For a space to be un-purposed, and therefore open, it must first relinquish a closed sense of function, which she achieves by adding indeterminate spaces alongside functional ones. This design strategy prioritizes the occasional user and local resident over the exigencies of commercial practice and is highly subversive, offering built forms of resistance to contemporary neo-liberal Macau. It suggests a practice of activism, of addressing Macau's chronic shortage of public spaces by adding, or "gifting", spatial value onto existing programmes. Bruni is clear that, despite her continuing fascination with Macau's urban informality, "the informal cannot be designed, but informality and disorder can be admitted through a surplus of space [un-purposed spaces] and rigorous architectural design."[4]

There was also a poetic aspect to the Urban Flashes project that Leão embraced, and this can be seen in his contribution to the 2002 symposiums held in Taipei and Linz where he presented "The Sky of Macau".[5] This project speculated on the city "as an organism of development that accumulates layers of invisible phenomena"—phenomena that are points of intense fragility and hidden processes that are waiting to be named so that the city "is theoretically mutated in a layering of even greater complexity, as the city is mirrored towards itself, and becomes more poetically understandable". Leão gives the example of electric cables which, because there are hardly any electrical poles, bounce from "wall to wall in a never-ending dance, establishing a random shaped diagram of curved lines over our heads". This network of seemingly random cables represents a "drawn-up sky" that has been domesticated by the city "and what apparently was a consequence, has become a communal art form". For Leão, the creative process was to be found through "looking, understanding, naming, transforming".

"Flashes" in the urban context became a metaphor for short, luminous, and ephemeral bursts of light that speak of communities of different networks that operate within the shadows away from the relentless glare of streetlights and empty office buildings. Pier Paolo Pasolini identified something similar in the fireflies, or *lucciola*, of his youth whose disappearance he lamented in his famous letter "The disappearance of the fireflies" of 1975[6]. This disappearance was the harbinger of a "totally, radically and unforeseeably new type of fascism" in Italy that had emerged in the 1960s. For Pasolini, fireflies and the flashes of light that they emit while they gather together represented both the search for love and the end of a period of innocence before the unremitting glare of an emerging consumption-based society that "modelled and deformed the conscience of the Italian people"[7]

It is impossible to speak of LBA without acknowledging the profound influence of Manuel Vicente who was their teacher, mentor, collaborator, and whose practice in Macau they ultimately inherited. Much has been written and said about Vicente, a Portuguese-educated architect who practiced in Macau for 30 years or so. His love for the everyday, the tawdry, and the trivia of Macau chimes with Leão and Bruni's experiences of Urban Flashes, whilst his absolute commitment to contributing an architectural vision for his chosen city must have been deeply inspiring. Vicente, although educated in Portugal, had also studied at the University of Pennsylvania where he graduated under Louis Khan in 1969. His exposure to the works of Kahn, Venturi and Scott Brown, Colin Rowe, and Andy Warhol, amongst others, framed his engagement with Macau which his colleague and collaborator Manuel Graça Dias has described as "the city of simplicity and naiveté, the city of "vulgar" love and card paper scenarios, the entrenched city of popular colors."[8]. Vicente carved out a unique role as advocate for both the realities and fantasies of the small Portuguese colony, designing and building many buildings without any of the sentimentalities and colonial indebtedness that might have been expected of him. These buildings speak of Vicente's fascination for the possibilities that postmodernism might bring in an extended dialogue with the diverse and dense fabric of Macau. At the urban and infrastructural scale, it is critical to distinguish his approach from that of his colleague and rival Álvaro Siza Viera, whose schemes for the NAPE and Areia Preta districts of Macau in the 1980s are straight out of a colonialist playbook, employing the layout of the 144m grid system that Siza had experienced on a recent visit to the Spanish colonial cities of South America. Ironically, the realities of Siza's static gridiron proved too inflexible for the commercial realities of Macau and it was disrupted by the insertion of major casinos.

At the urban scale, Vicente's Praia Grande Bay Closure Reclamation Plan of the late 1980s and early 90s marked a conceptual shift from both colonial tropes and the sterility of engineering-based solutions to infrastructural projects. The masterplan proposed a set of lagoons between the historic Praia Grande waterfront and the new reclamations, which Leão has described as a seminal urban laboratory, which "made a huge contribution to reminding the city of its historic relation with the coastline."[9] By pulling the new waterfront out by means of the curved geometries of infrastructure around the two lagoons, Vicente created possibilities for new public spaces such as Nam Van Square, which is organized, with a nod to Colin Rowe's Excursus to *Collage City*, around a reworking of Michelangelo's paving for the Piazza del Campidoglio in Rome. The way in which Vicente's visionary design was able to break out of its disciplinary constraints set a critical benchmark for LBA's later practice as an example of "how far the project can reach if the architect explores and expands on the brief that is given him by the client."[10] The extent to which LBA's practice developed in part as a vehicle to complete Vicente's project for the Nam Van lakes can be seen in the string of projects that they have completed around the lake, such as Nam Van Square and Sai Van Lake Park. In both cases, LBA extended their given brief by exploiting spatial opportunities in section and plan to create an expanded public realm. Their skills in prioritizing and fighting for architectural and spatial sensibilities in the creation of public spaces and landscapes in large infrastructural projects are remarkable in the Asian context. One is reminded of the vision and intricacies to be found OMA's 1988 project for Euralille. Yet whilst Koolhaas extolled the disassociation of such infrastructural projects from a specific place or city whereby abstract and disconnected programs "float and gravitate opportunistically around the place that offers the most connection,"[11] LBA have drawn strength and inspiration from the specificity of Macau and its flashes of informal, ephemeral, and subliminal moments.

In this age of precarity for the architectural profession in the West, LBA's achievements in Macau are remarkable. Underpinning their impressive body of built work, Bruni and Leão's commitment to expanding the role and practice of the architect and their engagement in urban and political activism in Macau to define their territories of operation are an example to us all.

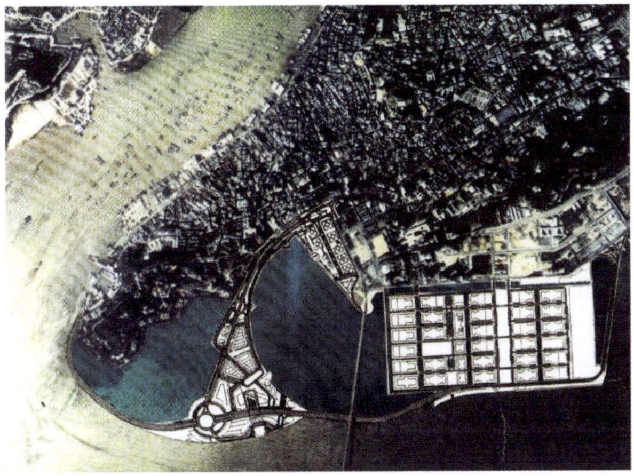

© VLB archive

1 Mary Douglas, *Purity and Danger - An Analysis of Pollution and Taboo* (London: Routledge, 2001).
2 Ti Nan Chi, "Introduction to Micro-Urbanism." In Urban Flashes Asia. *New Architecture and Urbanism in Asia*, eds Nicholas Boyarsky & Peter Lang, Architectural Design, Profile 165 (London, 2003). p.18.
3 Francesca Carlotta Bruni, "Shaping Macau's Un-purposed Space. Design in Context" (PhD diss., RMIT University, 2019), pp.241.
4 Ibid., p.249.
5 Rui Leão, "The Sky of Macau." In *Urban Flashes*, ed. Ti-Nan Chi (Taipei: Human Environment Group, 2002), p.167.
6 Originally published as "Il vuoto del potere in Italia" in *Corriere della Sera*, February 1, 1975.
7 Ibid.
8 Manuel Graca Dias "Architecture as a Gift to Others." In *Macau: Reading the Hybrid City. Discovering Manuel Vicente*, ed. Docomomo Macau (2016).
9 Rui Miguel Rebelo Leão, "Re-programming Infrastructure for Public Space. Opportunistic Planning as Urban Strategy for Macau" (PhD diss., RMIT University, 2019). p.88.
10 Ibid.
11 Patrice Goulet, ed., *O.M.A. Rem Koolhaas. Lille* (Paris: Editions Carte Segrete, 1990), p.15.

1.2. The role of the Architect

By Rui Leão

Rui Leão is an architect and co-founder of LBA, Arquitectura e Planeamento Lda. He studied at the Porto School of Architecture and earned a practice-based PhD from RMIT in 2019. Leão is the immediate past President of the International Council of Portuguese Speaking Architects (CIALP) and currently serves as Secretary General of the International Union of Architects (UIA).

Our exploratory trajectory as architects is strictly tied to the particular context of Macau, its political system and the unique relation of symbiosis that the Portuguese and local Chinese have developed in over four centuries of civic coexistence, and our deep knowledge of the city. We find design opportunities to challenge the installation of new major infrastructure meant to address the challenges of mass tourism and the constant issue of the lack of urban buildable land in Macau, which results in a lack of an acceptable amount of housing, infrastructure, spaces for sociability, and everything else.

We are creating alternatives for the procurement of architecture, by using every project as a trajectory of negotiation between architect, client, and other stakeholders. This approach has reconciled the often disjointed implementation of large public projects, by setting up precedent to sensibly adapt the insertion of major infrastructure into a city of heritage. The invention of a resilient infrastructural urbanism interprets infrastructure briefs into a multi-layered architectural apparatus that responds to large and complex site conditions.

Our contribution to the city spans several fields of action, inter-related and contributing to the empowerment of the project as an instrument to negotiate change in policy and urban typologies. These contributions result in an expanded field for the architect, demonstrated through an active role in the definition of the brief with the client and a subsequent engagement in negotiation and agency with other government bodies, outside the realm of the project, to achieve meaningful urban changes through design. This strategy confronts the statutory implementation of new infrastructure in the city through the production of opportunistic urbanism.

CRITIQUE AND OPPORTUNISM

Many of the briefs that we worked on seemed impossible to implement at first, seeming to lack the potential to work for the purpose for which they were being commissioned. Through our practice, we have contributed to improving procurement methods, which lead us to work on expanded sites and create additional opportunities with each project. Our reaction to this condition of working in Macau has allowed us to opportunistically insert larger agendas into the commissions, thus responding to the emerging social and civic gaps resulting from gaps facing Macau's accelerated development.

Our intervention in the city through the projects is proof that through a process of collaboration with the government and the decision-making stakeholders, designers have the opportunity to experiment and innovate at an urban scale. By sometimes acting as agents of change, sometimes as negotiators and policymakers, architects have an important role to play in changing both the culture of commissioning projects and the actual design solutions and spatial propositions for the future of the city—a place that faces constant challenges of new scales of users and new types of urban culture, arising from the tourism industry and the ultra-dense context of this territory.

PROCURING THE CITY THROUGH ARCHITECTURE COMMISSIONS

We believe that the scale of the commissions and the subsequent complexity that is inserted into the briefs has led us towards a process of incrementally planning large areas of the city, bringing together the spheres of architecture and agency. By this, we don't mean to say that the projects are incomplete or awaiting additions, but rather that the project-structure is made up of different components that interplay with different realms of the project, as site context and agendas brought in by us and by other stakeholders. We have come to understand the project as a platform of acceptance of all justified agendas, where the task of the designer is to operate and calibrate the different and conflicting intent into a designed solution.

OPPORTUNISTIC URBANISM

We are setting precedent by occupying the edge and the underneath leftover spaces, creating and discovering opportunities in the urban context, and by grafting additional uses onto the infrastructure of our commissioned projects for activities which aren't being addressed with current architecture procurements. We are using these projects to add a walking scale across the project sites, to allow the surrounding city to relate to the new context of our projects. We are also adding urban agendas to new infrastructure with the intent of integrating them with the logic of the historic city, demonstrating that the scale of the new infrastructure is compatible with the historic context.

In the particular political context of Macau, our contribution in raising certain aspects that are not foreseen in the policy and that are marginal to the public debate are critical to validate a system which has very few means to map the social realm. This leads us to take on many roles in advocating for certain agendas in a constructive way, to create checks and balances for a city that has to deal with very disparate scales of issues and design.

Our practice can be seen as having a certain political agility, underpinned by our desire to improve the civic, public spaces of Macau but also motivated to evolve a model of practice that can accommodate and respond to the particular "loose" political conditions of this place. This is evidenced through our ability and practice of "adding value" to commissions, expanding the scope of project briefs such that they address and respond realistically to the complex urban implications of the brief as well as the wider political context.

RESILIENT INFRASTRUCTURAL URBANISM

Following on from Manuel Vicente, our built work has set precedents and led to changes in policy based on the outcome of the work as an example for viable change, laying the foundations for future practices. Through the projects, we started to advocate for reclamations to be dealt with creatively to avoid passive offsets of the coastline and infrastructure destined for a single use. In the first project for the lagoons which we developed with Manuel Vicente, Nam Van Square, we made into a manifesto of our advocacy for a new agenda for custom-made reclamation, articulating public space, landscaping, and infrastructure on the waterfront.

We have learned through our practice that if we question the city as a bigger project, we can use any given brief as an opportunity to expand and work on the larger context of the site for greater issues lying beyond its strict physical limits, and we can act on a single project to use it to set precedents for future operations of its type. This avoids what could have been lost opportunities due to lack of good examples from which to draw and learn, from lack of specific urban policy, and the fact that other cities from where we could have drawn examples don't have the same set of gaps and freedoms allowed in our system.

INNOVATIVE PROCUREMENT STRATEGIES

We have been influencing policy on architecture by using our projects to integrate multiple use of public space into the briefs and engage with leftover spaces to make them work as alternate parts in the design of large-scale infrastructure. This experimental approach has led to government commissions starting to address the use of roof spaces and the commission of waterfront stretches for specific public space use. Both of these were first successfully tested in our designed projects, allowing us to take these agendas further by intertwining their components of added public space to engage with their urban context and allow these projects to respond to a new condition of mass tourism and a new type of place-making through the layering of three-dimensional public space solutions.

EXPANDED PUBLIC REALM

Not every public space is part of the urban public realm, as new peripheries and large development schemes aren't programmed to produce places for the public sphere. In new urban developments, public space is often forgotten or misplaced, and other infrastructure like car parks or gas stations may become ad hoc public spaces. This is why designed spaces are needed that create spaces of identity to anchor new urban developments to the notion of the city as a wider cultural sphere. Through our practice, we have learned to expand the public realm of the city when proposing alternative types of public space—related to public housing, to highways, and to other large infrastructure—where we make use of agency and the raising of awareness beyond the strict framework of the design process when the civic and the public realms aren't addressed in the commission. This has led us to envision teaching urbanism to kindergarten students, organizing tour guides in districts where there is heritage at risk and setting up urban planning and heritage awareness agendas for policymakers.

1.3. The un-purposed Space

By F. Carlotta Bruni

F. Carlotta Bruni is an architect, and co-founder and managing partner of LBA, Arquitectura e Planeamento Lda. She completed her master's degree at the Polytechnic of Milan and earned a practice-based PhD from RMIT in 2019. Bruni has shared LBA's work through lectures and conferences.

The un-purposed space is one of the focuses of our design research at LBA and our contribution to Macau's architectural and urban development as an implicit critique of Macau's profit-driven urbanism.

We have been re-evaluating the generally accepted architectural typologies as being too rigid for the un-formal kind of usage typical of the South Chinese. We have found alternatives with the purpose of freeing substantial areas in our projects to allow for other non functional possibilities of usage, blurring the boundary between site and context, public and private. We search for design ideas that allow us to offer a new set of spaces to the community. These spaces are a formalization of our urban intent and agendas—and have far-reaching implications in the wider territory of the city, allowing the context to permeate the design and the design to actively participate in its context through a seamless transition.

Un-purposed space has been a constant in our designs and generally conforms to one of four main configurations. The first configuration is the widening of the general circulation space in interior designs, thus creating extra areas. The second is un-purposed interim space as civic spaces for the neighborhood community as the result of our organization of the building mass. The third is un-purposed space as public spaces that exceed the project brief, while the fourth configuration is a broadening of the site context by extending the reach of the design beyond the physical site boundaries.

LBA understand the design context as a condition innate to the practice of architecture; a design always has a context and a relationship always exists between design and context. A design, while being informed by the context, changes the surroundings once it is in place, and both the new design and its surroundings become intimately inter-related. Thus, when we operate on a given site, we work on an objective physical and cultural context to create an intentional transformation.

There are two significant aspects to the notion of context: the first, physical and the second, cultural. A physical context constitutes the compositional, volumetric, and typological surroundings of the design, and is informed by the site's history and urbanism. Meanwhile, cultural context concerns the expectations of designers and users with regard to the potential future building, and relates to issues of identity; spatial memory; and, in the designer's case, training.

In addition to the obvious relationship between project and context, the background of a particular designer and his or her sensitivity to the given surroundings of the project might be a determining factor in the design outcome. LBA as a partnership have experienced the potential of cultural negotiation first-hand in their work, being both partners from different cultural backgrounds to each other and to Macau, the city in which they mostly practice.

We consider our origins and identities as a fundamental factor contributing to the outcome of our built work: as a response to our personal reading of the local context, we have developed specific strategies that stemmed from our formative years and identity. A sort of evolutionary adaptation has taken place both in our individual architectural methodology and cultural identity, as well as in the ways in which the city has adapted to the transformations that have occurred as a result of our built projects.

For the past 20 years, Macau has been LBA's context: our main relationship with the city is one of observation. Looking at a map of the Macau Peninsula, two features are immediately apparent: the compactness of the city grain and the lack of formalized public spaces. There is also a third, non-evident physical characteristic, which is the extreme density of certain areas of the city: the byproduct of continuous demolishing and rebuilding over the original city grain, where the plot size and its relationship with the city grid stays unchanged but the height of the new volume increases two- or threefold, sometimes even more, changing the street profile dramatically. In this over-densified environment, plots are systematically emptied and rebuilt, interstices are filled in, and additions to old buildings as well as the re-purposing of spaces are common.

LBA's spatial reading on the city of Macau focuses on three main issues—density, topography, and informality—which are all part of both the physical and the cultural context of the city.

Our observations on the issue of density constitute a critique of the profit-driven urban development to which Macau has been subject over the past 20 years. Our density-related agendas are meant to create as much free extra space as possible, and to free up space through a better fit of the programmatic part of the design within a given plot or design boundary.

In response to the issue of density, we have developed four main strategies. The first is to gain an understanding of the parts of the program that need to be organized in volumes and those that can be organized as a flow of spaces. The second is to design traditional circulation spaces such as corridors and hallways as alternative communal areas, through the discreet widening of their boundaries to allow for extra spaces and usages. Our third strategy is to overlay spaces with more than one function in a way that some free space can be gained through this economy. The final strategy is to efficiently fit together the programmatic areas of the designs to create empty areas that can be appropriated freely by the public.

Our observations on unleveled[1] cities of Portuguese origin are in fact an appreciation of their strategic use of section in public urban areas as well as in the design of buildings. These observations have led us to an implicit critique of the urban design of several recent land reclamations in Macau. These are significantly disrupting the cultural and phenomenological spirit of the place by offsetting the coastline and overlaying, on flat land, a series of orthogonal grids in various sizes that do not relate with the peninsula's original urban form. Our agendas concerning cities on unleveled terrain—as is the case in Macau—address the possibility of creating stacked, overlapping levels for public space thus simulating a topography.

The design strategies related to topography are in line with the phenomenological views of the most recent Portuguese architecture. Our first strategy developed to this effect is the definition of the void space through the design of its envelope. Our second strategy is to design topography to create a continuous flow of public spaces at different levels with the purpose of separating traffic flow from open pedestrian leisure areas. Our final strategy in this regard is to use section design to separate the programmatic areas of the project above and below ground to keep the ground level free for non-programmatic public usage.

Our observations on Macau's local, informal usage of public space define two specific agendas: the first is to design extra common spaces to promote non programmatic use; the second is to design these spaces so that they may freely be used but not occupied or annexed for private usage.

We have developed three strategies for the informality of usage of common spaces. The first is to make sure that the extra space is not designed to give privileged access to anyone, so that it cannot be appropriated by anyone or annexed to any private property. The second is to design these spaces in connection with the main flows of people; to never design a dead end. The final strategy is to make sure that the extra space is functionally needed, be it for light or ventilation purposes, regulation, or any other purpose.

We analyze the structures of the context and design accordingly, adapting to the local dynamic while pushing forward an agenda of fulfilling the programmatic requests of the project in such a way that extra space could be gained within the permitted volume of the design. This space, which we call un-purposed, is our contribution and a gift to the city. We are not only able to fulfill the economic expectations of the client through the understanding of local building practices, but are also able to give back precious open areas to the users and the city by organizing the program in a more orderly way through experimentation with different building typologies.

When questioning ourselves about the purpose of these spaces, we came to understand the disconnect between the urban spaces of our culture—which can still be found in Macau's Portuguese urban structure—and the way these urban spaces are used locally. We define our specific contribution to this issue in the discovery of the un-purposed space: a breathing compositional element that we have introduced into our designs at several scales, from interior designs to infrastructure projects; a notion that is part of a debate over new typologies for civic space.

1 I am using the word unleveled to address areas that are contoured, not flat.

2. Macau

By Rui Leão and F. Carlotta Bruni

LBA have been active in Macau under different names since 1996. Our practice started effectively in 2000 and since then we have been interested in developing projects which take on the issue of the city's identity as a hybrid of European archetypes for Asian use.

The chance timing of launching our practice in Macau just after the handover to China in 1999 provided us with a unique opportunity in that ours was neither a design firm from the colonial past nor was it perceived as part of the new Mainland Chinese status quo. Over the period through which we have practiced in the territory since the new political order came into effect, we have enjoyed establishing a close dialogue with the new political class through our built and speculative projects where we have tried to address issues of social identity, the role of the institutions, heritage management, and the new political narratives.

We appreciate how encounters between different cultures trigger processes of mutual influence and change that lead to original cultural forms and spaces.

Our knowledge of Macau is the result of our long interaction with the context as both architects and citizens. It is empirical and biased, and a consequence of design issues that have arisen during our practice in this context. The time span of our design practice in the territory, together with our living experience and our professional activities, has enriched the number and the quality of our observations which are autonomous and personal.

A series of considerations follow that have consistently informed our design agendas and which we feel are useful to illustrate and explain our current context and our point of view. These will help to frame the development of the political, social, and morphological context as we have perceived it during the period of our practice and will also act as a reference for our reasoning about design programs, regulations, and commissions.

HANDOVER TO CHINA

Both of us worked for Manuel Vicente in Macau in an initial collaboration that started in 1996 and ended in 1999. Our second collaboration with Vicente lasted until 2010, after which we set up our own practice. Just before the handover in 1999, Vicente received several commissions in Portugal and left his Macau office with little to no work. His Macau architectural practice closed around that time; likewise many within the Portuguese community—made up mostly of public servants, fearing the uncertainty of post-handover conditions—left the territory en masse.

We thought that whatever might happen in Macau would, politically and socially after the handover, constitute a far more unexpected and interesting reality than the life that we could find had we gone back to Portugal or Italy, and into a culturally stabilized Europe where cities already had a good share of planning and infrastructure in place.

The territory was handed over to mainland China by the Portuguese in 1999 after 12 years of negotiations, and did not enter into a post-colonial status. A joint declaration was signed by the Chinese and the Portuguese governments to allow Macau the possibility of retaining its political and social characteristics under the new rule. There was no traumatic takeover by the new Executive, and no revised set of economic, legal, and cultural strategies for an immediate reversion to mainland China rule of law and traditions. Instead, Macau was bound to live in an identity limbo for 50 years, with a definitive takeover by the People's Republic of China scheduled for 2049.

A curious state of affairs in relation to the practice of architecture emerged after the handover. On the one hand, the established local practices found themselves without a discourse to address the expectations of the new officials. Meanwhile, the new government itself was at a loss as to how to formulate an identity that it could project. It was clear that Macau society did not empathize with the culture of mainland China, but borrowing an architectural discourse from Portugal or Europe was also frowned upon. The city's models for the new development of Macau were found in Hong Kong and Singapore.

In the middle of this identity crisis, we found ourselves wanting to contribute to the definition of the specificity of Macau as a hybrid political and cultural space—a city that is Portuguese in form, Chinese in population, and with an administrative peculiarity. We understood that it was impossible to import models from our cultural origins and apply them to the local context in a colonialist fashion, as some of our colleagues had done until 1999. Instead, we focused on observing the way the population used the urban space and the way the city was designed and growing. We identified the relevant policies and hurdles. We then set out to design propositions for this peculiar identity that is the product of over 400 years of colonization, always reassessing our agendas in conjunction with the local authorities.

We took our cue from Manuel Vicente's design approach and political engagement. We took his militancy regarding dialogue with the city upon ourselves, both on the projects and on the public sphere, and the constant exercise of being critical of the context, the pre-conditions, the rules, others, and us.

He always kept an engagement with the local social context, exemplifying for us how an European type of public engagement could be received in a Southeast Asian context. He had the ability to adapt to the local building practice and an interest in understanding the phenomenological difference of Chinese culture applied to the art of architecture, through the qualities of light, color, scale, and spatial proportions. He also brought urbanism into the architecture of his projects.

The conceptual openness that we discovered in Manuel and his projects taught us that architecture can be infinitely inclusive, and that our affinities are not necessarily confined to our strict cultural framework. His understandings of Macau and China, or any reminiscence of a prosaic artifact that he chose to elect into the narrative of the project, were absorbed into it as much as his Portuguese baggage and any prosaic artifact reminiscent of a random narrative related to the site or the brief.

He had arrived in Macau in 1962 "as an adventurer rather than an explorer. He later returned to Lisbon to colonize Portugal as a Macanese."[1] His work had the intensity of a collective cry for freedom. The exhibitions that he curated in Lisbon on his built work in Macau were a critique of the restrictive approach to design in the context of Lisbon of the 1970s and 80s, and had a big impact on a younger generation of Portuguese architects.

Manuel's conditioned formal approach to a lot of his design agendas intrigued us, because in Macau, even before the handover, we felt we were dwelling in a highly hybrid condition whereas his approach seemed concerned with fixing narratives which might be too plastic for a social context which didn't follow the discourses of 20th-century architectural theory, cinema, or philosophy. We realize now that many of his projects were about the personal freedoms that he discovered and grafted onto the context of Macau before its time.

FRAMEWORK FOR OPPORTUNISM

Macau has a lot of money and no vision. The core of Macau's government budget derives from the 35 percent tax on gambling revenue. Since 2002, Macau's gambling profits have risen dramatically, with revenues peaking in 2013 at over 45 billion US dollars, three times the revenue processed through Las Vegas' gambling activity in the same period. This constitutes an enormous amount of money for the tiny scale a territory with a population of around 640,000 individuals. The annual budget is always under 20 percents of the casino tax collected yearly.

Macau has a deficit in policy and regulation that has to do with the scale of the city and a historical predominance of entrepreneurs in the urban development process, who prefer a loose system that is easier to navigate. That same loose system has a hard time deciding on distribution and setting up social policy. The passive role of the administration has been the main reason for social contestation in post-handover Macau. We have applied this same opportunistic thinking to the civic realm of the projects.

We believe that action will inform theory and that theory will, in turn, inform action. In our work we systematically expand and question the project briefs and use the commissioned projects to start a process of opportunistic urbanism, where the nonexistence of a masterplan and absence of urban policy becomes an opportunity to think freely about the public realm of the city and propose solutions that reconcile the civic and public dimensions of a very compact city. These agendas work like a time capsule, where urban intent is transported from one project to the next and our reaction to the lack of policy results in our engagement in a process of negotiation and dialogue with the clients and stakeholders.

As a result of our expanded role with the city, we build up a position that is more than design. Because we have grown into and become accustomed to this culture of constant negotiation and advocacy, our work is a consequence of the absence of a planning policy. Where most designers follow by example and work from a masterplan, in Macau we developed a masterplan through the individual projects that we were commissioned with, and a strategy that is more incremental than the usual top-down and predetermined approach, where each project is individual but not treated on a case-by-case basis.

POLITICAL SYSTEM

The political framework of Macau informs our practice orientation towards opportunistic urban activity. Our projects have led us to expand our role and act beyond the sphere of a strict design commission. Being a small territory with limited land resources and a very concentrated population, Macau poses a very particular set of issues which demand creativity and resourcefulness from designers and the local administration. Our opportunism works through this necessity and out of the lack of an organized system to procure efficient responses to the challenges that the city faces.

In the last decade of Portuguese administration, there was a halt in masterplanning in Macau, which marked a transition of the territory to China with no vision or discussion on urbanism.

During the first decade after the handover, Macau persisted with no policy for the urban sector, which left the urban planning of the territory at a standstill. In the first years as an SAR (Special Administrative Region) of China, Macau pulled the plug on all the planning departments in governance. The construction boom which resulted from the opening up of the gambling sector from 2003 onwards exhausted the existing land resources on the main land reclamation schemes from the 1990s. The absence of formal urban planning instruments and the lack of a housing policy started to affect our capacity as a city to work collectively towards a vision for the future. The lack of policy filtered through into the project briefs, creating an institutional void that delayed important social measures.

Being the gambling capital of the world, Macau directly follows neo-capitalist principles of development. This applies to the urban planning practices, where a laissez-faire policy has been the mainstay since the beginning of the 20th century, when the city started to grow in competition with the economic rise of Hong Kong. Adding to that, Macau's political system is poorly regulated by comparison with other cities. The lack of concise legislation and planning policies, gives rise to a situation where designers can work opportunistically and strategically and in direct response to the circumstances and the site conditions they face. Rules and systems for urban design are negotiated and determined on the go and case by case, and design strategies emerge from incremental moves and direct experience on the ground, as well as from negotiations and discussions that take place around projects with politicians, the media, and policy groups. This process in turn builds precedents and exemplars for future projects and urban development.

After the handover, the fields of architecture, urbanism and heritage have all become essential in the struggle for identity and social equity issues in Macau in many social debates. Public discussion on policy is key to a political system where there are no publicly elected roles in the whole administration. For a small-scale city with a single layer of decision-making, public opinion on future policy is crucial in creating complexity in the commissioning of public projects. This is a context that can easily become very efficient and produce great examples if there is a new type of agency, a new breed of engaged and outspoken professionals, supported by public opinion-making.

The city emerged from these initial years of denial when it published a new urban planning law and a heritage protection law, both passed in 2013, and founded two committees made up of representatives from the professional sector: one to review the planning policy and the second to address heritage protection; finally, a (very generic) masterplan was approved in 2020, and detailed plans are still being commissioned.

The lack of a planning discourse and the apparent absence of a vision for the territory has allowed us to insert our agendas, through a series of different actions to improve a condition that disqualified the whole apparatus of the construction sector, and to create an important platform for sharing a joint social vision and a joint project for our role in the "One Country, Two Systems" policy.

At the peak of the first post-handover gambling-industry construction boom, the lack of ongoing formal urban planning instruments and the absence of a housing policy generated a state of instability due to the lack of design commissions to local practices which, like us, didn't want to get fully absorbed into the casino projects. Architectural competitions became very rare in the post-handover period, which led to alternative ways of procuring architectural commissions. In this period, we learned to negotiate and establish critical discussions with government agencies. We began to propose our visions for the city in specific ways to find consensus and commissions.

MACAU'S URBAN DEVELOPMENT

The specificity of Macau's urban and civic structure is the result of the influence of two different cultures, the Chinese and the Portuguese, as is apparent in the city's built form. The urban history of the city is a testament to this.

Since the time it was established, at the beginning of the 16th century, the size of the territory has been fixed by an agreement with the Chinese authorities. At first, it corresponded to the area of the peninsula as far as the border gate at the end of the causeway. Later in 1864, it came to comprise some of the island next to the peninsula, with a final agreement that extended the territory on to Taipa and Coloane islands in 1887.

The peninsula was naturally divided by a topographical elevation that stretched between the inner harbor and the Praia Grande Bay; like other cities that are designed on unleveled terrains, Macau has adopted urban design techniques that adapt to its morphological conditions—mostly involving the extensive use of section in the design as a means of overcoming the difference in levels between the plots.

The city was historically constituted by two settlements developing concurrently. The Portuguese city to the southeast was built along the southern bay, the Praia Grande, featuring its typical Rua Central, a street traced at the top of the main hill, to organize and defend the Outer Harbour. The Chinese city to the northwest developed along the Inner Harbour, which has shallower waters but is closer to the other shores of the Pearl River Delta, offering additional short connections if traveling locally by sea. The two cities eventually met and mixed, the Portuguese city starting to descend on the side of the Inner Harbour and the Chinese city coming up as far as Rua Central.

In a way that is similar to other cities of Portuguese origin, Macau has traditionally adapted its built structures to the geographical conditions of the site context, thereby creating public spaces that are generally not of a regular shape, built, as they are, within the topographical limitations of the site; the city grid is distorted according to the terrain and public spaces are shaped accordingly.

The opening of Almeida Ribeiro Avenue around 1920, cutting through Macau's main topographical elevation, was the first deliberate urban act to connect the two harbors in an attempt to unify and democratize the city. Nowadays, the transition between the Portuguese city and the Chinese city is seamless, recognizable only by the different sizes of the city blocks and the typologies of the historical buildings.

Typically, Portuguese urbanism is inclusive and adapts to local customs of occupying urban spaces. It can thus be argued that Macau is a city where the cultural hybridization of public space has been ongoing for over 500 years. In the case of Macau, we can also attest to the way these spaces, which are the formalization of a European way of using the city, adapt to the culture into which they are inserted. The main differences are the informal manner in which the population uses these spaces and the generalized private appropriation of public space, which is a well-documented characteristic.

In terms of cultural hybridization, even the most recent urban developments demonstrate that Macau has an intrinsic flexibility in accepting foreign urban models, as the new casino strip referenced to American urbanism demonstrates. It appears that Chinese informal usage of public spaces allows for the free appropriation of any typology, from any background.

CITY EXPANSION

The first urban masterplan for Macau, drawn up in 1927, shows proposed alterations to the city centre with the opening of Almeida Ribeiro Avenue, the planned expansion of the city towards the border gate, and a first planned reclamation. Until this point in time, the process of land reclamation had been slow and mainly followed the opportunistic usage of the extra land resulting from soil deposits along the coastline as part of the urban territory. At the beginning of the 20th century, building on the peninsula of Macau started to expand as far as its physical limits and beyond – it transformed into a fluid territory always negotiating its boundaries. The processes of actively reclaiming land—which started to increase exponentially during the last decades of the 20th century—had begun.

Being an offset of the original coastline, each new reclamation imposed a new grid, plot size, investment size, urban identity, and a place on the original peninsula. By 1999, the peninsula had become a patchwork of different urban propositions, with the old city centre completely surrounded by taller and larger buildings. In the 1990s the city was quickly modernizing and expanding.

We were hopeful that after the handover there would be a reflection on which model the city would adopt to strengthen its identity and direction for subsequent development. Contrary to our expectations, after both the handover in 1999 and the new gambling concessions in 2002, the City of Macau, determined to become a worldwide gaming attraction, made another dramatic change towards losing its local identity and gaining a global one. We witnessed a new American model and identity being imposed on the new reclamation areas between Coloane and Taipa, an area known as COTAI, as well as on areas very close to the city centre in NAPE.

Macau has increased its size through reclamation by almost 50 percent since the handover and is planning on doubling its population by 2030. The vision of the city that we try to implement is one of a tightly connected urban network which, despite its urban density, can offer designed public spaces flexible for appropriation.

ON LAND RECLAMATION

Land reclamation in Macau is a political phenomenon expressing the cultural and social construct of the people who make up the city.

Macau has no land reserves. New reclamation schemes have always been subject to political approval granted by the Chinese Central Government. This fact results in Macau not having a strategic vision for its future urban necessities, as they need to be negotiated politically before being technically addressed as a design brief. Approvals of reclamation schemes were always dependent on good political relations with China, which was also the only source for soil. As Macau never owned any territorial waters during the colonial period, the Portuguese had to come up with convincing agendas—either for a bigger sea port, new large-scale infrastructure, or better road connections—to negotiate the new land requirements with the Chinese authorities.

The fact that new land procurements are a political deliberation of the Central Government in Beijing and cannot be decided locally leaves urban planning as a marginal practice, leading to reclamation plans being piecemeal and never understood as holistic instruments of policy implementation. This particular condition, inherited from the colonial period and the political respect that Portugal held for China, compelled architects to speculate on the future development of the city. Because Macau is in constant need of new reclaimed land, speculative plans are a useful tool to create a vision and discussion on development scenarios at every cycle of the city's development.

Commissions to the private sector have ceased since the handover aligning with the practice in centralized planning of mainland China, in the hands of large design institutes that follow top-down policy. The plans have grown more elemental and incomplete, defining only the minimal volumetric constraints and the space between urban plots as simplistically calculated fluxes of mobility and sidewalks. In this post-handover system with more central decision-making and less dialogue at the masterplanning level, our contribution to incrementally "feed" these planning standards with various layers of additional urban content has been in most cases to retrofit the formal planning through commissions for added urban content that are plugged into the initial masterplan.

In Macau, there is also a constant struggle with an expanding population in a very compact territory, and an exponential growth in tourism, which daily tests the saturation point of public spaces, transportation, restaurants, and basic supplies. The government confines itself to producing new reclaimed land, only addressing the elementary preconditions of securing accessibility and producing new saleable urban plots to satisfy the urban engineering of the Central Government, which wants accelerated growth in Macau. The planning in all current reclamation plans isn't comprehensive or sustainable in defining demography, mobility, quality of life, public space, or access to sociability. The process of reclamation in Macau is critical for us, because it is rich in opportunities to redeem the city of its faults and gaps through a process of accretion, through which informal interventions agglomerate over and around the infrastructure. Our projects are part of our opportunistic, incremental planning approach, mostly located along the edges of newly reclaimed land where the projects are opportunities to retrofit, re-program, landscape, and micro-plan the raw territory of the reclamation.

We understood that the Central Government's policy of One Country Two Systems[2] and the 50 years of integration into mainland China implied regional planning agendas, like the urban and infrastructural integration of Macau into the larger context of the Pearl River Delta region, nowadays referred to in political terms as the Great Bay Area or GBA. We started to look beyond the border of Macau, something that was a taboo for any non-Chinese in the immediate post-handover period, leading to an invitation from the Macau SAR Government for Rui to write on urban strategy and on long-term urban policy. Part of our advocacy in working with this think tank was around how Manuel Vicente's Praia Grande Bay closure masterplan constituted a genuine understanding of Macau's urban development and a good example of understanding the urban insertion of reclamation into the old city, with the prospect that future masterplanning in Macau could retain Vicente's legacy as a tradition, a sensible urban gesture, comprehending the dialogue that it had to establish with old Macau and the different scale of the lots, thus providing the resolution of scales that is both possible and needed in the urban development of Macau.

PROFIT-DRIVEN URBAN DEVELOPMENT

Macau's urban development policy continues to be profit-driven and now has a very generic masterplan lacking detailed plans. This fact, together with the very basic level of planning regulation, is a major obstacle to the implementation of an urban idea for Macau. To work without a masterplan means that, as an architect, you are always guessing the expectations, if any, of the government. It means that there is no shared plan, no consensus between the government and the community on the development of the city. Consequently, the only common agenda is financial. The consequences are twofold. For one, there are no planned public spaces in the redevelopment of the city. Secondly, private developers do not exercise any initiative in inserting public spaces in their buildings, which would be to the detriment of the achievable gross floor area. This situation is transforming the city into an unrealistic urban scenario with streets and sidewalks as its only open areas.

The opportunities of the real estate market have created a local community of practice dedicated mostly to housing schemes and casino developments. Only a few practitioners—such as LBA, Arquitectura e Planeamento—engage in public and infrastructure works because these kinds of projects are very demanding and this is not reflected in the designer fees.

The main characteristic of Macau's recent development has been unregulated urban growth. Several factors are responsible for this. Macau residents have become wealthier due to the rise of the gambling industry. Accompanying this has been a certain mobility of the population from older housing projects to newer buildings, from smaller to bigger flats, with a consequent increase in the available living areas per person and the real estate bubble created by mainland Chinese investment in Macau's properties.

Macau's real estate market has grown exponentially since 1999 through demolition and rebuilding in the consolidated urban fabric and by building new properties in newly available or reclaimed plots. We refer to the practice of demolishing and rebuilding as "urban cannibalism." It is a historical tendency shared by Macau and Hong Kong alike, probably a consequence of limited space resources or the scarcity of prime-site plots. The main consequence of this tendency is an increase in urban density. Since all new developments are profit-driven, there is no space for social, common, or empty space. A secondary consequence is the loss of the character of the city's traditional spaces.

DENSITY-RELATED URBAN STRATEGIES

Looking at a map of the Macau Peninsula, two features are immediately apparent: the compactness of the city grain and the lack of formalized public spaces. There is also a third, non-evident physical characteristic, which is the extreme density of certain areas of the city: the byproduct of continuous demolishing and rebuilding over the original city grain, where the plot size and its relationship with the city grid stays unchanged but the height of the new volume increases two- or threefold, sometimes even more, changing the street profile dramatically. In this over-densified environment, plots are systematically emptied and rebuilt, interstices are filled in, and additions to old buildings as well as the re-purposing of spaces are common.

An increase in density in a fixed volume corresponds to an increase in mass. We see this as a literal expression of Macau's condition, where the boundaries of the city are always negotiated with China, even now that Macau owns the water that surrounds it. Nowadays, Macau Peninsula has completely grown to fill its boundaries. The old fabric has been transformed into a flat slab into which the roads are carved. Almost no communal space remains because all the open areas have been filled in with long-standing temporary constructions, a sign of the informality of appropriation of common space. A portion of the traditional built fabric has been demolished and replaced with taller buildings that reach or exceed the maximum gross floor area allowed. In the most recent reclamations, the plot sizes

© LBA archive

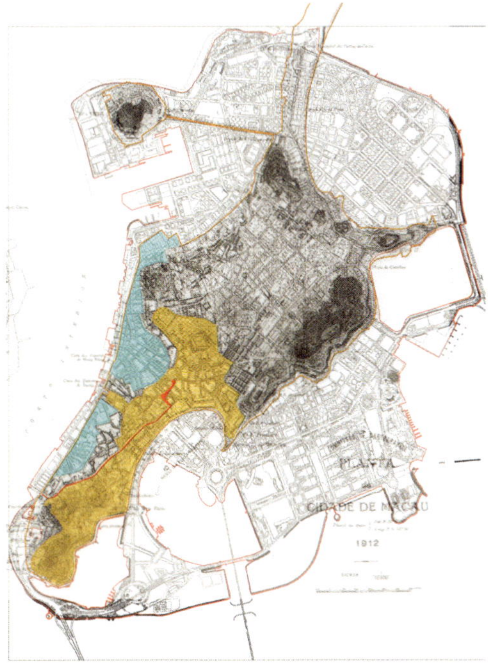

© LBA archive

↑ Contemporary Macau with the recognizable historical morphology: the main areas of the Portuguese settlement in yellow and the main areas of the Chinese settlement in blue. Rua Central marked in red.

are so large that they can each fit the whole area of the city center inside their boundaries.

In addition to this and in response to the need for extra space, the population traditionally resorts to strategies of building over the formal urban fabric, in interstitial spaces, within gaps in the public realm. Some of the most common examples of these strategies, which contribute to some of Macau's particular urban characteristics, are rooftop additions, protruding windows grilles, advertising panels, as well as shops that expand into the street and free-standing street hawkers. This is a demonstration that culturally in Macau—in a manner that also occurs in some other parts of Asia—public space is considered up for grabs by whoever has direct access to it, and within this appropriation we find examples of the general informality of usage of common city space.

This free appropriation is a way of overcoming the lack of private space, which works, in general, to the detriment of existing historical public areas. Now that population and tourism-related pressures have also increased, this cultural aspect of the misuse of common urban space has started to conflict with necessity for wider, uncluttered public spaces. A city with a fixed area, Macau has neglected building programs for open and public spaces in favour of a mantra of greed by developers for greater gross floor area.

1 Eric K. C. Lye, *Manuel Vicente: Caressing Trivia* (Hong Kong: MCCM Creations, 2006,

2 The principle that defines the political framework of the Special Administrative Regions of Hong Kong and Macau in the context of the People's Republic of China.

3. LBA: Caressing Entropy Macau, 1999-2049

By Jorge Figueira
CES, Department of Architecture, University of Coimbra

Jorge Figueira is an associate professor at the Department of Architecture, University of Coimbra (UC); researcher at the Centre for Social Studies, UC; and curator of the exhibition "O que faz falta. 50 Years of Portuguese Architecture in Democracy," Casa da Arquitectura, Matosinhos (2024—2025).

1999

Rui Leão and Carlotta Bruni's biographical circumstances are in themselves extraordinary. That the two architects have been working in Macau since 1996, and as LBA Architecture and Planning since 2008, only amplifies the fascination and intensifies the narrative and critical possibilities. Since the arrival of the Portuguese in the 16th century, Macau has been a mythical point of convergence between cultures , a phenomenon which accelerated in the 20th century and multiplied in the 1990s in preparation for the "handover" to the People's Republic of China, which took place in 1999. Not long after, and without wasting a breath, Macau—now known under the designation of "Special Administrative Region—reached stratospheric heights with the liberalization of gambling in 2002. There was SARS (severe acute respiratory syndrome, in 2003), as there would be other moments (the crisis at Lehman Brothers, which put a stop to casino construction in 2018); and, more recently, Covid-19. Nonetheless, Macau is a resilient place, as it has proved throughout the centuries, and gambling—or architecture—are powerful. RL and CB are at the turning point of the colonial era towards this post-colonial period; a "limbo"[1]— in CB's own words—of 50 years, the expected period of transition. We are roughly halfway through it.

The two theses they presented in 2019 at the School of Architecture and Urban Design, College of Design and Social Context, RMIT University are the fulcrum of my reflection: "Re-programming infrastructure for public space. Opportunistic planning as urban strategy for Macau," by Rui Leão, and "Shaping Macau's un-purposed space. Design in context," by Carlotta Bruni.

They are, in fact, indispensable pieces of work because they are akin to listening to both architects closely, intimately, in opposition to the noisy and hyperbolic explosion happening in real time and in which they are also involved—in which they act as both agents and critical observers. The way in which each of them approaches the "problem" is enlightening; their biographies and respective backgrounds—which intersect somewhere between Porto and Lisbon—mean different yet complementary ways of understanding and projecting Macau.

Though RL and CB occupy this "limbo", simultaneously a transition and a highpoint, it is to Manuel Vicente (MV) we must hearken back, the indomitable architect who arrived in Macau in 1962, with whom they worked, with whom they were partners, and whose pioneering spirit and boldness is necessarily the reference point for the two young architects. In Macau, MV felt what Frank Gehry concluded when he arrived in Los Angeles in the 1950s, after some experimentation with the modern canons: that it was necessary to find another way. For MV, this other way translated itself, of course, in Robert Venturi and Denise Scott Brown's approach, perhaps more so than in the work of Louis Kahn, with whom MV had worked between 1968 and 1969. But what matters is this genealogy of radical mismatches, be it with the "canons" (any of them) or between one's training and one's work, for this is also where RL and CB meet: in a process of "unlearning" or, at least, of dealing with the migration of learning.

There are still notable Portuguese architects working in Macau today. But MV was unique, as I have pointed out many times.[2] Not only was he an *enfant terrible* of Portuguese architecture but he also incorporated Macau's otherness into his own trajectory.

By taking advantage of the path opened up by MV, both literally and conceptually, and with the expanded and specific contributions I shall highlight, RL and CB are especially well suited to occupy the effusive space that the post-handover has created in Macau. In any case, their task is as daunting and complex as it is exhilarating: to create a "local" identity for Macau's new global geoculture; to deal with the abrupt scales and new density created by the invasion of casinos and mass tourism; to fix, via architecture, the transient and the ephemeral in a relentless, ever-changing place.

When the pieces permanently change places—mobility and décor, new and old, fake and authentic, earth and water—architecture is an arduous exercise for those looking from this Western side of the world. And what is the architect's job anyway? RL devotes part of his thesis to this question, first in "role of the architect"[3] and then evolving into "the expanded role of the architect".[4] As an existential problem, however, it is always present in the work of both architects.

It is therefore very moving to see how CB sees the creation of "un-purposed" spaces as an act of redemption for architecture; or how RL looks to political dialogue to create opportunities ("opportunistic planning") for transforming infrastructure into public space. At the end of the day, they are both trying to spatialize beauty, as architects have always done, even in the face of the intense *star wars* between Asian and American casinos.

To paraphrase "caressing trivia"[5], Eric K. C. Lye's beautiful turn of phrase to characterize MV's work, perhaps RL and CB are "caressing entropy".

ONE TERRITORY, TWO ARCHITECTS

Look at the expressive diagrams that RL and CB present in their doctoral reflections. Perhaps that's what they're aiming to do: to "caress entropy". Those on page 49 of RL's work, "Re-programming infrastructure for public space..." aim to show "the use of different project strategies" and the "use of different political hats" as a "set of expanded actions over and around the projects working to expand the projects' ambit."[6] On page 91, another diagram shows how "the first lagoon projects" functioned as a "testing ground" for "different political agendas" in which RL breaks down his role as architect into those of "advocate," "advisor," "agent of change," "negotiator," "policy-maker," "lobbyist," and "opinion-maker."[7] The diagram on page 191 focuses on the Barra PTI (Public Transport Interchange) project and outlines "strategies for an expanded role of the architect in the design process". Essentially, as well as demonstrating the project's programmatic and administrative complexity, it aims to stratify the negotiation process that allows us to go beyond."[8] The diagram on page 215 allows us to map RL's "shift of practice" by articulating together the various project experiences towards the aforementioned expansion of the "architect's role," which includes "engaging agency, advocacy and lobbying."[9]

On page 18 of Shaping Macau's un-purposed space...," CB proposes a "conceptual diagram of the dissertation."[10] Though made with the specific purpose of guiding the research process, process, here too the need to properly sort and organize references, projects, and strategies appears like a diagrammatic volcano, a graphic device which also functions as a kind of paper architecture.

Though presented as a complement to the texts, drawings, renders, and photographs of the projects, these diagrams stand on their own as conceptual pieces. They have a character that could be said to evoke the Japanese Metabolism of the 1960s, a reference to which I will return: they are the expression of architecture metabolizing itself in the transition from Italian and Portuguese references to another "paradigm," with the force of nature leading the "buildings" to curve, bifurcate, divide without a centre—perhaps even without direction—and yet, apotheotic and visceral in their desire to find it.

Perhaps a first sign of the transition from "trivia" to "cherished entropy" can be found in the Areia Preta Fire Station designed by MV (1991—1998). In the structure's "reptilian" character, built in layers, in perpetually paralysed movement, this work is already "something else" in the Portuguese exit from Macau. But it is with RL and CB that the big bang takes place, in Nam Van Lakes and Nam Van Square: a derision of the "Western" after decades of work *in between* the two, whose comparison with Álvaro Siza's neighboring plan for the NAPE (*Novas Áreas do Porto Exterior*, New Areas of Outer Porto, 1984) renders the "metabolization" of Classicism/modernism towards the global Chinese 21st century even more evident. In that regard, RL's words are particularly trenchant: "The remoteness of the NAPE masterplan helped me realise how congenial Manuel Vicente's Nam Van Lakes masterplan is to the culture of Macau, through its more complex articulation between the volumetric plan, infrastructure and the construction of a new territorial landscape with the invention of the lakes, which are a sort of emptied balloon around which density is defined"[11]. This complexity, expressed so assertively, ultimately describes a particular handover: as if the political and administrative handover were matched by an architectural handover.

The Nam Van Square project is therefore a sign of things to come: it is practically impossible to compare this experience with the European models that RL and CB describe as formative in their doctoral reflections. It is remarkable, moreover, how in this theoretical work they carry out an exercise in transposition, translation, and adaptation which explains Macau to us essentially by opposition, rarely by convergence. Perhaps one possible convergence is the concern with "public space" as a result of a European sensibility: when CB talks about "un-purposed" spaces, there is an echo of Ignasi de Solà-Morales' "Terrain Vague"; RL's repeated concern with negotiating and projecting infrastructure as "public space" is as much pragmatic as the European culture of the turn of the century, formative years for both.
In fact, beyond RL and CB 's biographical aspects, which in themselves reveal a remarkable multicultural trajectory as I have already mentioned, it is interesting to note their academic experiences in order to understand Macau's projects—by proximity or distance, almost always by opposition.

CB reflects on her "neo-rationalist"[12] training at the Politecnico di Milano; RL stresses the social vocation of the "Escola do Porto" (Faculty of Architecture of the

University of Porto) and is marked by the way the city is understood as an "object of observation, from which a direct process of learning through observation could be devised".[13] CB tells us about the "locus", based on Aldo Rossi, as the physical and cultural context with which she looks at Macau in the post-handover period, and the "identity" as her own—a "scientific autobiography," I might add. For CB, "the circumstances of my practice in Macau and the fact that I have been able to keep my architectural identity is the result of two specific conditions: the fact that Macau is historically accustomed to cultural hybridisations and the fact that I have been trained to be very respectful of the context in which I operate".[14]

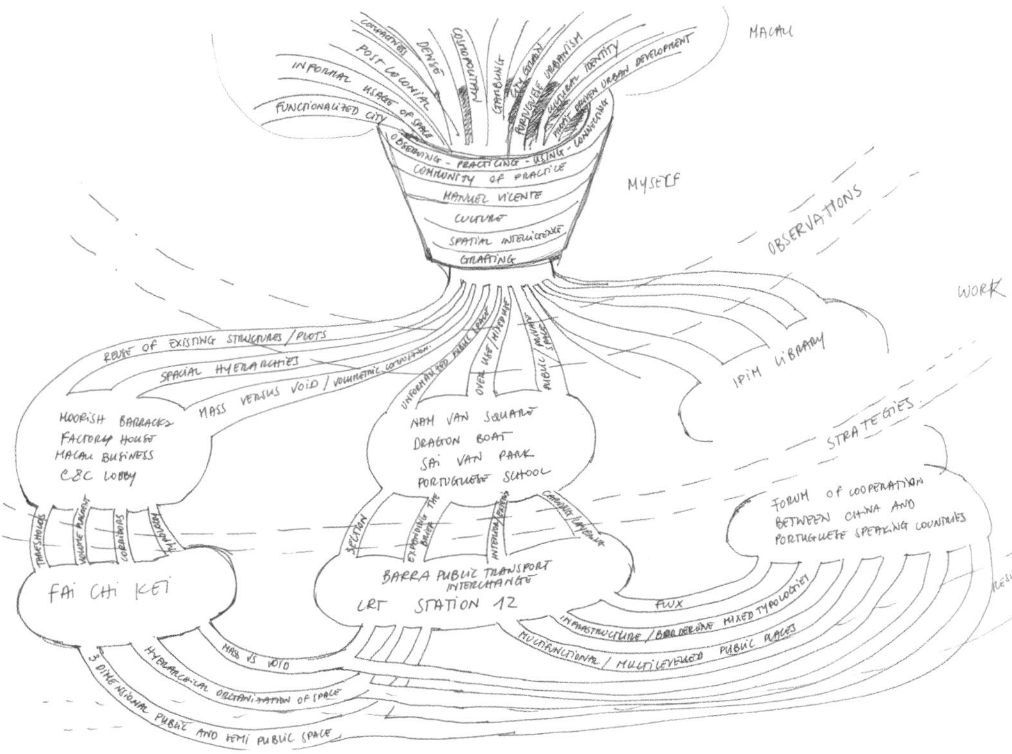

© F. Carlotta Bruni

As foundational formative periods, very much defined by the debates of the second half of the 20th century, and with results that are celebrated and followed globally (Rossi's and Siza's works, for example), it's hard to imagine approaches that are more distant from Macau's moving cartography, from its growing architectural volatility. If anything sets Macau apart, it's that architectural archetypes, whether Classical or modern, are *phantasmagoria* brought on by visitors, which go back with them. "Neo-rationalism" cannot be imagined without a radical "disciplinary autonomy" which means going down to the bones of architecture (the "type"); and "place" in Porto does not exist without the modern project that truly founds it (a possible synthetic definition of Kenneth Frampton's "critical regionalism"). In that light, and cruelly put, "neo-rationalism" and "critical regionalism" are two cul-de-sacs as far as Macau is concerned. Macau doesn't lend itself to nostalgia for the cener, for the Classical or modern order—something which MV discovered after the Helen Liang Orphanage (1964), which is still influenced by it.

CB and RL are very cognizant of that.

In any case, the 20th century is slipping further and further away from us; Macau is only moving closer and closer to the 21st century.

It's curious how CB describes the environment she found in Portugal when she arrived there in 1992: "I discovered a country that was in a highly energetic and dynamic phase of its history ... As a result, modernist theories and typologies were being reassessed across the board. I found this a breath of fresh air compared with the theoretical nature of the Italian panorama. Everybody was experimenting"[15] outside of the "analysis" and "typologies" of the Italian school—not exactly a "blank canvas", but a first stage in approaching Macau. On the other hand, and beyond ever-lingering doubts from then on, what RL takes from the Porto experience is the "social" dimension: "I believe that my socially orientated attitude

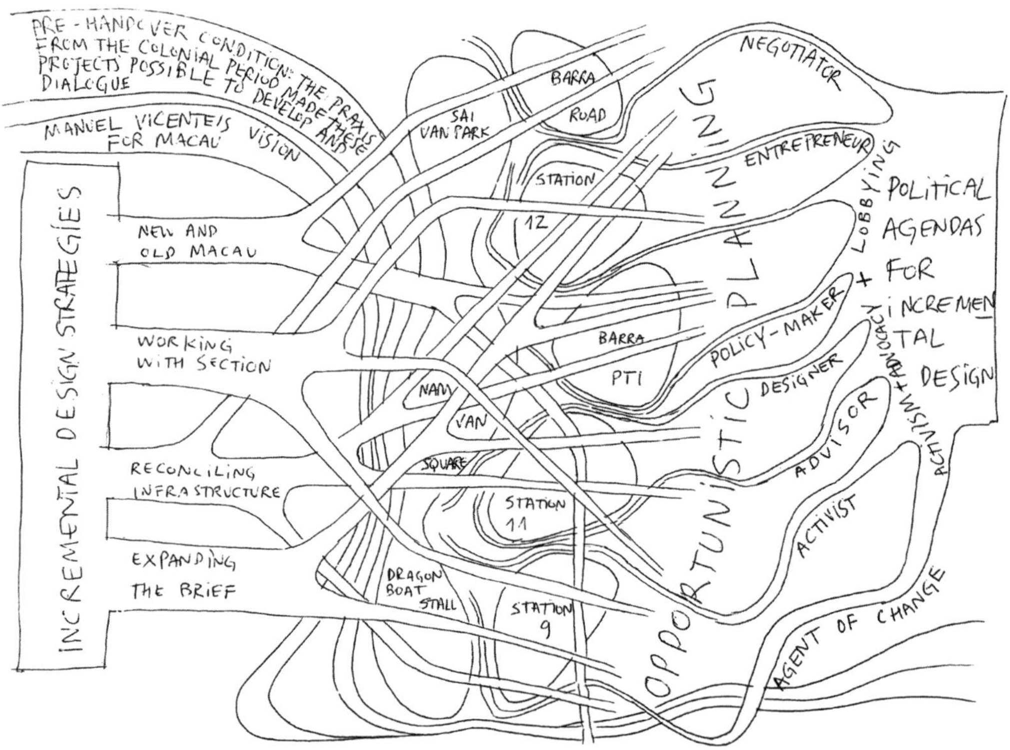

© Rui Leão

to making public space, my pursuit to relate the old in the new in the ambit of every project, and my tendency to understand the project more as a system than a structure, is tied back to my learnings at Porto".[16]

In any case, it is the best of the European experience (at least in the south) that RL and CB bring to Macau, though perhaps only as imagery or autobiography. The way they argue and project perhaps doesn't give up on having the physiognomy of the Teatro del Mondo or the poetic asceticism of Bouça, Porto, on their horizon. But the horizon is where they remain: the archetypes re-imagined in "neo-rationalism", and the "place" re-imagined with the heroic architecture of the 1920/30s in Porto, refer to "permanences" that are foreign to Macau's transient reality. It is perhaps necessary to have the 'hybrid cross-cultural identity'[17] that RL ascribes to himself in order to deal with the phantasmagorias of the West in the face of Macau's complexities and the "gaps"[18] caused by the handover, as he also tells us.

It is true that beyond the Portuguese pre-handover experience, particularly MV's, the presence of influential figures in contemporary architecture in China—Rem Koolhaas, Zaha Hadid, Steven Holl, to name but a few—allows us to find some coordinates for Macau's "permanent-transient" collision, the force field where RL and CB act with temerity. Many things at once, in a small dense space, which they compare with Las Vegas, where once there was a desert.

FROM THEORY TO WORK

As mentioned, the Nam Van Lakes masterplan for Macau's southern expansion and the ensuing Nam Van Square project symbolize the transition from the Portuguese experience to the territory's new status and a decisive attempt, as RL writes, "to demonstrate Macau's capacity to think differently, a cultural legitimacy that needed to be reassessed".[19] The project's success, recognized internationally with the ARCASIA Award, and the massive and varied use of the spaces created, later expanded and complexified in the adjacent Sai Van Lake Park, allow us to pinpoint the moment when this story begins anew. The intertwining of infrastructure and architecture, the emergence of public space with an ornamental and participatory commodity. This demand is summarized by CB on a methodological level: "I see the programmatic part of the design as a threedimensional mass of spaces that need to be fitted together as a volume. I execute the design exercise of organising the mass of the building in the aim of increasing the size of its empty spaces".[20] In the same vein, RL emphasizes the use of "section as a tactic to resolve the complexity of the urban insertion of infrastructure".[21]

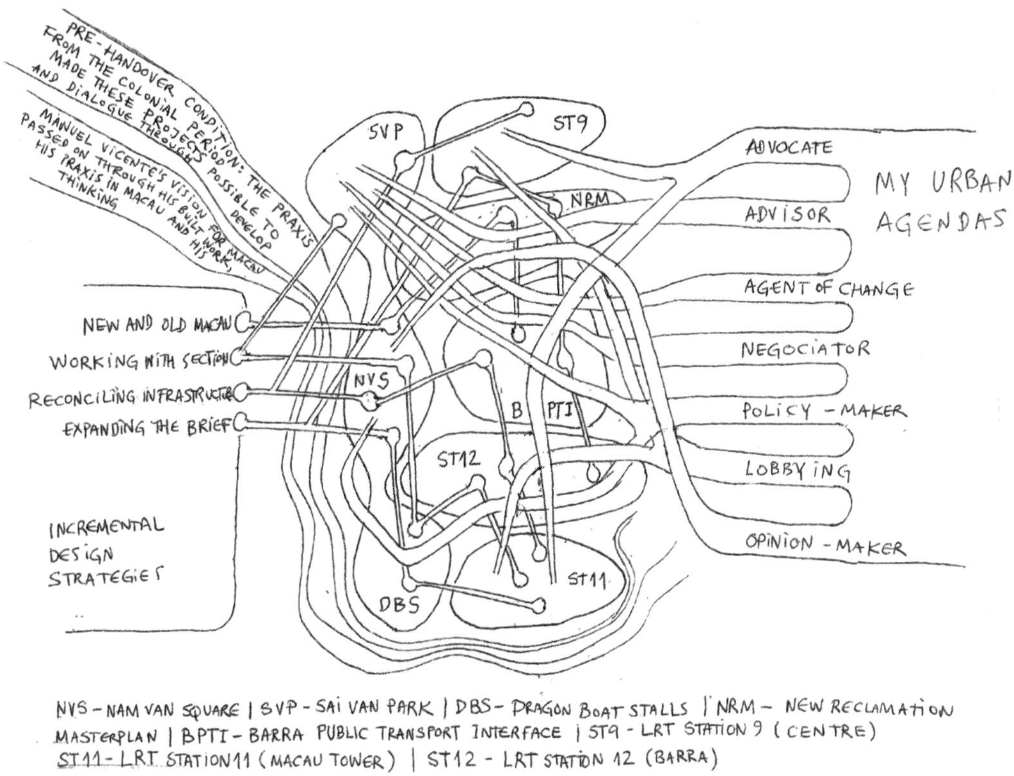

role—as a character all its own, not merely a backdrop —from this point onwards take place according to a hybrid, "opportunistic" model, in search of a spatiality that can keep pace with the speed of the territory's growth. This is RL and CB's launching pad, drawing up scenarios for future expansions, with or without "land reclamations", trying to take advantage of Macau's "laissez faire" and exponential growth. From the emergence of new mobilities and new uses, "public" or "civic" space can be reinvented. In these new topographies that cross land and water, soil and "space"—that old "protagonist" of modern architecture, now not exactly "open" or "organic"—is a scarce

But it is not only in the disciplinary field that transformations are underway. The "opportunistic" dimension or, perhaps, or perhaps RL's proposed "agile political urbanism,"[22] means that a "topography to thicken the floor and give it a scale to domesticate the bridge infrastructure that was designed by traffic engineers too close to the delicate historic skyline of old Macau" is created right from the Sai Van Lake Park project onwards.[23] In other words, every infrastructural or landscaping operation, which tends to have an essentially technocratic slant, can be reversed or at least redirected towards a more effective "public" dimension, which RL and CB understand as being in tune with the history, scale, and uses of the territory; with the culture that has resisted the transformations of the last 20 years; or, ultimately, with the culture being forged as the 21st century unfolds.

RL and CB's motivations are clear and lucid, as is the approach they take—a more "disciplinary" approach in CB's case, a more "interdisciplinary" one in RL's. But how do we project beyond "archetypes" or "languages," or "space" as it has been understood in the modern era? Fai Chi Kei and the Barra PTI/LRT Station 12 projects were big challenges for RL and CB, in both cases showing the fingerprints of Portuguese colonization/administration, and great examples of Macau's acceleration. In the Barra neighborhood, the sophisticated new interventions coexist with the three Barra Towers designed by MV, the state of the art in collective housing in the 1980s. The new Fai Chi Kei (vertical and dense) replaced the Fai Chi Kei that MV also proposed during that golden period (two horizontal bands with a street/piazza in between), which weren't able to withstand new Macau's real estate pressure. This comparison with the present/absent past of 40 years ago is a window into Macau's rapaciousness—and that of contemporary architecture.

Rather than any "archetypes" or "languages" being rescued, what can be seen in the new interventions at Barra and Fai Chi Kei is an architectural polysemy based on a theme—everything is a curved line at Barra, everything is a straight line at Fai Chi Kei. As if they were exercises in the reinvention of architectural form itself, aggrandized by the need for the programme and complexified by what RL and CB want to add to the brief. Where Fai Chi Kei is peremptory and dramatic in its vertical and horizontal lines, Barra's infrastructures are liquescent. In the sense of the tower; in the sense of the shell. There are no archetypes—no composition; only performance, strategy, concept, calculation.

"Curatorship" has replaced "composition"; this might be a possible definition of the condition of contemporary architecture.

With the Fai Chi Kei project, the scale of the order has changed profoundly, and RL and CB are facing a new challenge. Firstly, they are trying to subvert the traditional layout of the tower over the podium, and find "un-purposed", unprogrammed spaces on the ground floor that will allow them to retain some of the urban experience of the demolished structure. But the new structure's high density necessarily precludes another model. It is also in the "porosity," the connections between the blocks, the "variety and richness of the common spaces"[24] that they look for the "opportunity" of architecture to emerge from the infrastructure. Or perhaps the distinction makes little sense, and another name needs to be devised.

The Barra PTI/LRT Station 12 projects are the highlight of this itinerary that I've been describing, where RL and CB's various approaches, doubts, and certainties I've been exposing ultimately converge. It is also a work that deserves to be recognized as one of the most extraordinary of our time, whatever the geoculture we might be considering. Infrastructure-architecture, anti-monument and iconic, space-logistics, Barra PTI/LRT Station 12 is all of these things. As CB writes, "we added a civic dimension to the logistics of people movement by adding extra areas for purposes other than just pedestrian flow".[25] The technical issues, mainly flows and ventilation, the treatment of the roof and excavation, are negotiated to create a "public park". A park that hyperbolizes the impossibility of a centre, a hierarchy, or a finish: everything is a fringe, a gap, an interstice, a residual. Everything is the sculptural-other. RL writes: "After the handover, the fields of architecture, urbanism and heritage have all become essential in the struggle for identity and equality issues in Macau, taking centre stage in many social debates".[26] These strategically diverse interventions are a decisive contribution to the creation of Macau's identity in the post-handover period. What comes next?

2049

In the projects he carried out in Macau, Manuel Vicente sought to bring other arts and worldviews into architecture, particularly cinema, by recreating a sense of drama that combated the "anonymity" to which the beloved "abstraction" of trivialised modern architecture had led. "Form must follow fiction", in Heinrich Klotz's ironic words. Rui Leão and Carlotta Bruni had to take the opposite path, one might say, finding architecture in the midst of technocratic briefs, but in any case full of the fictional fever with which the government and casino authorities map out Macau's future. MV designed buildings pretending that they were still architecture, when they were something else. RL and CB take the opposite route, by trying to establish a living form of architecture in an almost surreptitious way, in the face of density in height, width and horizon, flows and statistics—as we have seen, without the nostalgia for the "archetype" or the naivety of imagining an anthropological "place" in "land reclamations."

Macau's political, economic, cultural, and social circumstances in the 21st century, as it adapts to the premises of global China, even as a "Special Administrative Region", lead to an architecture that necessarily reflects them. RL and CB therefore make an extraordinary intermediation between the gigantism of the '"mainland China" models, the best "iconographic" examples of recently arrived contemporary architecture, and the

Macau doesn't have a predominant cultural model. People learn to suspend judgment as they learn to live in the presence of another culture that may be predominant in some context in an overall shared space. This kind of freedom, typical of multi-cultural societies, allows for each group to retain its identity and co-exist with others'[28].

They're both correct, but the so-called years of "limbo" (1999-2049) will be decisive in establishing Macau's "post-colonial" identity; a particular "metabolism"

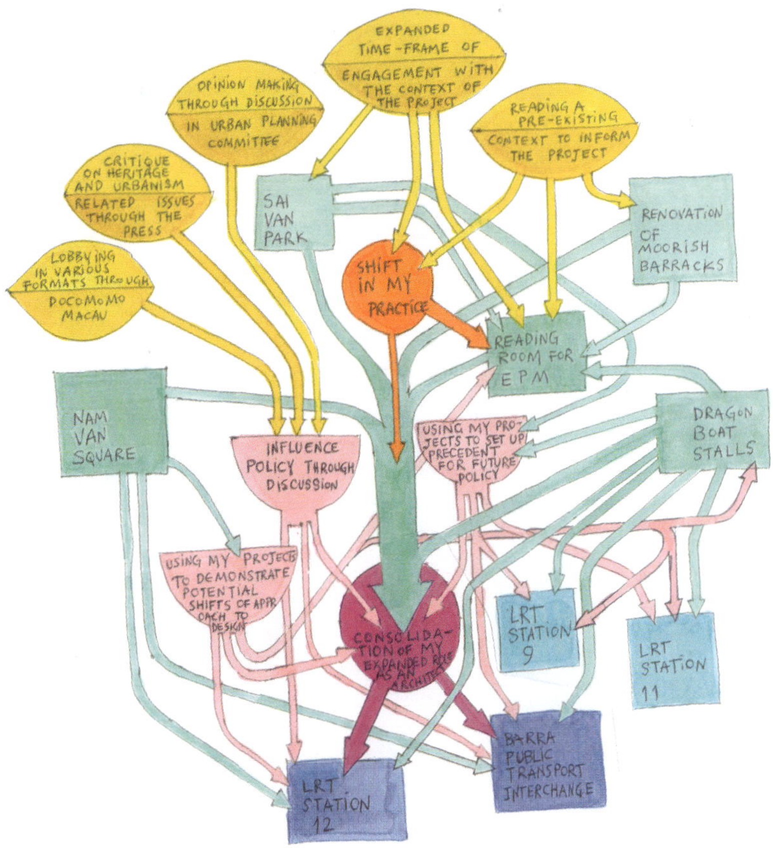

© Rui Leão

training they assertively expose in their reflections, as I was able to highlight.

It's interesting to see how, in that regard, CB has harsh words to share about the culture of "profit" that governs Macau, which she goes so far as to deem "cannibalism",[27] while RL prefers to emphasize the territory's cross-cultural, historically hybrid availability, now exacerbated by globalist movements in a struggle against nationalist ones: "Like all post-colonial territories,

between infrastructure and architecture has by now been made evident, one possible definition of RL and CB's work. Traditionally, infrastructure tends towards the generic and architecture towards the particular; here there is no such predictability, no order, no hierarchy, and the resulting entropy, as I said at the beginning, needs to be "caressed".

Macau's "metabolist" condition means that dimension is always larger than it should be and always smaller than it needs to be. Here, "scale"—shattered as a concept by the American 20th century—has an even more unstable definition: are we talking about the streets and buildings that RL claims to know one by one;[29] or the Venetian, the "second largest casino in the world", or the Salvador Dalí sculpture outside the MGM Grand Macau?

It is unavoidable to conclude that the irrepressible "iconic" vocation of RL and CB's work is a response to a territory that is itself becoming cartographic iconography, with the succession of land reclamations, bridges, and strips. In particular, the Barra PTI/LRT Station 12 projects transcend the immediate locality of what was previously known as Bairro da Barra, and aim for an "iconographic" global quality, densifying density, fragmenting fragmentation, challenging entropy to coalesce into a design.

Is this the translation of a "post-colonial" condition, or just literal eccentricity in the manner of the best and most eccentric contemporary architecture?

Going into the history of architecture just for a moment, it's possible to imagine that Macau's casinos, especially the American ones, are a literal translation of the postmodernism that erupted in the 1980s, like a tsunami followed by a fire. In that sense, RL and CB's projects would be like to a throwback to the radical architectures of the 1960s, without a "face," without a "scale", eruptions and calligraphies sprung from the ground—the "utopia of quantity" instead of the "utopia of quality." (Archizoom).

But, of course, we're not in the history of architecture. We're in a future being designed by Rui Leão and Carlotta Bruni in Macau, which we're following with excitement—waiting for "2049," the real second *Blade Runner*, a sequel and the end of "limbo" (which will go on enduring).

1 Carlotta Bruni, "Shaping Macau's un-purposed space. Design in context" (thesis, RMIT University, 2019), p.57.
2 See Jorge Figueira, "Arquitectura em Divagação. Manuel Vicente em Macau", *Review of Culture, Macau*, "Cultural Heritage", 50 (2015), pp.72–83. Jorge Figueira, "Manuel Vicente: Pop goes Asia!" In *Macau: Reading the Hybrid City, Discovering Manuel Vicente*, coord. Rui Leão (Macau: Docomomo Macau, 2016), pp.14–17.
3 Leão, "Re-programming infrastructure for public space," p.8.
4 Ibid., p.264.
5 Eric K. C. Lye, *Manuel Vicente, Caressing Trivia* (Hong Kong: MCCM Creations, 2006).
6 Leão, "Re-programming infrastructure for public space," p.49.
7 Ibid., p.91.
8 Ibid., p.191.
9 Ibid., p.215.
10 Bruni, "Shaping Macau's un-purposed space," p.18.
11 Leão, "Re-programming infrastructure for public space," p.88.
12 Bruni, "Shaping Macau's un-purposed space," p.9.
13 Leão, "Re-programming infrastructure for public space," p.16.
14 Bruni, "Shaping Macau's un-purposed space," p.20.
15 Ibid., p.44.
16 Leão, "Re-programming infrastructure for public space," p.23.
17 Ibid., p.8.
18 Ibid.
19 Ibid., p.78.
20 Bruni, "Shaping Macau's un-purposed space," p.10.
21 Leão, "Re-programming infrastructure for public space," p.96.
22 Ibid.
23 Ibid., p.128.
24 Bruni, "Shaping Macau's un-purposed space," p.154.
25 Ibid., p.211.
26 Leão, "Re-programming infrastructure for public space," p.77.
27 Bruni, "Shaping Macau's un-purposed space," p.137.
28 Leão, "Re-programming infrastructure for public space," p.15.
29 Ibid., p.16.

4. Infrastructural urbanism: Agendas for an opportunistic planning

By Rui Leão

The process of reclamation in Macau is critical for us, because it is rich in opportunities to redeem the city of its faults and gaps through a process of accretion, through which informal interventions agglomerate over and around the infrastructure.

Our projects are part of our opportunistic incremental planning approach, mostly located along the edges of newly reclaimed land, where the projects represent opportunities to retrofit, re-program, landscape, and micro-plan the raw territory of the reclamation.

We understand the Chinese Central Government's policy of One Country, Two Systems[1] and the 50 years of integration into mainland China as a process of integrating regional planning agendas in the territory of the Pearl River Delta in order to optimize the urban and infrastructural integration of Macau and Hong Kong into the so-called Great Bay Area of the Pearl River Delta.

Rui started to write about regional integration, looking beyond the border of Macau, something that was non-existent for any non-Chinese in the immediate post-handover period. This led to an invitation from the Macau SAR Government to write on urban strategy and long-term urban policy, whereby he started to reflect on policy and regional urban integration. Most of the projects that we have selected in this publication are built inside the Praia Grande Bay masterplan, which is defined as a sensible urban gesture, comprehending the dialogue that it established with old Macau and the different scales of the lots, thus providing the resolution of scales that was both possible and needed for the urban development of the city at that time.

Over the past 22 years, through a process of add-ons to the city fabric, the work produced by our practice in Macau has developed as an opportunistic urbanism adapted to the implemented reclamation masterplans for the south of the peninsula of Macau. It has built up invaluable design knowledge and examples, which in turn has established new territory from which further civic and public spaces are realized through the projects. We work using methods to design an elastic, opportunistic model of practice that facilitates a complex layering of intent onto the projects to add value to the civic realm of Macau, provide examples for future practitioners to deal with the confrontation of the water and the integration of large infrastructure projects into the fabric.

Through design and through agency, we have been addressing the development of Macau based on our urban vision, consisting of a set of urban agendas which we graft onto our commissioned projects. The projects demonstrate how change can come about in Macau and denote the urgency with which these urban agendas need to become the policy for future urban planning. The awards that we have received for the projects serve the role of validating our urban agendas as a response to the current urban planning challenges—addressing the opportunities of shifting towards a responsible infrastructural urbanism, inclusive of peoples' daily needs, their mobility, socializing and recreation.

We have *a vision for the public realm*: to create as many opportunities as possible to slot more and better public space into the projects to expand its civic realm, making each site work for the city in a context where development is led by developers not interested in the civic and institutional dimensions of urban space and decision-makers who lack the understanding that producing architecture means setting out a basic framework for the culture of the city.

For each of our urban agendas, we utilize a set of different *urban and political strategies*, which we build onto the projects and beyond them, in order to implement these urban agendas, as we have found that design is not enough to respond to the potential of large-scale public commissions in Macau. In the context of Macau, practitioners may be better equipped to understand how policy can best adapt to the city, but when addressing typical large-scale design briefs, designers are systematically being asked to respond to the wrong questions, on the wrong sites, with unsuitable frameworks. We had to *become political* to gather the tools and to use our projects as a contribution to the social and environmental response that the city and its condition demands.

We use these agendas to make opportunities out of different and unrelated project commissions and articulate an evolving urban system that uses architectural moves and scales to insert new programmatic infrastructure, adding a layer of public space to the whole set of almost contiguous sites. What connects the projects conceptually is their ability to operate incrementally in a physical and chronological dimension, by being open and proposing new agendas for the future of the site context and by allowing for a large degree of interpretation over time because of their non-purpose-specific nature.

DIALOGUE BETWEEN NEW AND OLD

We are *reconciling the old and new Macau*, reflecting on how the historic city makes use of space and what makes it work, and trying to bring those qualities into our projects. There is also the issue of resolving the contiguity of the Chinese and the Portuguese urbanisms, which in Macau have coexisted as different bodies in collision, but which can have new expressions in the new territories and scale of the city.

With each project, we respond to a larger set of issues that speak back to the city's fabric—a city struggling to deal with the challenges that it faces, a city still coming to terms with the importance of procuring architecture as a response to social, cultural, and urban policy.

To articulate between the new and the old is to understand how the pre-existing context can be re-signified through its relation to the new presence of the project.

When we were commissioned to design the landscape under the Sai Van Bridge, our first concern was what could be done to mitigate the negative impact that the infrastructure would have on its surroundings. We understood the commission as an opportunity to intervene and mediate the impact of the infrastructure, which had just been erected. We realized that by curating the site in section and choosing the places where people walked and stayed, the system of viaducts could be used as framing devices and could have new uses to provide protection from the sun and rain for the future users of the park.

More importantly, we thickened the floor from its flat configuration at street level to produce a topography that created platforms at many levels and made landscaped pockets cut away from the noise and sunlight. This new topography was rigorously shaped to allow for walking under the viaducts, a basic infrastructural requirement for pedestrians and joggers, making the overscaled viaducts useful, and thus good, through this new human usage of the site.

We worked to *rediscover the civic dimension of the water space*[2], through a designed integration of infrastructure, architecture, and landscaping. Here *the new reclaimed land works like an organic extension of the old waterfront* and *infrastructure is an opportunity to create complex public realms* for urban life to happen and be generated, liberating the community from its daily struggles of overcrowding and lack of spaces to socialize and dwell.

THE ARCHITECT AS AN AGENT OF CHANGE

We have come to realize that Rui Leão's involvement with various networks and different interest groups form part of our strategy to influence policy and agendas related to urban planning, architecture, and heritage policy. Rui's network is a lever for pushing for policy that allows the practice to succeed in innovation, setting precedence for both the community of designers and for policymakers, for whom our design works as a proof of achievable standards.

His advocacy on and off the projects is a contribution to a city whose society was not prepared to deal with the complexity of its political agenda in the period of its integration with China and the huge development associated with this. He took a step forward when he understood that his advocacy and lobbying roles and our agenda as designers are part of a same strategy of action that builds resilience and an expanded field for the projects.

The Dragon Boat Stalls project is a good example of this. It demonstrates our ability to form precedent in Macau, developing strategies to create alternative forms of spatial occupation for public space within a specific functional brief, and by adding important functional layers to the project, like the car park, the coach parking, the wooden deck and the rooftop promenade, which have an exponential uses when articulated into an integrated sectional organization, where they transcend their functional role to become part of a totally new urban proposition. **(p. 173: Dragon Boat Stalls)**

The Dragon Boat Stalls project takes the sectional articulation of the two linear pedestrian levels and transforms them into a covered civic space by adding a large roof; a third, sunken level for a bus terminus; and a fourth, raised level as a viewing deck. Here we were acting as agents of change. In more recent commissions, we have seen the result of this dialogue as some of the design tactics from Dragon Boat Stalls started to become policy for newly commissioned large-scale infrastructure in Macau, and part of some of our future client's briefs in later projects like LRT Station 9 and Station 12 and Barra PTI.

© Serena Bruni

INTEGRATING INFRASTRUCTURE

We want to *integrate infrastructure* successfully *into the urban fabric* of the city, and use the projects to demonstrate how the briefs can operate on any given site to incorporate new design programs by expanding the main functions of infrastructure with additional architectural implementations that resolve the tie-up of the scale of the program onto its site context with added civic space modalities. The scale of the infrastructure usually has leeway to allow smaller spatial agendas that we undertake as autonomous design briefs responding to typically un-commissioned social concerns.

The initial proposition for the Nam Van Square project had an improbable brief to design a square inside a traffic node and a highway alignment. Our proposal for the project takes full control of the design of the roads and viaducts, making them act with the space and become part of the architecture of the place. Our response is proof that almost any place can be occupied and interpreted as public urban space. We learned with this project that a top-down commission of a formal program could be questioned and re-elaborated into a process of negotiation. **(p. 41: Nam Van Square)**

In the Nam Van Square project, the commission of the square coincided with the planning for a new bridge to the islands, which implied an increase in the road profile. The causeways had to be enlarged and the roads had to be pushed to the side so that the bridge could fit in the center. This meant that the intersection had to adapt, so we added lanes and made the site bigger by pulling out the roads and increased their radius to have faster traffic. The roundabout was enlarged and overlapped the edge of the lake at the lower level. It was a real challenge to design a piazza in the midst of a major road intersection. Instead of making further reclamation for the new roads, we planned a set of flyovers, which we then designed. The flyovers define a new typology of space where the infrastructure creates a series of architectural layers. When designing these flyovers, in section, we pushed the structure as much to the center of the structure as possible, so that the viaduct could be used as a roof, rather than an underside of a beam. As a result, we discovered the possibilities of working with infrastructure, and realized that we have to design the actual Infrastructure in order to make architecture out of an infrastructural function, to make it meaningful in the civic realm as an urban event.

The Nam Van Square project shows how we added the civic to this new area of the city, by integrating the Macau Tower into the urban fabric and creating a notional sense of place. With this first commission for a public space amidst this road system, we saw the possibility to engage with this new infrastructure around the Nam Van lakes through the design of appropriate civic architecture.

We discovered during the process, that if we could design a public space in a roundabout, we could do much more. This set out our future agendas.

In the Sai Van Lake Park project, we discovered that by filling up the structural base of the pre-existing revetments we could add a continuous walkway along the whole perimeter of the lake front. We just filled up the structural base of these revetments on all the extensions of the causeway, creating a walkway aligned with the water level and with this, the existing linear promenade along the old fort was mirrored to define a new walking experience along the Sai Van Lake.
(p.51: Sai Van Lake Park)

INCREMENTAL PLANNING

As a result of our expanded role with the city, we build up a position that is more than design. Because we have grown into and become accustomed to this culture of constant negotiation and advocacy, our work is a consequence of the absence of a planning policy. Where most designers follow by example and work from a masterplan, in Macau, we developed a masterplan through the individual projects that we were commissioned with, and a more incremental strategy than the usual top-down and predetermined approach, where each project is individual but not treated on a case-by-case basis.

We make use of incremental design strategies to propose new ways of connectivity, alternative modes of inserting the new infrastructure of the city into the lagoon reclamation—always with a desire to make the city by incorporating the old and new. This process of informally planning the infrastructure and landscaping has resulted in an intense sequence of public spaces, reflecting the culture of density of usage that all urban plots are subject to in Macau. The novelty of the density and layering of our water's-edge projects is that it deals with voids and the invention of new ways to decompress and heal the lack of socially scaled public space, and the opportunity to interpret in the new reclaimed land the typologies of urban space that are congenial to the people of Macau based on the observations on how they use public space in the historic city.

This was very evident in the Dragon Boat Stalls project, where the brief only called for a simple public stall for the dragon boat races, and where we managed—through a series of negotiated moves—to add architectural features that added up to a large-scale multi-use infrastructure able to handle festivals, open markets, live concerts, and multiple parking lots.

Incremental planning strategies are taken as a deep approach in the design of the LRT Station 12 where the building's roof becomes an autonomous public park. We designed the station as an overlap of two infrastructures: the train station running underground, and its connection to the ground floor piazza, and a roof park infrastructure, creating a new car-free urban layer running across the district. The landscaped roof was not designed as a green occupation of the roof, but rather assumed as a topography, with different levels that connect it to the PTI rooftop shops to the west, to the lower level of the piazza in the east, and across the road towards the waterfront park. By covering the entire footprint of the station with a public park, this incremental function of the building reconciles the initial impact of the building's footprint, where two thirds of the area houses inaccessible ventilation equipment and the station atrium occupies only a third of the building's footprint. **(p.79: LRT Barra Station 12)**

MAKING LAND

We want to refocus Macau's civic dimension onto its water's edge, as the city's organic and ritualistic interaction with the water has progressively been eliminated through a sequence of land reclamation offsets, which have repeatedly erased the urban typologies of interface between the people and the water. These are never understood as significant cultural marks, leading to the effacement of people and their rituals with the waterfront. This can be resolved through curating the design of new reclaimed land and using the opportunity of the extension of land to re-evaluate the section of the existing spaces and reassess their use. We are designing the reclaimed land as an extension of our projects, focused on the sectional articulation with the pre-existence and working to make the new reclaimed mass a rework extension of the urban space before it.

We figured out that we have been using every project to test and relate our thoughts around the design work with our urban visions, aiming to expand the framework of architecture. This has allowed us to negotiate and curate the projects from a set of points of view which contribute to making significant shifts on the briefs, the impact and the scope of the projects—expanding the briefs, the intervention sites, and the wider discussion on the urban approach to infrastructure, leading to an expanded role for the architect.

The system of public space and parkland designed by our practice along the shores of the two lagoons of Sai Van and Nam Van constitutes an architectural experience at the city scale that added roughly 40 percent of open and accessible public space to the peninsula of Macau. The elements of the water and the roads, which delineate the project sites, have been understood far beyond the status of their limited sites. The water, unreachable until then, was used in the projects to connect people to a phenomenological territorial dimension—becoming a collective, vital space. Our projects have reworked the platforms of the causeways along the southern reclamations of the peninsula, where only roads existed previously, to include systems of spaces that recover the territory for the infrastructure to the walking public, so that both types of user can use and occupy the territory.

These linear parks have incrementally been extended around the perimeter of the whole Sai Van Lake, connecting the old districts with the new causeway park. They work to restore to the city its past glorious qualities of sociability, which have been lost in the current process of globalization brought about by the rescaling of the gambling industry. **(p.51: Sai Van Lake Park)**

1 The principle that defines the political ambit of the Special Administrative Regions of Hong Kong and Macau in the context of the People's Republic of China, under a centralized single-party governance on the remaining continental territory of mainland China.

2 The connection with the water is the primordial relationship that both the Chinese and the Portugese established culturally within the territory of Macau

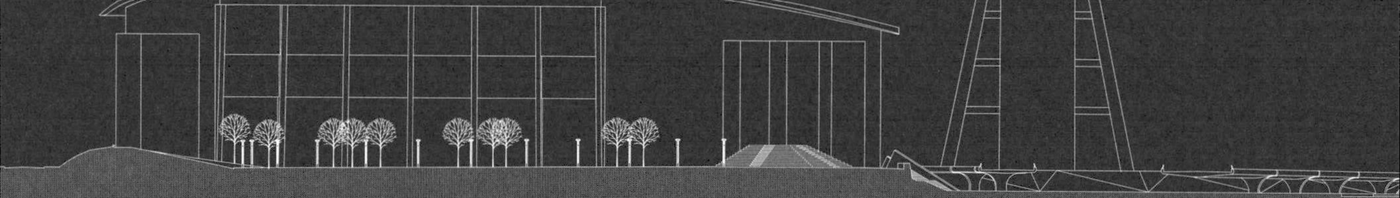

4.1. NAM VAN SQUARE (SAI VAN LAKE)

DESIGN DATE	GROSS FLOOR AREA
2001	**30,600m²**

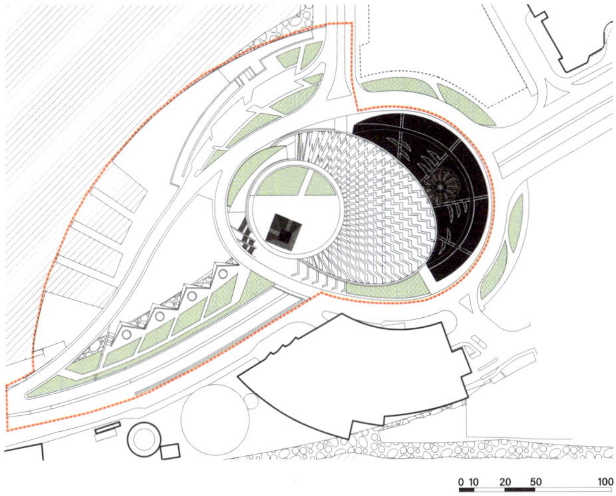

The site is a roundabout located at the crossing of the two main roads of the Nam Van reclamation, with a highway passing below it, an intersection at grade, and to the west of a high-speed traffic bridge under construction. Apart from the specific request to mitigate the impact of the traffic infrastructure of the new Sai Van Bridge on the future square site, the only functional specifications in the brief were for a formal piazza, with seating across from the Macau Tower mega-screen, and a main space capable of hosting large outdoor events.

The initial proposition for Nam Van Square, to design a public space inside a traffic node and next to a highway alignment, was an improbable brief. In addition to designing the square, LBA took control of the designing of the roads and viaducts, making them become part of the architecture of the place. This architectural response is proof that almost any place can be occupied and interpreted as public urban space.

It was an opportunity to design a civic space as an anchor and a center for the future development of the whole reclamation area, and as a statement of a new identity for a city that—due to its specific size, scale, and density—has had to unfold in unconventional ways to propose public space for its new social order.

A piazza needs to get the scale and connectivity right. In the case of this site, however, the sheer amount of adjacent infrastructure meant that the traditional European models weren't an obvious typology to be transported to the project. In this project, we started to develop agile political urbanism by concurrently designing the infrastructure, the reclamation, and the public space—and by working in section as a tactic to resolve the complexity of the urban insertion of infrastructure.

The project addresses the water's edge, being the first spatial proposal in contemporary Macau to reconnect the people with the water. The square is a civic occupation of the new land reclamation which extended the leisure promenades of the old Macau waterfront into the new territory of the reclaimed causeways, stitching together the old neighborhoods and the new, reclaimed districts by developing a lower level for the square.

The traffic road network is detached from the main body of the square through two flyovers that allow for the insertion of a connective tissue between the upper and the lower square areas, where the stairs and ramps become major elements to connect across all the site levels. The flyovers become a positive presence over the pontoons at lake level because of their shaded linearity and their sculptural quality. This sectional design not only resolved the car flow but also provided shade for the platforms at lake level below.

We worked in section to liberate spaces and voids, discovering design moves to organize comfortable coexistences between the infrastructure and the people. The design of the section resolves the dense condition of different requirements throughout the site, enables more layers of use, and allows the practice to understand and act on the city and its path of transformation, leading to innovation and new policy.

In the Nam Van Square project, as mentioned above, we organized comfortable coexistences between infrastructure and people by finding ways to add more layers of use that make the site a conduit in its wider urban context.

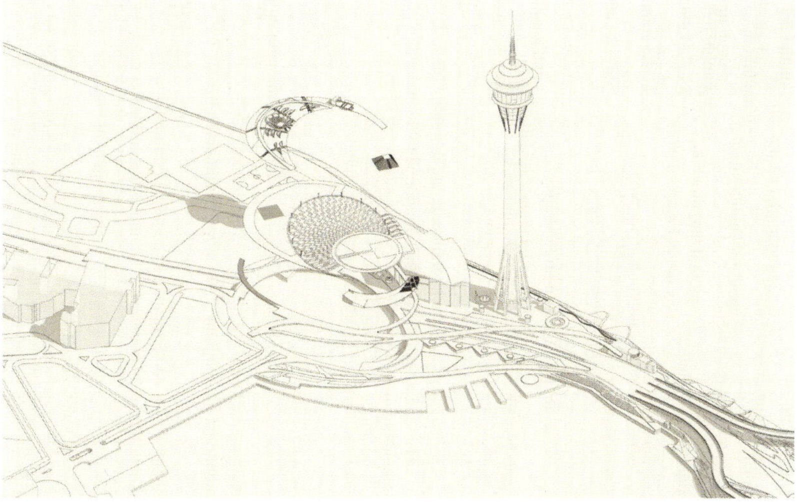

4.2. SAI VAN LAKE PARK

DESIGN DATE
2004

GROSS FLOOR AREA
42,450 m²

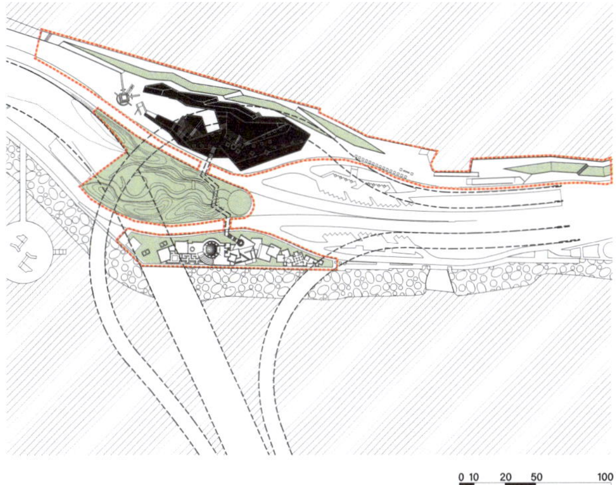

The brief given for the Sai Van Lake Park project was to embellish through landscaping the access to Macau's third bridge crossing to Taipa. Macau, like most cities in the Global South, is in a process of improving its main infrastructure systems to optimize accessibility and expand its regional footprint; as a result, the urban fabric is full of voids left over by infrastructures that aren't reclaimed by the city for other uses.

The intervention fell on the unconnected strips lying between the lanes of the ring road, under the flyovers that connect to the new bridge platforms. There was no agenda for the public's utilization of these areas in the original commission. LBA wanted to prove that public spaces could coexist with the raw infrastructure: our proposal for the park was to make a place for people amongst a highway environment; thus the project became about domesticating the infrastructure and converting the site for public usage.

Spaces around large infrastructure often become barriers because the infrastructure cuts across the territory, limiting possible appropriations of the leftover spaces which don't have the scale to be developed separately. The site was unique, with two stretches of water, the lagoon, and the river, parallel to the park's longitudinal side. We saw the project as a crossing point to link these two unconnected shores. We wanted to design a crossing, a connection between the two shores, that would be part of the park experience to further mitigate the strong presence of the cars' movement: we created a human-made topography to thicken the floor, allowing a smooth transition between the park and the pedestrian overpass and giving it a scale to domesticate the bridge infrastructure that had been designed by traffic engineers too close to the delicate historic skyline of old Macau.

We made use of section to separate people flow from the traffic, taking the pedestrians to a higher level where the views open up towards the outer landscape of the lake and river; the moving cars below thus become part of the scenery. The pedestrian territory is a complementary system of lively spaces away from traffic, to be appropriated by people walking through the site. The park is an inclined sequence of spaces, with high platforms on both sides of the road stepping down towards the water. On the higher platforms, the project is topped with a pedestrian flyover crossing the highway from one water body to the other. On the river side, the water could not be accessed and the project had to be cut off at street level due to typhoon impacts and the lack of legislation on territorial waters; but on the lake side, we took the park right up to the water level. LBA lowered the levels and pushed the land mass towards the lake with a composition of triangulated planes that organize a system of ramps and platforms along the lake. These replaced the dull, horizontal line of the bridge reclamation dike. The design of the raised pedestrian floor is an artifice of hiding and transforming the expressway into a sunken space and reducing the size of the Sai Van bridge viaducts, which was a successful strategy to make the whole infrastructure less imposing on this delicate historic location at the southern tip of the Macau Peninsula.

The resulting design is another urban hybrid: a park surrounding a highway. It is LBA's tribute to the local strategies of exploitation of space and the capacity of adaptation to atypical conditions; it resulted in the transformation of a nondescript space into a public place where we offered varied spaces to allow for several types of occupation, from fishing to jogging.

Demolished part

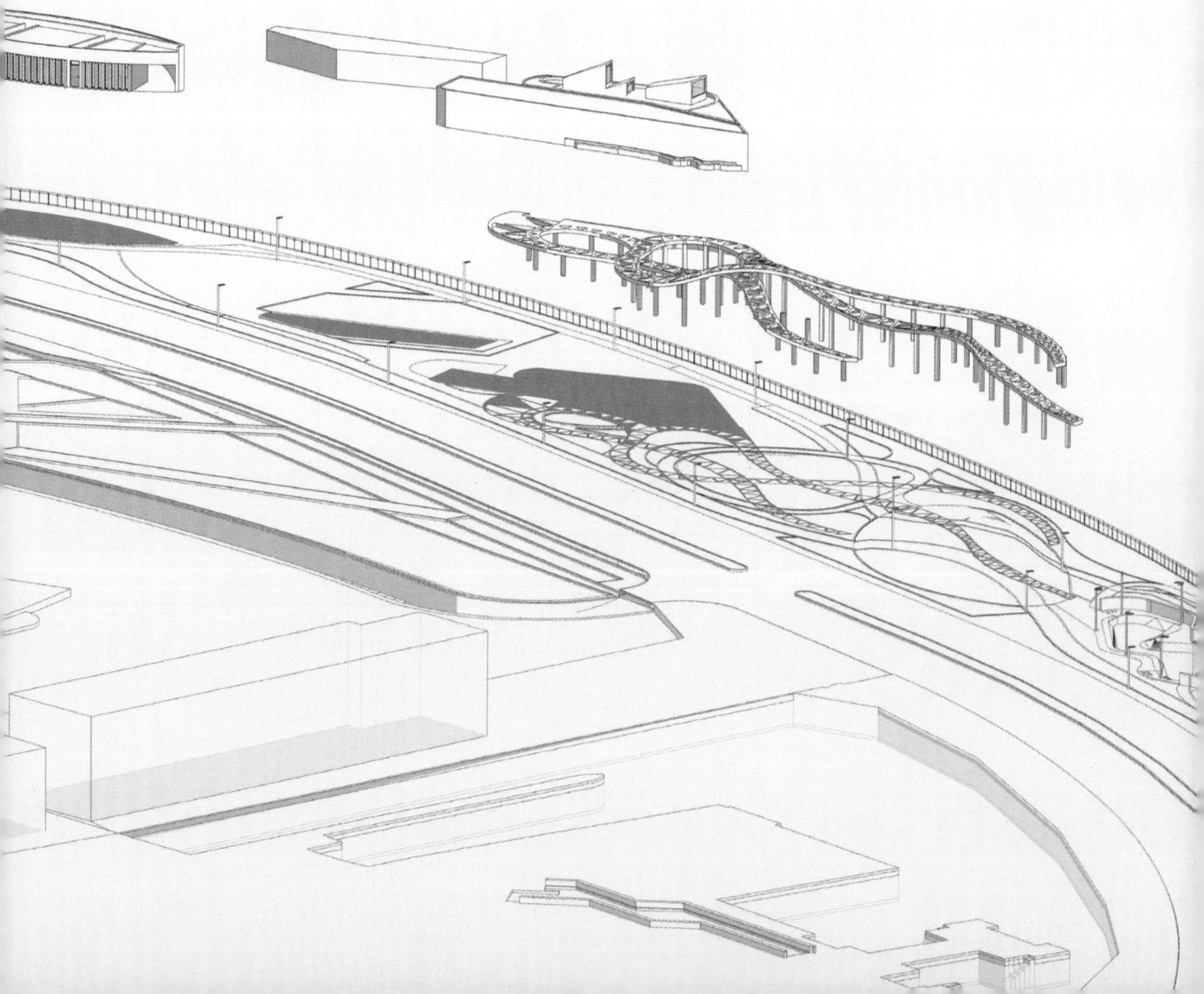

4.3. BARRA WATERFRONT PARK

DESIGN DATE
2015

GROSS FLOOR AREA
14,935m²

The site is located in the coastal zone of Barra facing the shipping canal and Wan Chai Island. Towards the south, it is connected to Sai Van Lake Park; to the north, the site extends to Rua do Almirante Sérgio and A-Ma Temple square. The Macau circular high-speed road of "Avenida Panorâmica do Lago Sai Van" separates the site from the main pedestrian urban network.

The site presented significant constraints of public access, with only one connection to the city at its northern end. During the design stage, LBA proposed two overpasses to connect to the three-dimensional pedestrian network designed at Station 12 and Barra PTI, to extend the concept of seamless pedestrian movement from the transportation hub to the waterfront park. Not part of the design brief, these proposed connections would improve the accessibility of the three government projects in the district and transform the the riverfront, lakefront, and new landscaped areas into an integrated park at a city scale for its location and articulation with respect to Station 12 and the Barra PTI. This urban park could become an example of a panoramic leisure park slotted through a transport hub complex.

The intervention is divided into three areas. The first one to the north is a stretch of promenade facing the small pond of the Maritime Museum and connecting the A-Ma Temple square to the future Station 12 and PTI through the proposed overpass. The second one, in the middle, is the main intervention area where all the programmatic features of the design are located. It corresponds to a long curve of waterfront edge facing the river at the southwest. This strip of land has a very irregular depth, ranging from 31 meters to only 5.5 meters at its southern tip. This presented the design with the challenge of how to distribute the programmatic functional areas; how to provide passage for strolling, jogging, and cycling; and how to define the different garden and leisure areasareas. The third area, to the south, comprises the land beside the access to the new Sai Van Bridge and a stretch of riverfront walkway connecting to Sai Van Lake Park at its southern end.

In order to separate the functional areas, and create intimate clusters and a variation in the views and experiences of the users through the park, LBA organized the site with a series of naturalistic hills that define the main feature of the garden area, enhancing the presence of the planting, acting as a focal point for people walking along to Station 12. The main functional areas of the park are located in the valleys. The riding and jogging tracks run up and down the hills to allow for exercise with varied intensity.

Located above the hill garden, the pergola generates shadow along several pathways, creating a Chinese garden-type of experience with a comfortable shade from pergola and trees. Additionally, the wavy pattern of this tentacle-pergola will become a visual focal point for drivers on the main road or canal-boaters.

Dotted throughout the park are cafés, public toilets, a public events area, skateboarding track, dog exercise area, children's playground and gardens.

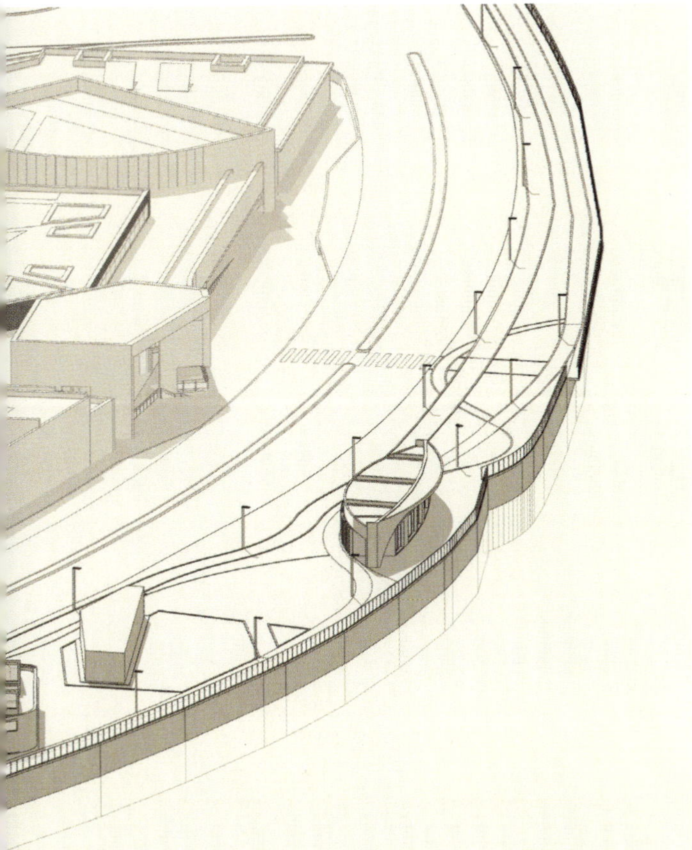

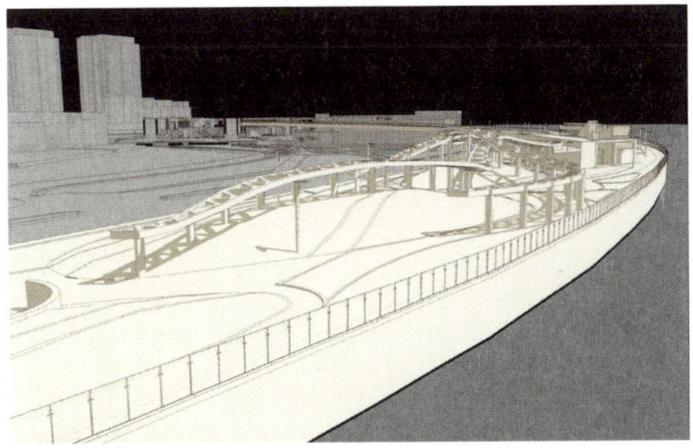

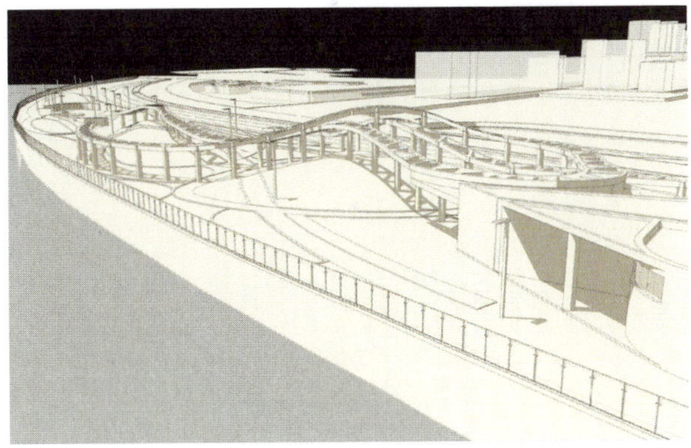

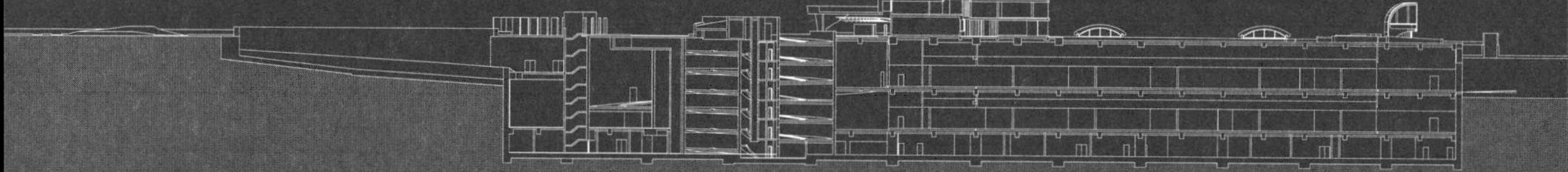

4.4. BARRA PUBLIC TRANSPORT INTERCHANGE (PTI)

DESIGN DATE
2013

GROSS FLOOR AREA
38,225m²

The Barra site is an area of historical urban discontinuity. Macau's two harbours used to converge at this point, but were effectively separated by the topography of the site. To the south, we can find the Portuguese S. Tiago Fortress that defended the southernmost point of the peninsula and, to the west, the A-Ma Temple, one of the most important religious sites for the Chinese community. In between the two heritage sites is the D. Carlos Dockyard. The two harbors are just recently connected by land reclamation. The Barra PTI site is inserted here.

The Barra PTI is a public transport interchange for public and private buses and private cars, with a connection at first-basement to the LRT system. It is a complex building with an ambitious program: to be Macau Peninsula's main traffic interchange hub. It comprises a private car park, two public bus pick-up and drop-off halls with bus parking, and a seamless connection to the LRT line.

Due to its density and scale, Macau's planning generally lacks buffer areas for large-scale infrastructure, leading to a juxtaposition of program and scale. The Barra PTI site is one of these cases, turned into one of the main areas of the peninsula where traffic infrastructure is concentrated after becoming home to the arrival of the main deck of the Sai Van Bridge, a public transport interchange, and an LRT interchange station.

We considered the urban implications of having this type of program adjacent to the historical city and arrived at the conclusion that transportation infrastructure has to be considered as a type of public space, being a place of arrival and departure with a large concentration of travelers. We focused on efficiency and logistics on the one hand, while also trying to improve on the chronic lack of public spaces in the city by proposing spaces that could be used in ways other than their functional purpose—in other words, un-purposed: we focused on the changes that these public spaces will bring to the context and how we can un-typify them to be able to offer the city new, contemporary public areas.

Our design focus centered on emptying out the core of the site and creating an outreaching pedestrian network: by sinking the bus terminus and shifting the ventilation infrastructure to the side, we allowed the project to build around an urban void and designed the roof to incrementally unfold, to lay out a rooftop park connecting all the public buildings planned for the district. This translated into a built connecting tissue that would link the old waterfronts of the lakes to the new waterfront park and across to the old inner harbor waterfront without having to interface with the traffic flow.

The design of the main space doesn't assume this public square as a formal space, nor does it subject to a clear geometrical order, as the space is the result of a planning process and not a prerogative instructing the design. The Barra PTI square was defined as a centrality with extending walking passages in all directions. These extensions correspond geometrically to the territorial extensions towards the east, west and south. The public square is anchored on the design of these walkways that connect to it, in order to become a meeting place and a significant urban space beyond the hosting of the LRT station and the PTI and their functional interface. The urban strategy of designing these public walking corridors validates the location and scale of the square. It ties it into the urban fabric and creating a large gathering space in a place with historical significance where new large infrastructure is being introduced that will shift the scale of users and its centrality as a leisure and cultural neighborhood.

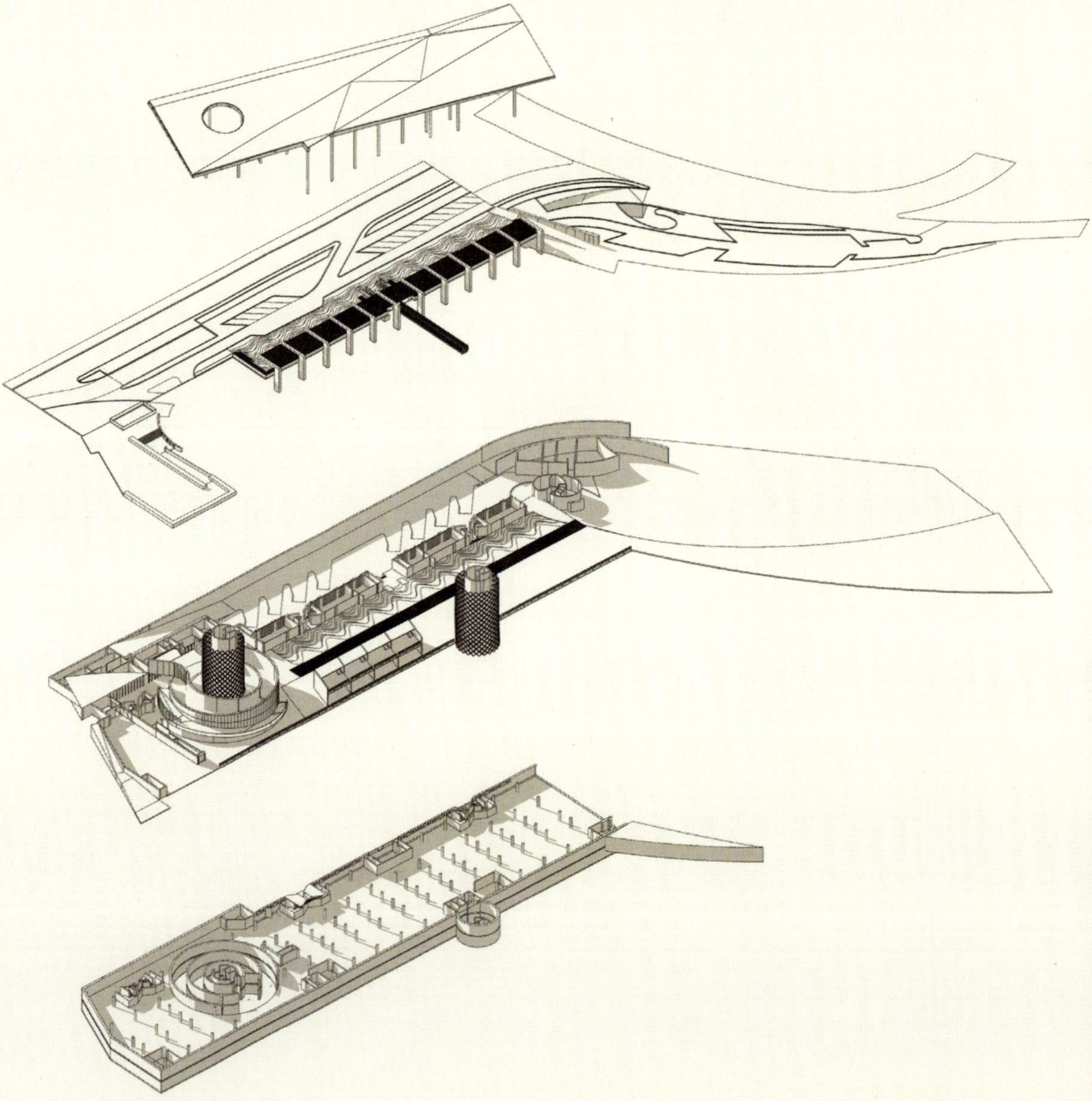

4.5. DRAGON BOAT STALLS (SAI VAN LAKE)

DESIGN DATE
2004

GROSS FLOOR AREA
19932m²

The Dragon Boat Stalls are located along Sai Van Lake on the northeast side of Nam Van Square as a natural extension of its public space program.

After the construction of the square and the commission by the government of a new fire station along the lake perimeter, we understood that it was critical to consolidate the lake's edge with leisure infrastructure to avoid any extra reclamation or appropriation by private investment. Thus we proposed to the government the design of a new public facility for the viewing of the dragon boat races on the remaining un-designed perimeter of the lake, exploring the design of infrastructure and public space concurrently.

In this case, LBA developed an innovative procurement strategy, to generate and auto-commission a civic space, with a public car park, coach parking, and retail from a very simple architectural brief for outdoor seating stalls for an ephemeral event. We decided to over-densify the design with several public facilities because we knew that these necessities would not be addressed in the future design of the private plots in the Nam Van reclamation.

In the Dragon Boat Stalls project, we took on the exercise of the sectional articulation of two pedestrian levels started with the Nam Van project and added a third, sunken level with a bus terminus and a fourth, raised level on top of the roof with the dragon boat race viewing platform. The structure of the project is a circulation diagram where the architecture works to transform the different zones and their connections into recognizable scales of spaces that are all interconnected.

We proposed a build-up of sections to relate the different spaces and create thresholds to mediate the water, the infrastructure, and the cars. In the Dragon Boat Stalls project, the focus is on working with multiple zones and developing strategies to connect the different levels of the site.

In summary, we moved the newly proposed programmatic part of the design over and below ground level—effectively stacking the program vertically, to be able to keep a free area for public use. This was an exercise of mass organization in section instead of plan, and, once again, we availed ourselves of the unleveled terrain to achieve our proposed agendas. We designed the void space in section by designing the slab of the stalls as a shading device and a large cover for the areas below, thus using the built structure not only functionally but also as a spatial device. Its shape has a double crease that is visible from underneath, which also serves to make its appearance slimmer.

The focus of the project is the large roof, projecting shadow over a considerable deck, and not the actual grandstand for the dragon boat races. The centerpiece of the project is this new space with the versatility of being used 24/7 all year round as a result of its proposition as a wide covered space, usable during both the rainy and hot tropical seasons. We used this project to create a new centrality on the lake shore. The project demonstrates LBA's ability to form precedent in Macau, developing strategies to create alternative forms of spatial occupation for public space within a specific functional brief, and by adding important functional layers to the project—like the car park, the coach parking, the wooden deck deck, and the rooftop promenade—which have an exponential use when articulated into the same sectional organization, where they may transcend their functional role to become part of a totally new urban proposition.

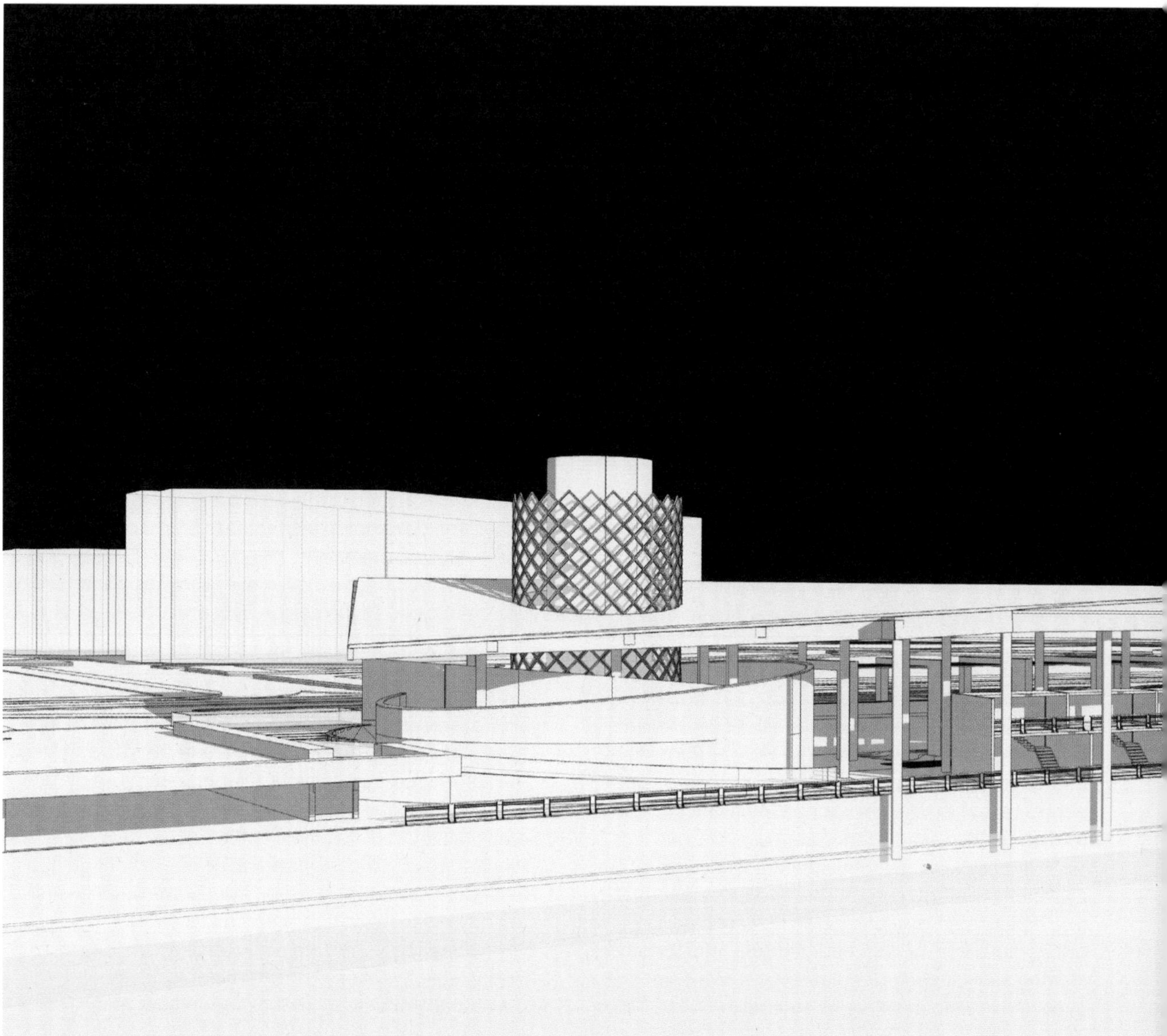

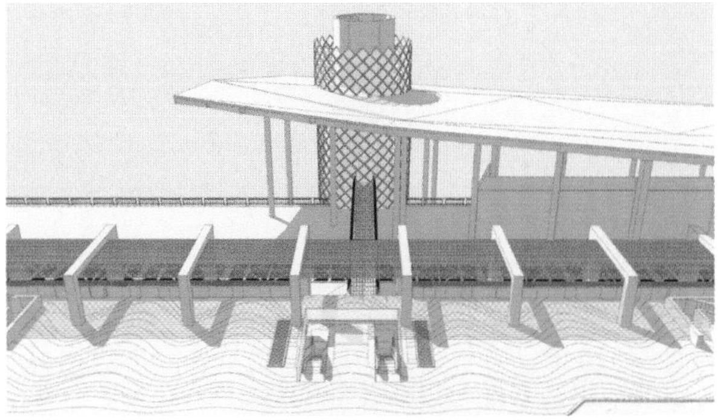

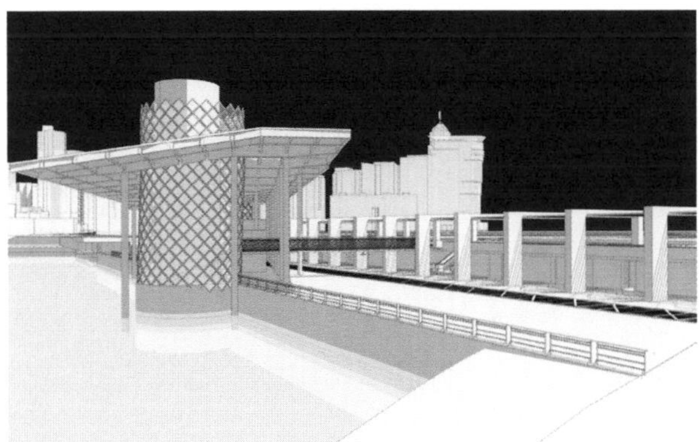

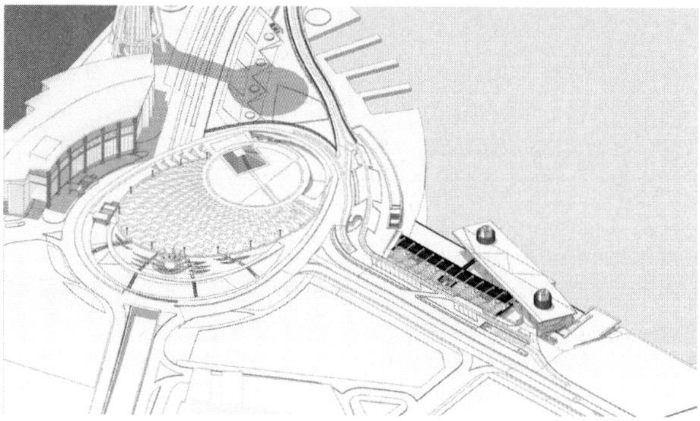

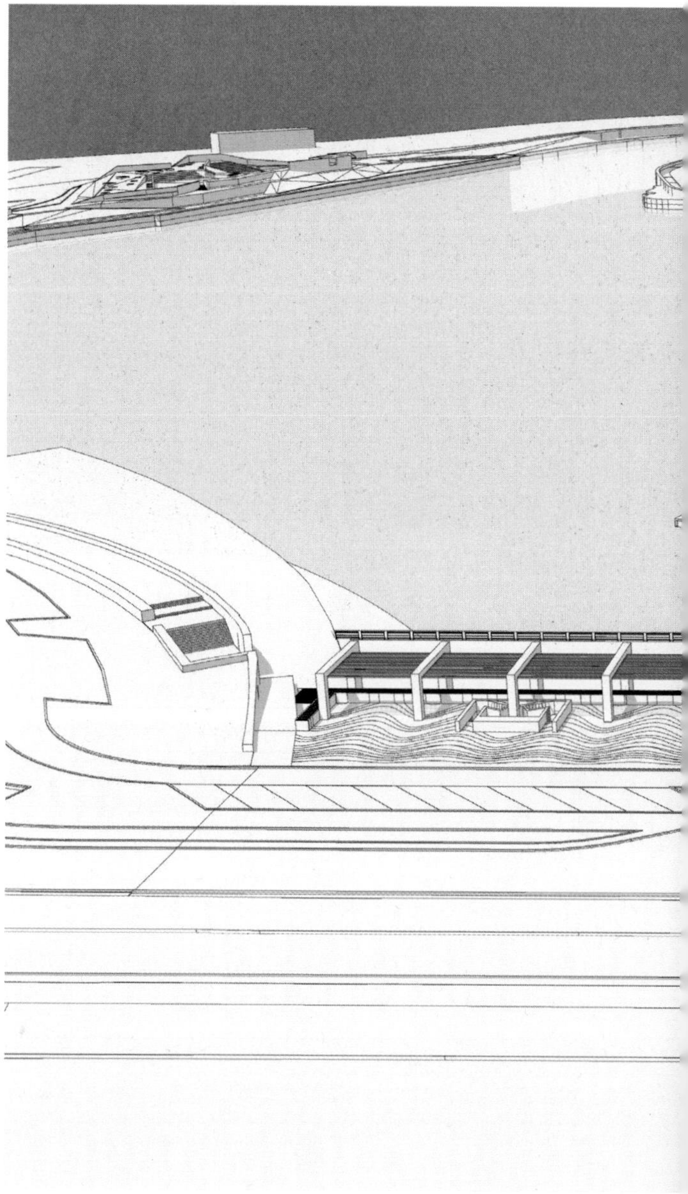

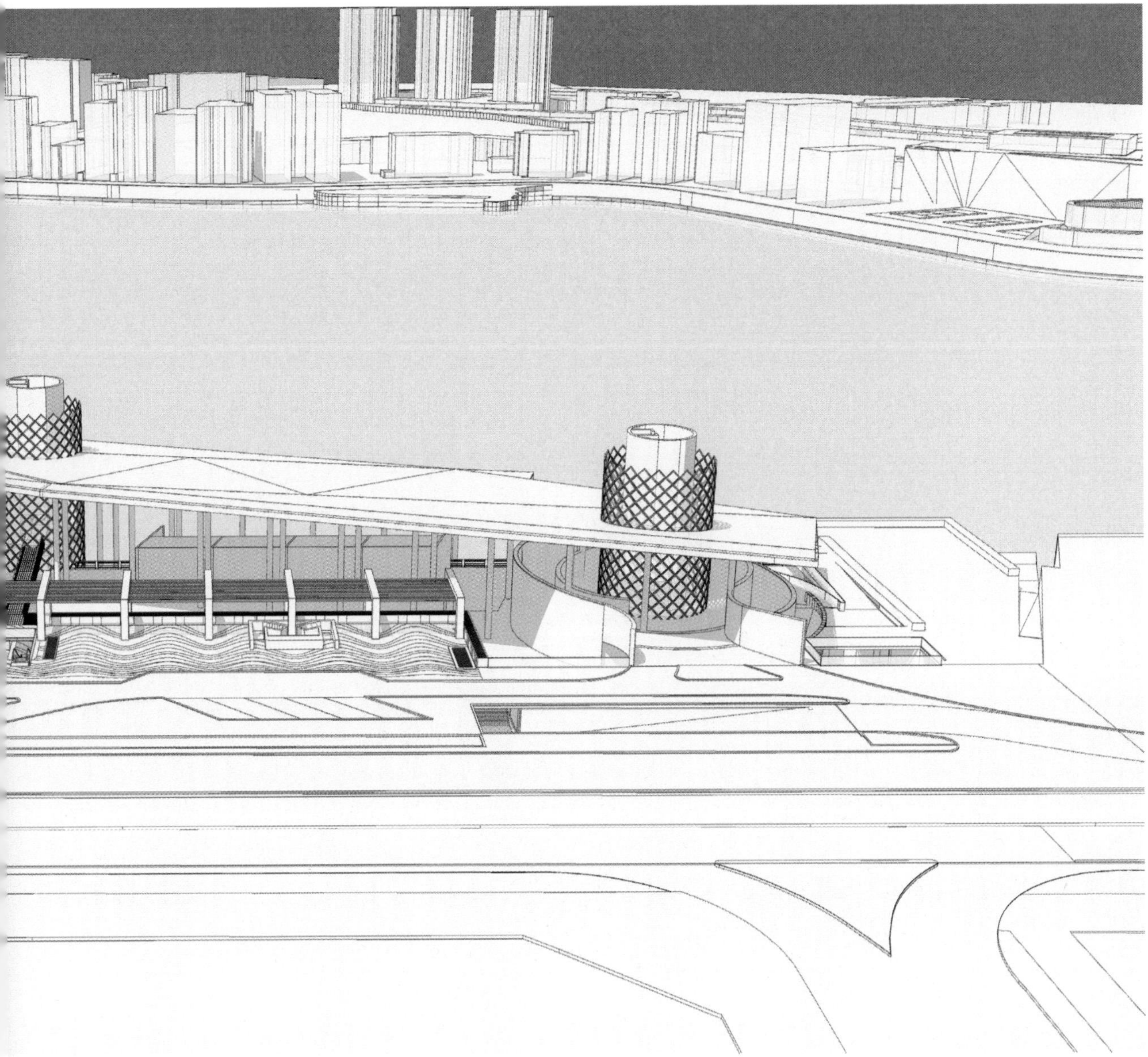

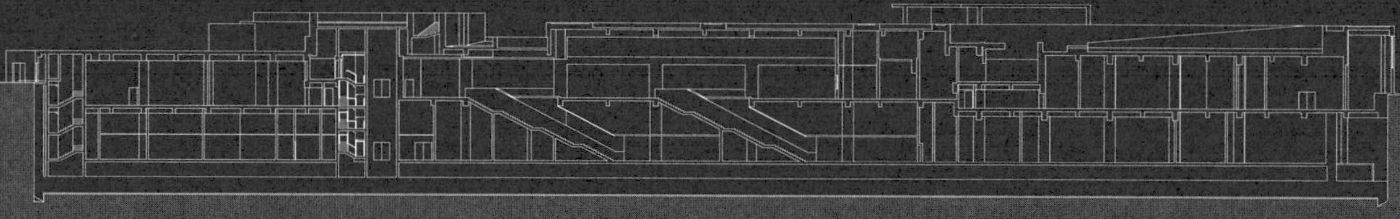

4.6. LRT BARRA STATION 12

DESIGN DATE
2017

GROSS FLOOR AREA
14,430m²

Station 12 is the terminus station of the Taipa line, located at Barra on the Macau Peninsula, and is the only underground Macau Light Rail Transit station.

The urban purpose of Station 12 is twofold: to connect the commuting population of Taipa Island to Macau's bus system, operating from the adjacent Barra PTI, and to increase accessibility to the heritage district of Barra, which is centered around the A-Ma Temple.

With the aim of improving on the chronic shortage of public spaces in the city, the design enhances the typology for public transportation infrastructure by incorporating substantial public spaces while keeping efficiency and logistics in mind. This exercise provided us with the opportunity to design both a public space and the functionalities of the building as an intertwined system.

The design for Station 12 constitutes an experiment in resilient infrastructural civic urbanism. It makes use of the main function of the building as a transportation hub to generate multiple zones for public space. It articulates the piazza designed in the adjacent PTI plot with the sunken station's atrium, and molds the station volume as a topography for an urban park that uses the roofs of both the station and the PTI to establish an independent public space layer. This is a continuous terraced garden that takes people across the whole Barra district, establishing direct access from Sai Van Lake towards the A-Ma Temple and the riverside boardwalk.

Station 12 is formalized into a three-dimensional connection building between three means of transportation—bus, metro, and pedestrian—and two areas of the city—the riverside and historical coastline. The agenda is to overlap open public spaces within the same plot in order to over-densify the public areas and allow for seamless pedestrian flow.

We designed the station as the vertical stacking of two infrastructures: below ground, the transportation infrastructure with the train platforms and concourse and its connections to the bus terminus and the ground-floor piazza; above ground, the roof park infrastructure that creates a new urban car-free layer running across the district, where the public space and the three-dimensional connectors became a programmatic part of the design.

The station concourse is the main space of interface for users. We wanted the concourse to be part of a ritual of arrival, so we sunk it two meters below the PTI square level. This vertical move, allows the project to define a grand hall with plenty of headroom for the station concourse in an otherwise small surrounding urban scale. The shift in scale from the station atrium to the PTI piazza has this effect of compressed space, as a strategy to receive hordes of visitors and still retain a sense of void in the station atrium.

The landscaped roof is molded as a built topography; the different levels are connected by stairs and ramps that create a landscaped form of continuous and dialoguing spaces—rendering the roof a territory to be explored, with various views out towards the river and towards the hills and the heritage points on the opposite bank. The multiple points of vertical access to the ground organize a system of routes and cross paths that reconnect the roof spaces back to the piazza, to the station, to the PTI, to the taxi stand, and to the sidewalks around the site, making the roof a natural extension of the street level and the lower functional levels. Additionally, the whole roof is stepped down to piazza level on the northern side of the site, fully merging the roof garden with the main public space.

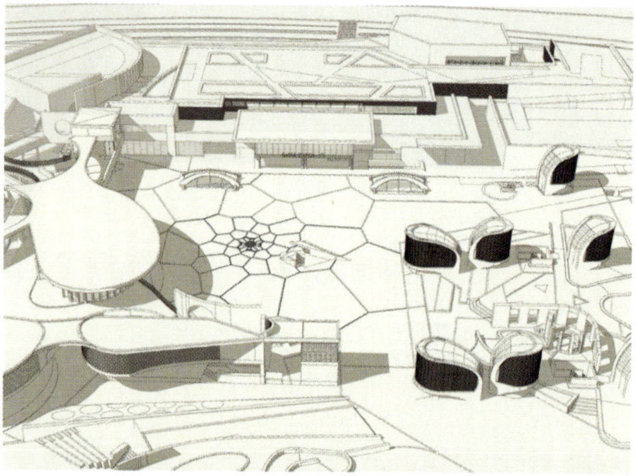

南灣 氹仔
NAM VAN TAIPA
南灣 氹仔
NAM VAN TAIPA

5.1. Free space: agendas for density

By F. Carlotta Bruni

Macau's well-documented extreme urban density (as the combination of limited land resources, profit-driven urban development, and informal strategies of public space appropriation) is the condition that has triggered LBA's main design agenda of inserting breather spaces as a typological characteristic of our designs, irrespective of the commissioned design programs.

Macau is a city-state with a fixed area established 500 years ago and no natural space for growth; territorial expansion has been historically achieved through land reclamation plans, painstakingly negotiated with China due to the fact that Macau until 2015 did not have jurisdiction over the water that surrounds it. The physical result of this historical constraint is that nowadays, Macau—namely, the peninsula—has grown to completely fill its boundaries.

The way that the population has increased in Macau corresponds to an increase in mass within a fixed volume, that is: more density. This is a literal expression of Macau's condition: a city with a fixed area and increasing population.

During the most recent city development, Macau has neglected the commissioning of urban public spaces and the integration of open common spaces into private developments to favor the greed of developers for greater gross floor area. With the rise in population (21,340 inhabitants per square kilometer) and number of tourists (35,000,000 a year), this cultural aspect of the misuse of common urban space has started to conflict with the necessity of wider, uncluttered public spaces.

The handover to mainland China in 1999 was the moment when Macau could have reassessed and redefined its urban strategy while implementing overall urban growth and tourism policies; a substantial change in the design of its public spaces might have arisen to reflect a newly found identity. This was a significant point in time for LBA because from this moment forward—starting with the design of Nam Van Square, a major post-handover public space—we began to question what would be a suitable proposal to reflect the uniqueness of a territory that was starting its post-colonial journey. We begun by studying the hybrid relationship between the Western spatial heritage of public spaces in Macau and its local type of appropriation and cultural use. From this, we postulated that this may be one of the main identity traits of the city and worked within this principle to develop a public space that could identify with this context by being at the same time monumental and informal. It could also keep the underlying discourse on the consequences of building in a dense environment visible though the negotiation of the third bridge access routes, the traffic roundabout and the pedestrian connection to the lake level.

A second turning point for the practice in relation to the understanding of extreme density in urban settings was the Fai Chi Kei Social Housing commission, a residential block for low-income occupants where we were confronted with our desire to increase the common areas in the building to overcome the lack of space of the housing units while creating a sense of community within the building. The final result is the design of an atypical podium and tower block that hosts a series of communal open spaces, from the sidewalk patios to the wide common spaces at each floor level to allow for community engagement at several levels.

The practice since then has developed a set of specific architectural strategies applied to Macau's context to achieve un-programmatic empty spaces within a fixed architectural program and to increase public space areas that have the potential to inspire the development of other architectural typologies and be applied in diverse urban situations.

When thinking of density in our designs, we immediately think of order. Maximum density within a fixed volume is achieved through the natural organization of the entities that fill that volume until there are no leftover spaces in between. The meaning of "order" that we apply in our practice to overcome the constraint of density can be explained by an experiment: empirically, when we fill up a tin with coffee beans, we usually shake it to make space for more beans. We are packing together the particles inside the tin, reducing the space between beans, making the particles fit better together. The result of a better organization is the optimization of the empty spaces in the tin. Our reaction to the density of our surroundings has been to shake the coffee beans, to organize the programmatic mass of the project in such a compact way that we can achieve sizable open spaces, instead of scattered voids, within the same volume.

Translating this experiment into an architectural strategy, we have realized through our personal experience that order and hierarchy in the design—the exercise of fitting all the programmatic parts together with an economy of corridors, halls, and connecting tissue—maximizes the free space in the design. LBA has become very good at fitting area schedules in the design and has come to understand that the purpose of this exercise is to maximize empty space within a dense environment—in other words, to create a release.

We found also two main characteristics in the traditional Macanese public space that have been inspirational to our work and have helped to unlock some of the density related strategies employed in our designs while contextualizing the architectonic exercise: the overlay of Western models on an Asian city and the attributes of Portuguese urbanism.

Regarding the first characteristic, we have observed that the local population in Macau—similarly to other post-colonized regions in Southeast Asia—is not intimidated in the appropriation of public spaces of Western typology, to the point that the free appropriation and commercial use of communal areas and public spaces is widespread; the identity and typology of the urban public space thus changes due to its use. This observation led to the development of designs that are critical of their Western-inspired typologies and propose hybrid alternatives.

On the second characteristic, Portuguese cities built on unlevelled terrain generally display a full set of creative urban typologies and strategies to overcome such differences in level; hence, is not uncommon to have buildings with two main ground floors, at two different levels, in addition to urban devices that connect different levels of the city. The organic shapes of Portuguese urban public spaces are a byproduct of building on steep terrain. The irregularity of Macau's city spaces, inherited from Portuguese urbanism (roads and squares), is itself an inspiration towards the design of a new type of urban connecting tissue that is formalized according to flow and volumetric composition and that, even if designed over flat reclaimed lands, could make use of several overlapping levels of public space in the design to simulate topographical variety.

Through these observations on Portuguese cities, we have discovered that in an overly dense environment such as Macau, where one is always negotiating how much area to assign to the given program of spaces and how much to assign to circulation and extra space, we can transform this exercise from plan view into a three-dimensional exercise—thus multiplying the communal areas over several levels.

We have consistently applied a strategy of shaping empty space to make it substantial and available to the user. One of our responses to density has been the insertion of non-programmatic public space in the projects, achieved through the mutually dependent design of mass and void.

Conscious of the distinctive characteristics of Macau's city growth, we have developed specific design strategies that respond to three main agendas. The first and most obvious agenda has been to include in each design all the necessary urban features to ensure an autonomous quality of life for the building and its immediate surroundings, given that we cannot foresee how adjacent areas will be developed. The second agenda is to consistently propose strategies to free up the ground floor for the development of common urban areas that can be easily plugged into the main city spaces such as sidewalks and squares. The third one has been to find strategies to stack common spaces vertically over the height of the buildings, to make up for the lack of space at ground floor and to foster the growth of different community usages within the buildings.

Through our projects, we wanted to demonstrate ways of finding equilibrium between built areas and public or open space, stitching a neighborhood context together through the design of public space and dignifying the designs with public and semi-public space.

ORGANIZE MASS

LBA believes that the design of a building mass is an integral part of overall city-making.

We began Fai Chi Kei by organizing the project's programmatic mass of spaces to address the lack of communal areas due to excess density in built environments. The purpose of this strategy was to free up a significant void space that could be used as common area.

At the beginning of our practice, we were using this strategy only in plan; little by little, we transformed this exercise from a two-dimensional to a three-dimensional operation inspired by the Portuguese urbanism strategies referred above. On one hand, we explore fitting the volumetric mass of the design program better within the constraints of a limited plot or a fixed, enclosed space; on the other, we find solutions to the programmatic request and expand the design to include extra non-programmatic areas at several levels.

In Macau, communal space is never accounted for in the building program, nor is it ever a government requirement for developers. However, in several of the following designs—such as the Fai Chi Kei and B10 Social Housing, and the LRT depot—the client did not object to the proposed scheme of inserting programmatic communal areas in the design, providing that the rest of the program would fit in the proposed land plot or built volume. This freedom in the commissioning of the buildings is what allowed us to explore alternatives to common housing and infrastructure typologies.

While in the Fai Chi Kei Social Housing the large communal areas are mostly interior and repeated in the same place every floor, in the B10 social housing we explored the design of hanging gardens that span 2-3 floors located randomly along the building façade. These effectively give a stronger sense of belonging and vertical neighborhood due to the differences in the floor plan of every level.

In the LRT depot, the decision to combine all the necessary functions into a single building allowed the opening up of three large courtyards on the second floor that created a natural light source and a domestic scale, in an otherwise industrial setting, for the office staff that occupy the top floor.

In all three examples, we organized the mass of the program in volumes that could embrace the open space through the clever fitting together of the programmatic areas. The void is, thus, part of the design of the volume itself, as if the volume is being designed by its mass as well as by the empty space that surrounds it.

VOLUME PLACEMENT

Sometimes the simple act of positioning a volume in space creates a very interesting change in its surrounding context and rich spatial connections between the common areas.

Every project is an opportunity to dwell on the thematic of the relationship between the given site and the overall urban situation.

The strategic placement of volumes in an open space (construction plot) can be an exercise in finding new meanings within the context of the design: the volumes are a device that helps to demarcate the empty spaces and at the same time creates spatial hierarchies and connecting tissue.

As an example of this, in the Fai Chi Kei and the B10 Social Housing, we started by creating an urban hierarchy of spaces through the simple act of positioning volumes. We used the street as a corridor and attached our patios to it as a widening of the sidewalk. We created a so-called open courtyard, a public space that belongs to the building, whose spatiality is defined by the building volume on three sides, but that also comes into direct dialogue with the surroundings.

The open courtyard, therefore, becomes an accident of space and light in an otherwise compact city continuum. Bridging the gap between a public square and a private courtyard, the resulting space is European: Italian in its form but adapted to the local informality in usage because it does not have a focal point or a specific orientation; (there are no main entrances or noteworthy urban entities to speak of).

LBA uses the composition of volumes and the placement of the building mass in space as a way to create urban spaces of different sizes and shapes, discovering that these connecting spaces, when designed with intermediate sizes and irregular shapes, can be transformed into spaces that don't belong to the standard typologies of road, square, or sidewalk. Somehow, this intermediate scale—broader sidewalks, open patios, narrow squares—gives them the quality of being spaces of free interpretation and appropriation.

This is a strategy of breaking the barrier between what is volumetric and what is spatial. It goes beyond the definition of the wall as a limit. It is a mass-versus-void relationship. Communal spaces are organized and separated by the placement and shapes of volumes and the thresholds are defined by changes in the size and scale of connectors, giving fluidity and logic to the whole design: the logic of connectivity, perspective, and phenomenology.

This is evident in the design of the CEM Dispatch Center and in the China-Lusophone Cooperation Building, where we set out to design the volume and the void simultaneously, like a yin-yang exercise to signify and intertwine public and private space through connections between interior and exterior and between buildings and their surroundings.

BUILT TOPOGRAPHIES

One of the consequences of stacking people in high-rises is that there is not enough space at street level for everybody. Designing overlapping public spaces allows us to shift some of the activities to higher ground while creating a sense of community around the shared common space.

This strategy when applied to a public building program introduces into the design the responsibility of allowing for empty areas to be designed in a way that can be appropriated by the community in a non-permanent manner. The final result is an alternative typology of porous blocks with multiple connections at several levels to bring the communal space theme three-dimensionally to the higher floors, thus enabling connections and semi-public spaces in a vertical setting.

This technique was adapted from the housing projects when we started to work with public buildings such as the IPM Library, the Tap Seac Youth Center and Macau's Central Library. In these three examples, we worked with a mass of soil and differences in level, carving and thickening as well as designing continuous vertical floors for our areas of connectivity: a set of slabs located at different heights and connected to their surroundings through ramps and stairs.
(p. 95: IPM Library; p. 121: Tap Seac Youth Center; p. 99: Macau Central Library)

The methodology used on this family of projects is three-dimensional and involves the systematic use of sections to create independent but interconnected public spaces at different levels. We discovered that it is possible to overlap open public spaces within the same plot in order to over-densify the public areas. In the typology of public buildings, the un-purposed space is partially used as a connector and partially used as a public space, with a consequent blurring of the separation between interior and exterior. The space gains in complexity with many areas that are covered but not enclosed.

In the designs for these projects, we are actively pursuing an agenda of a three-dimensional, stackable series of public spaces, taking advantage of the lessons learned from Nam Van Square and the Dragon Boat Stalls to design the empty space both in plan and in section.

PEOPLE FLOW

LBA translates the strategy of molding the surrounding space of a built volume to the urban setting to induce movement and behaviors in the user in the search for new typologies of urban spaces.

The previous strategy of building topographies leads to the overlapping of open public spaces within the same plot in order to over-densify the public areas and allow for seamless people flow. One of the main inspirations for our design were the three-dimensional pedestrian links found in Hong Kong, which are strategies for dealing with extreme density by stacking pedestrian and vehicle circulation. In the Barra PTI/Station 12 projects, however, we added a civic dimension to the logistics of people movement by adding extra areas for purposes other than just pedestrian flow.

It is a technique to inversely employ the teachings of unlevelled Portuguese urban spaces by creating a difference in level where there is only a flat surface. The lesson learned from this project was how to use section not just as a passive means to deal with the topography of the site but as an active technique for creating different levels in public space to facilitate connections and differences in use. Design-in-section became a necessary tool to achieve this result: the section is used to overcome the spatial confinement of a public space or of a city block.

In the design of the GIT Museum the technique of building topographies effectively designs the visitor flow of the museum, from the main entrance to the exit in a continuous loop.

In our urban infrastructure projects such as the LRT Station 12 and the Barra PTI, the design of the flow of people and three-dimensional connections are a deliberate strategy. We use these to overcome the inevitable conflicts of a congested environment. We avail ourselves of techniques from Portuguese urbanism combined with our own perspective on logistics management of human and traffic flows in an urban setting, joining functionality with the design of the connecting space.

The research in these cases focused mainly on formalizing passenger and pedestrian flow and how movement has created comprehensive three-dimensional dynamic designs where the strategies of carving and layering are used in conjunction with the extensive use of section. The result is a very a-typological ensemble that has the characteristics more of a land form than of a building.

OVERLAPPING FUNCTIONS

One of the observations frequently made about dense cities is that, due to lack of space, important infrastructure has to coexist with more mundane urban areas, and main urban events—such as public buildings or public spaces—have to accommodate more than one function into their design.

The idea of stackable public spaces or overlapping of functions has been developed by LBA mainly in the Macau Central Library, IPM Library, and the Tap Sec Youth Center, which were tendered just after the completion of Fai Chi Kei Social Housing. These designs were the starting point for a decisive shift in our practice towards a very different type of architectural approach: the design of layered buildings.

This possibility for multifunctional use of a single building has been inspirational and has helped us to domesticate big urban "events" such as bridges and other traffic-related infrastructure in later projects—and to make use of their presence in the design, focusing not only on their functionality but also on their spatial qualities.

The Dragon Boat Stalls was the first instance where we explored the design of infrastructure and public space concurrently. Designed in partnership with Manuel Vicente, this was a visionary proposal and a summary of our (Carlotta's, Rui's and Manuel's) agendas for the urban development of the city of Macau.

Our design idea was to organize the programmatic part of the project, both under and over ground, to be able to keep the ground level completely free for public use. The clever use of section allowed us to design an open public space on two levels, a higher one at road level and a lower one at lake level. Below the first level, we fitted a public bus parking area; below the second, a car park. The slab for the stalls is raised at a third level over the two large public levels and is oriented, at an angle, according to the dragon boat racecourse, thus creating a variation in the atmosphere of the levels below.

In summary, the newly proposed programmatic part of the design over and below ground level, effectively stacking the program vertically to be able to keep a free area for public use, this was an exercise in mass organization in section instead of plan.

This project constituted a major shift in our practice because the exercise taught us that we could overlap large public spaces, and that, in the kind of climate we have in Macau, the protection of porticoes or extensive slabs is welcomed as shelter from both rain and sun. We also learned to design voids in plan and section—a technique that convinced us that, in an environment like Macau, every design has to be an opportunity to develop not only the proposed program but also, if possible, other functionalities that can be accommodated within the design brief. We systematically bridge the gap between public space and infrastructure, and, by making use of the synergies of both programs, are able to enrich the spaces that we design in dense environments.

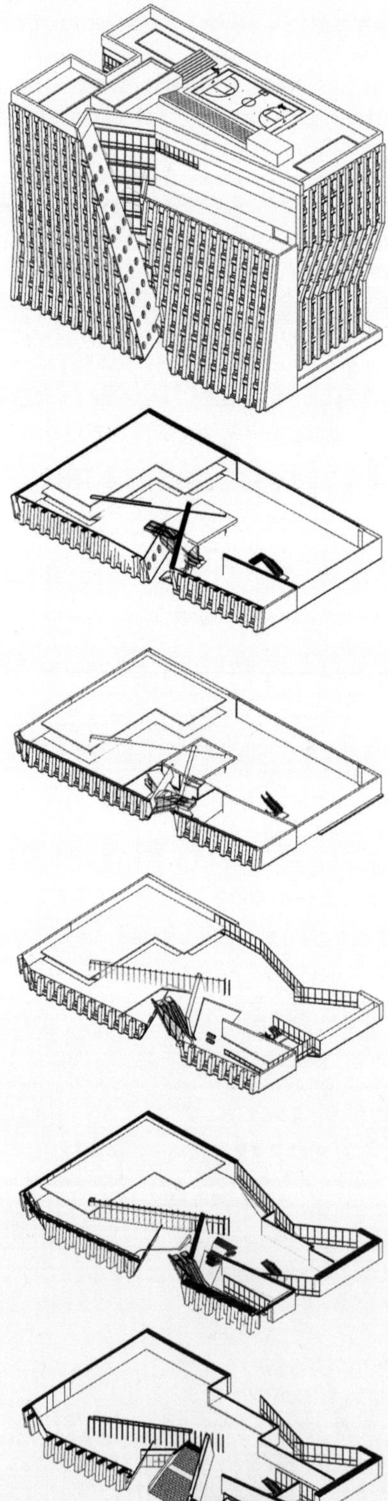

5.1. IPM LIBRARY (POLYTECHNIC UNIVERSITY OF MACAU)

DESIGN DATE	GROSS FLOOR AREA
2016	**47,979 m²**

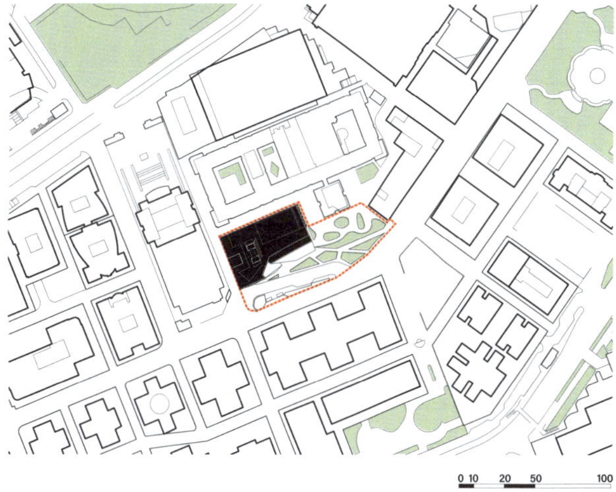

The new IPM Library is part of the renovation of the IPM University City campus. It is located along a curving street with a variable profile, Rua de Luís Gonzaga Gomes, that features large uniform buildings on the opposite side of the campus with continuous pedestrian porticoes on the ground level. On the campus side, the buildings are stand-alone structures and with significant differences both in height and architectural style.

As it is situated next to the bend in the road, the new library is placed at a slight angle, creating a large informal piazza at ground level to allow easy access to the rest of the university buildings behind it. This makes the new volume appear more prominent and elegant in the context of the street even though it will have the same height as most of the urban blocks on this road.

Due to the extensive public program, which exceeds the footprint of the building, LBA decided to distribute the main functions vertically across the first six floors of the building and design a three-dimensional connection space along the building elevation to allow for independent use of each of the floors of the library. The street being a privileged place in the city, the place where the city really happens and reinvents itself, we thought it would be a luxury for the focal space of the new campus to be a vertical street—overlooking the main campus entrance and the river to the south, and the lighthouse and the hill to the north.

LBA's proposal configures the building as a single volume with a fractured main elevation that divides it into two façades developing in a slightly angled position. The project takes great advantage of this— firstly by designing two slender and light volumes instead of a single block, and secondly by organizing a central void between the two façades where the main entrances of the library and the campus are located as well as all the vertical connections to the public floors. This empty, narrow section allows the passerby to glimpse into the program of the building, its public and reading spaces, as well as the human movement within it.

From the inside, this vertical void allows the library's most public areas to maintain views of Macau's urban landscape. We see this act of looking at the city during the periods of study and reflection in the library as a way of connecting higher education with the human and social culture of its city as the cityscape remains visually present during the permanence in the building.

There will be a number of public access areas in this building that will house the book storage, reading rooms, a student service office, computer rooms, multimedia rooms, two auditoriums, rehearsal rooms, cafés, exhibition spaces, and more. On top of the first six floors for the public, there are eight floors dedicated to the university and library offices, and a rooftop sports field.

In the IPM Library, LBA decided to explore the vertical extension of public space. Along the main elevation of the building, several escalators, stairs, and ramps compose a pedestrian route to access the main public programs at different levels. This connective space is a vertical public space and is intended as an extension of the sidewalk; it is a public space intertwined with the main building's architecture.

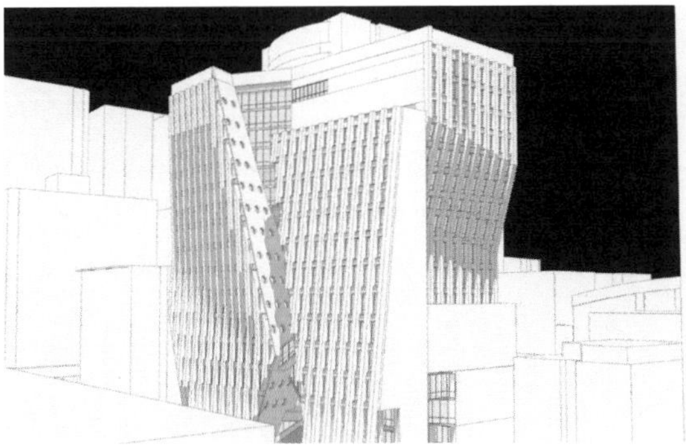

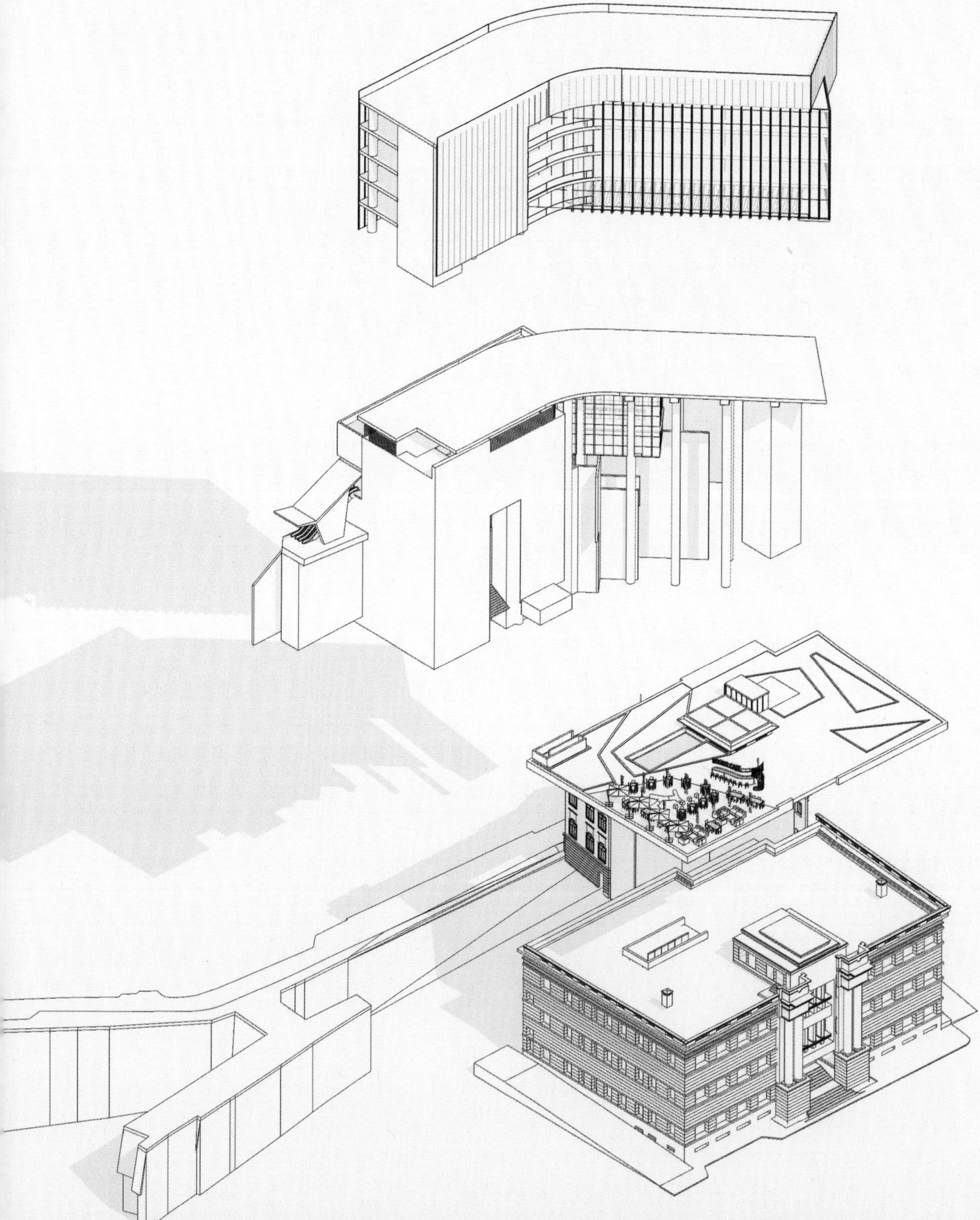

5.2. MACAU CENTRAL LIBARY

DESIGN DATE
2018

GROSS FLOOR AREA
18,264 m²

The proposed location of Macau's new central library is a lot with great historical and cultural relevance that merges the land of the old courthouse building with the plot of the former judicial police. This place is the focal point of the former civic center of Macau, at the elbow of the old Bay of Praia Grande. The plot lias between Avenida da Praia Grande and Rua Central, Macau's two main historic urban axes. The first runs at the lower part of the Bay, the Portuguese harbor, and the second follows the ridge of the hill, effectively separating the Portuguese and the Chinese settlements; both roads housed the main institutions and activities of the historical civic center of Macau.

Geographically, this lot has enormous potential, because it allows a rethink of the centrality and institutional role that this location had in the memory of the city and its convertion into a contemporary setting. The competition brief requested an interpretative restoration of the most significant heritage buildings within the plot and the insertion of a high-rise volume to complete the functional requirements of the library program.

LBA proposes to create a strong pedestrian connection between the three urban perimeters of the lot, transforming the main spaces of the unleveled ground floors of the existing buildings into a space-pivot of the pedestrian movement in the city center; with the clever placement of its access points, the building is set to become the meeting point and cultural and social hub of the city.

The users find entrances at grade in each street surrounding the building. Due to the difference in levels between the entrances, a network of ramps and escalators allows the spaces at ground floor to connect freely with each other and be used as public halls.

A staircase is designed along the west façade of the old courthouse that connects Avenida da Praia Grande with Rua Central at the exterior of the building; designed to replicate the scale of the old city, in the style of a "ladder street" characteristic of ancient Macau, this new connection will serve as a gateway to the world heritage circuit along Rua Central, while also serving as a new link between the city center and the residents along this hill.

The design is treated as a collage of three parts: the two historical buildings, with their autonomous elevations and levels, and the new high-rise building that stitches the program together. Every construction is kept volumetrically independent from the others. The new building entrance at ground level is at the back corner of the plot and is designed as a symbolic column, holding up the curved volume that overlaps the old courthouse at the sixth floor, two floors above the courthouse roof. The second footing of this new elevated volume occupies one of the courthouse patios.

The strategy is to design a piece of city where the new and the old communicate with each other and to avoid a clear stacking of the new program over the historical building façades. The insertion of the program of a library in such a complex lot has been done through the redesign of the lower volumes in a way that lets the surroundings infiltrate—thus designing porous structures that establish connections between the street and the interior of the plot through people flow, locating all the open and public parts of the programs at these levels, such as exhibition spaces, cafeteria, museum, and theater entrance. The study and research areas are located away from the bustling lower areas in the elevated volume that oversails the plot.

Socially, the building program referred to all layers and social groups of the city, allowing the establishment of a building of universal access and bestowing all citizens with equal weight.

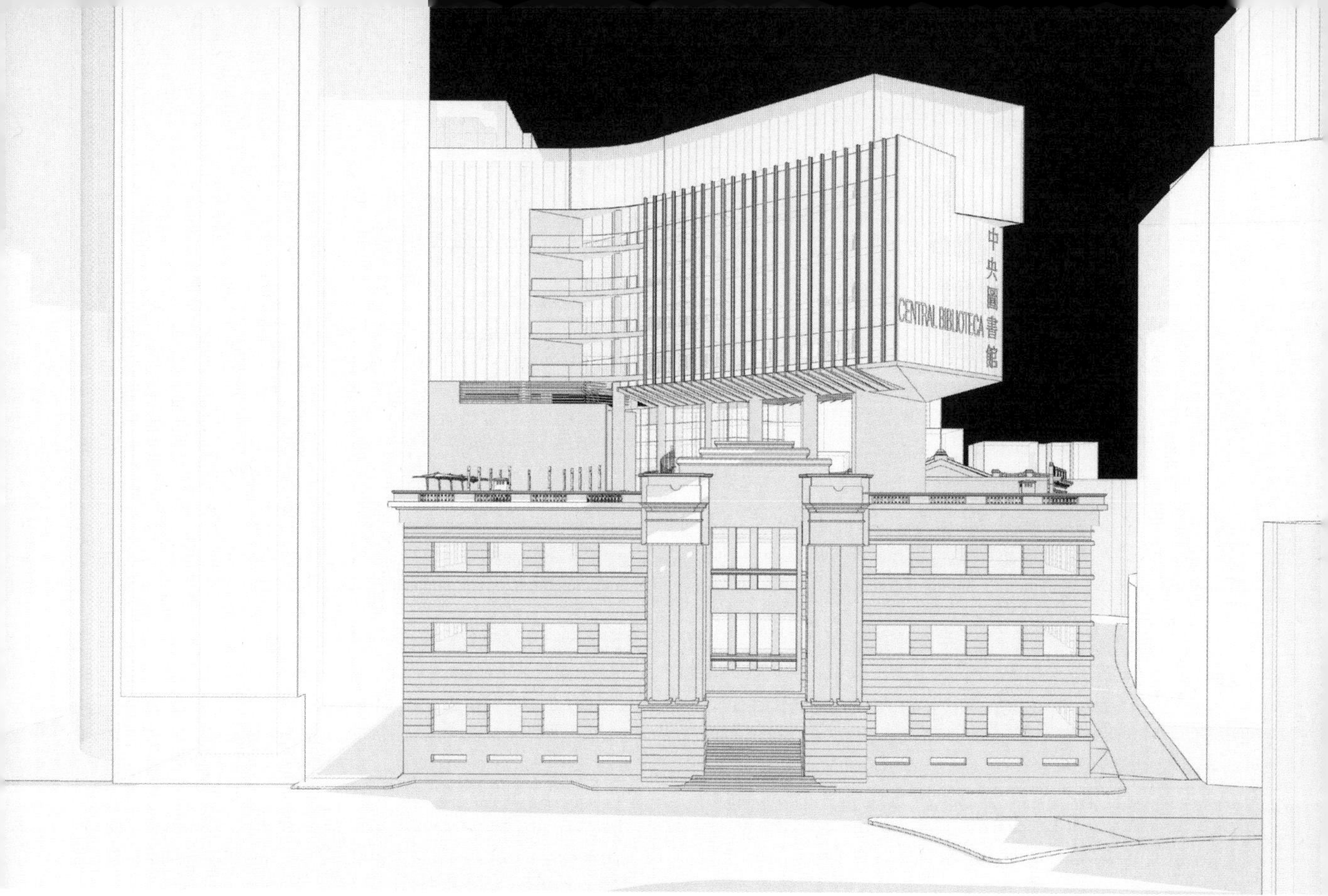
中央圖書館
CENTRAL BIBLIOTECA

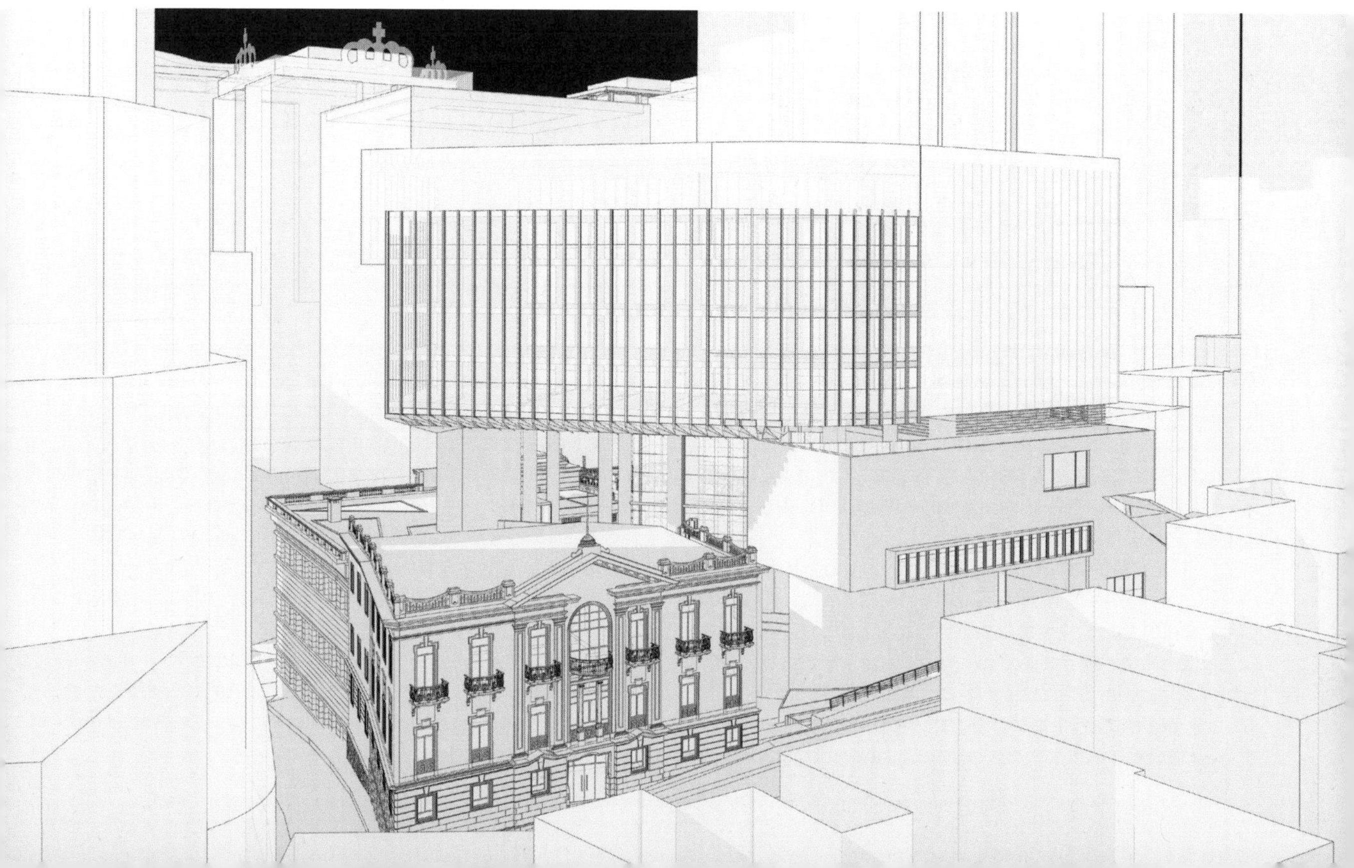

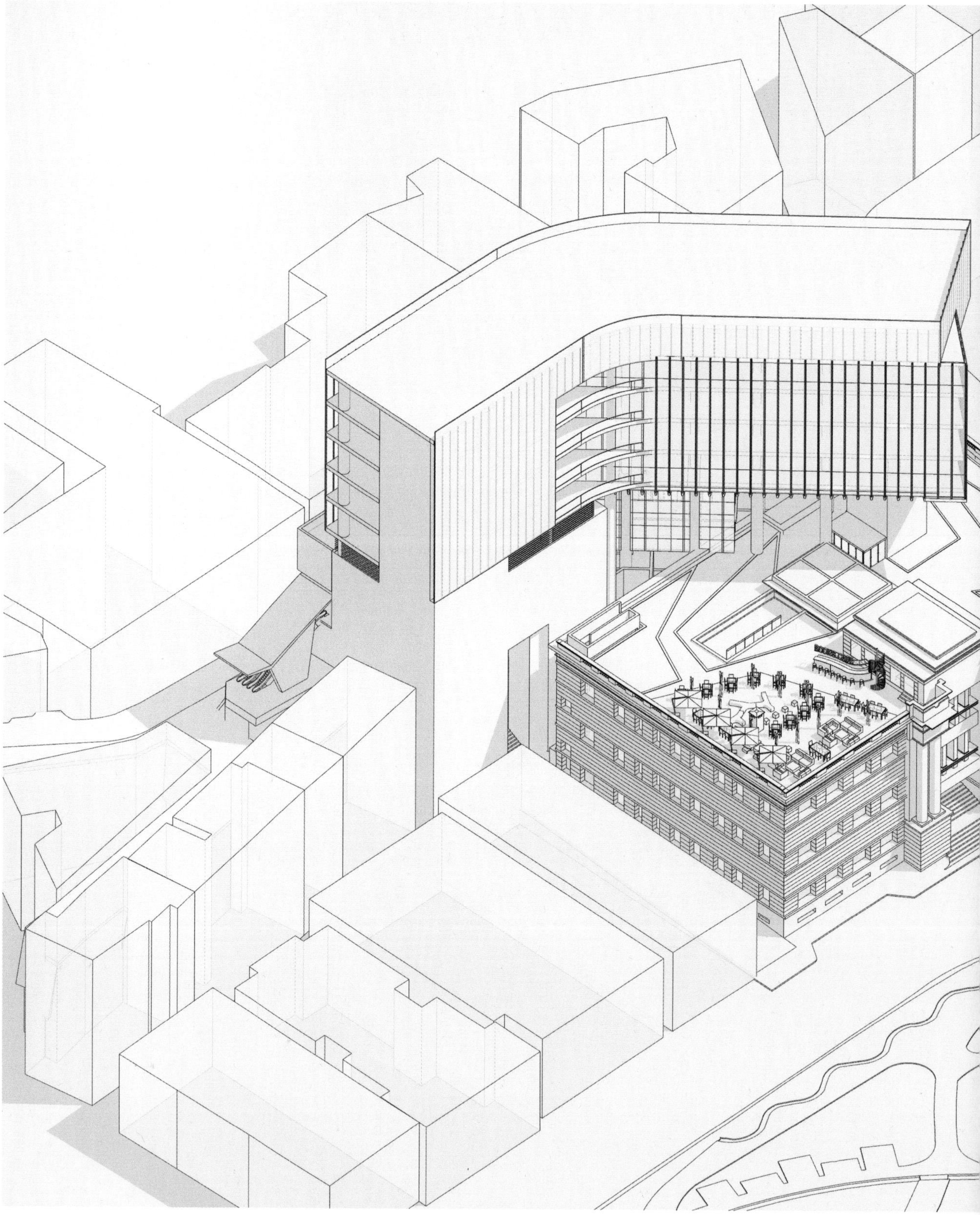

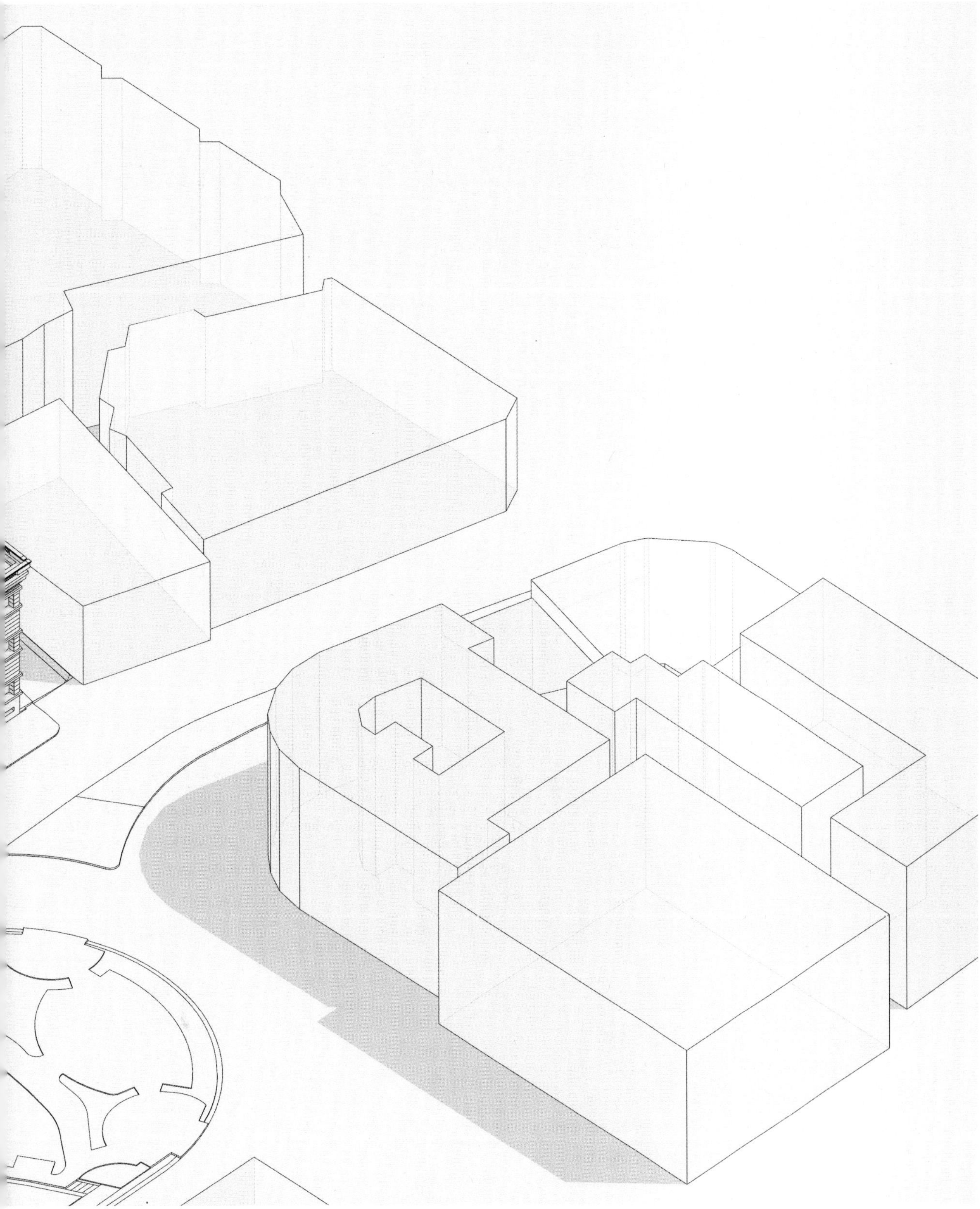

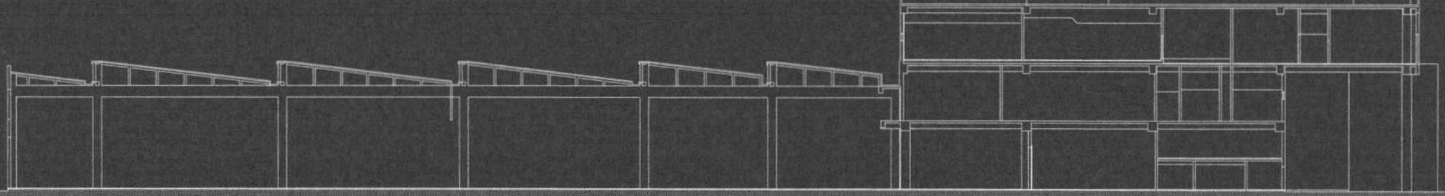

5.3. MACAU LRT TRAIN DEPOT

DESIGN DATE
2016

GROSS FLOOR AREA
144,567 m²

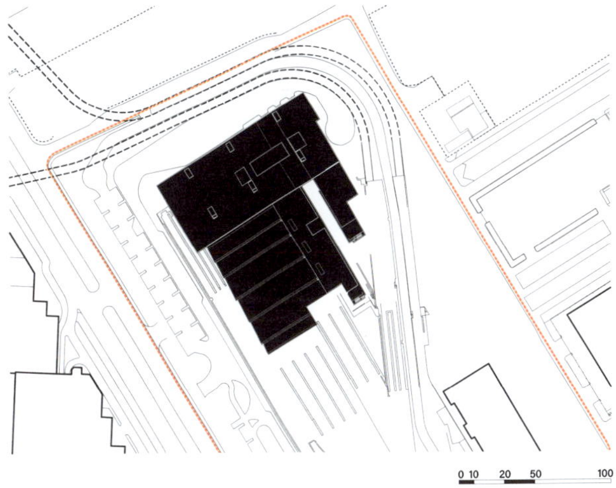

This large train depot for the LRT system is situated on an undeveloped landfill site in a logistic zoning near Macau International Airport. It is a semi-peripheral location for Macau, set along a main avenue, Av. Do Aeroporto, at the back rear of one of the main university campuses and two large casino complexes. As a result of its length (660 m), the depot creates an urban barrier for any development that may take place around it in the future.

This facility is designed to stable trains; store equipment; and power, maintain, and manage Macau's light rail network. The design brief called for scattered independent buildings to fulfill each of these functions. Instead, we decided to pursue a compact solution: by stacking the programmatic areas on top of each other, we were able to make better use of the land and give the building an institutional quality that reflects the scale and dimension of the LRT operation (this is the only headquarters of the Macau Light Rail system management company, MLM).

Since the landfill soil was particularly loose, we had to build the entire depot site on top of a slab 66,000 m² large, raised 4 meters from grade level; to counter this, we provided a 35m-wide hilly green belt around the entire facility.

To achieve the compactness of the building volume, we started by stacking the major part of the program, assigning to each piece of the building its autonomous visual characteristic. The maintenance area in the middle of the complex is divided into two sections: an office and storage area in two floors a double-height workshop area with an industrially inspired sawtooth roof connected at ground level directly to the stabling, cleaning, and the train test track.

To the southwest of the complex, designing the main entrance is the LRT visitors' center in over three floors with an exhibition area on the first two floors and the connection to the control center on the third. On the opposite site are located the power transformer facilities on two floors, and the rescue train and line maintenance facility separated by a maintenance vehicular access.

The first two floors are organized as independent volumes; the third floor, where the administration is located, bridges over all the structures with a one floor horizontal block bringing unity to the whole complex. With this stacked layout, we managed to develop a building with a good networking environment between all the stakeholders of the Macau LRT: the management company, the operator, and the rolling stock supplier and maintainer.

The strategy used for this design allowed for an integrated building and economy in road and pedestrian access to the different programmatic parts of the building, enabled a better layout of the train tracks along the rest of the depot site, and minimized obstruction of the views of neighboring casinos and hotels.

2
1

cem

5.4. CEM DISPATCH CENTER

DESIGN DATE
2016

GROSS FLOOR AREA
5,049 m²

The main electric power plant compound of the CEM concessionary, built on the north shore of Coloane Island, was originally located on the shoreline and has now become an urban confrontation on the south side of the COTAI urban reclamation.

Within the power plant, next to the entrance gate, is the new CEM Dispatch Center, the only administrative building in the complex. It is situated in an alignment of small buildings facing the water that structure a first row of built volumes. Separated by the plant's main road is a second row of buildings containing the older generators that outline the backdrop to the dispatch center.

The building's location will define the front and main entrance of the power plant complex from COTAI, thus redefining the public image of the facility. As a result, LBA designed a building that integrates the site planning context while following a new architectural premise. The proximity to the water is a quality of the site that should be enhanced by the building. We address this by making a set of important spaces dialogue with the water landscape. The main hall and the exhibition space are located in the water's edge.

Due to the depth of the site and the character of the surrounding environment, the design took the option of organizing the building around a central courtyard to create a self-defined exterior space. The program is thus distributed on two volumes with independent functions that form the dispatch building.

The north-facing volume faces the outer landscape of COTAI and the power plant entrance. It was defined as a three-level building with regular openings, with the intent of integrating with the simplicity of the power plant architecture and planning. The south-facing volume is located along the main road and has four levels. It is mostly raised off the ground, allowing views of the central courtyard from the main road. The southern volume traces a curve that creates a welcoming gesture from the complex gate towards the plant's main road.

The two volumes meet on the western part of the plot, where the Dispatch Centre control room is located, which is where the program articulation requires a deeper section. To the west, the twin curves of the two volumes form an eye-shaped courtyard where the main entrance and guest entrance are located.

The circulation spaces have been concentrated around the central courtyard to create human visibility within the building. Most of the circulation will have full-height glazing to fill these spaces with natural light and relate the circulation spaces to the exterior as much as possible. The building has been organized around two vertical cores, which will work with a high level of autonomy. One is the Dispatch Center proper, and the other is the combination of the public spaces—namely, the auditorium, the conference rooms, the canteen, and the common area—which form a multi-purpose facility, well connected to the central courtyard and the future footbridge across the main road.

The footbridge to cross the main road, requested in the brief as a future development, was designed as an integral part of the building. It is aligned with the external circulation of the NDC proper, which was configured as an exterior space, to reduce consumption in both stretches of the footbridge. A stair to access the footbridge from the ground level was included, well articulated with respect to the central courtyard. This will allow, in the future, the central courtyard of the NDC building to be connected directly to the first floor of the future building across the street without any type of intermediate control point or barrier.

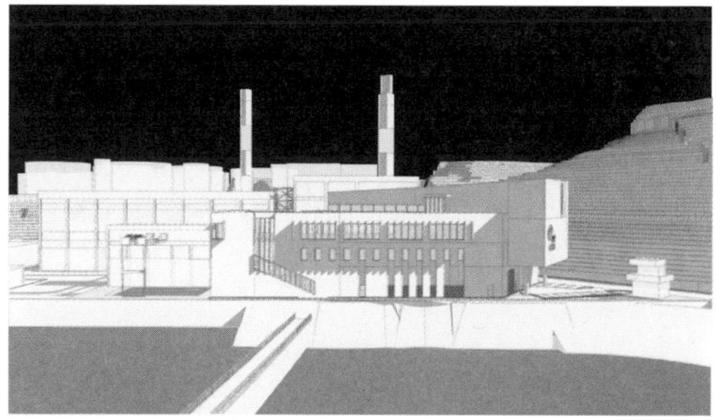

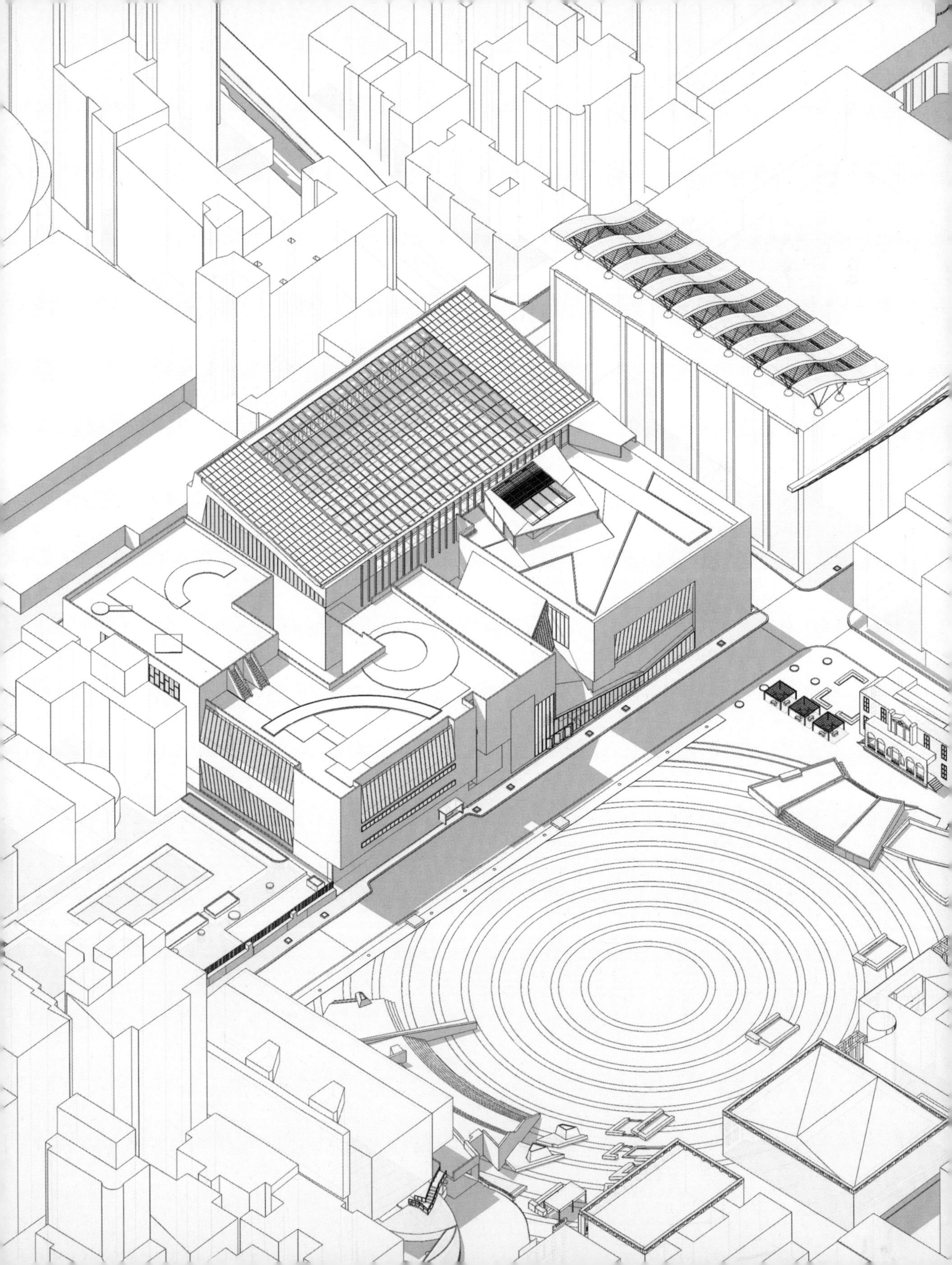

5.5. TAP SEAC YOUTH CENTER

DESIGN DATE
2018

GROSS FLOOR AREA
59,487 m²

The location for the Tap Seac Youth Center is the lot of the former Estoril Hotel, the first purpose-built hotel-casino in Macau. The lot overlooks Tap Seac Square, one of the main public squares in Macau's historical fabric, around which we find a row of historical buildings converted into a public library, a health center, Macau's historical archives, Macau's cultural institute, and exhibition spaces. In the surrounding area, there are several schools and a sport center.

The site stands at the bottom of Guia Hill, with a significant level difference between its front part along the square and the back road where several nearby schools are located.

LBA developed a design concept wherein the specific location of the plot was used to extend the public function of the square though the youth center's cultural program and pedestrian connections, contributing to additional informal public spaces to the young population for the surrounding schools.

Due to the four main segments of program needing to be fitted under the same roof, we designed a building that projects a strong unified volume and architectural image along the main square but at the same time is porous in its core, to develop strategies of functional distinction and segregation.

We seek to recreate within its interior the atmosphere and scale of the historic patios and alleyways of Macau through the design of the connecting tissue between the two roads and the four programmatic entrances. These are structured as a network of public areas of different sizes and purposes within the design, creating the opportunity for the building to be used by the population as a connecting device between the two unleveled roads.

The building program is varied and complex: it hosts a theater, the Macau Music and Dance Conservatory, a youth center, and a public swimming pool on the roof.

As a cultural, educational, and sports center of prime importance to the city, the buildings' image and spaces must reflect the urban and spatial culture that distinguishes Macau from other cities in the region. This culture resides in a strong civic sense of public space; in the complexity of how spaces connect and articulate, making architecture participate in the city and vice-versa; and in the architectural distinction of institutional spaces, which must be much more than just functional to elevate Architecture to Art, fulfilling more than strict spatial functionality.

Fitting in the overall program of the Tap Seac Youth Center design is a three-dimensional exercise that allows for interior and exterior communal areas to connect all the different programs.

On the façade facing the square, a strong and rhythmic ensemble is designed, in a composition of masonry and glass. The conservatory's dance rooms, the theater foyers, and the pools on the roof will all be oriented towards the square, becoming part of the life of this public space. From the square, you can get a glimpse of the activities unfolding in all these spaces, making it a more lively and participatory place in the institutional and cultural life of the city.

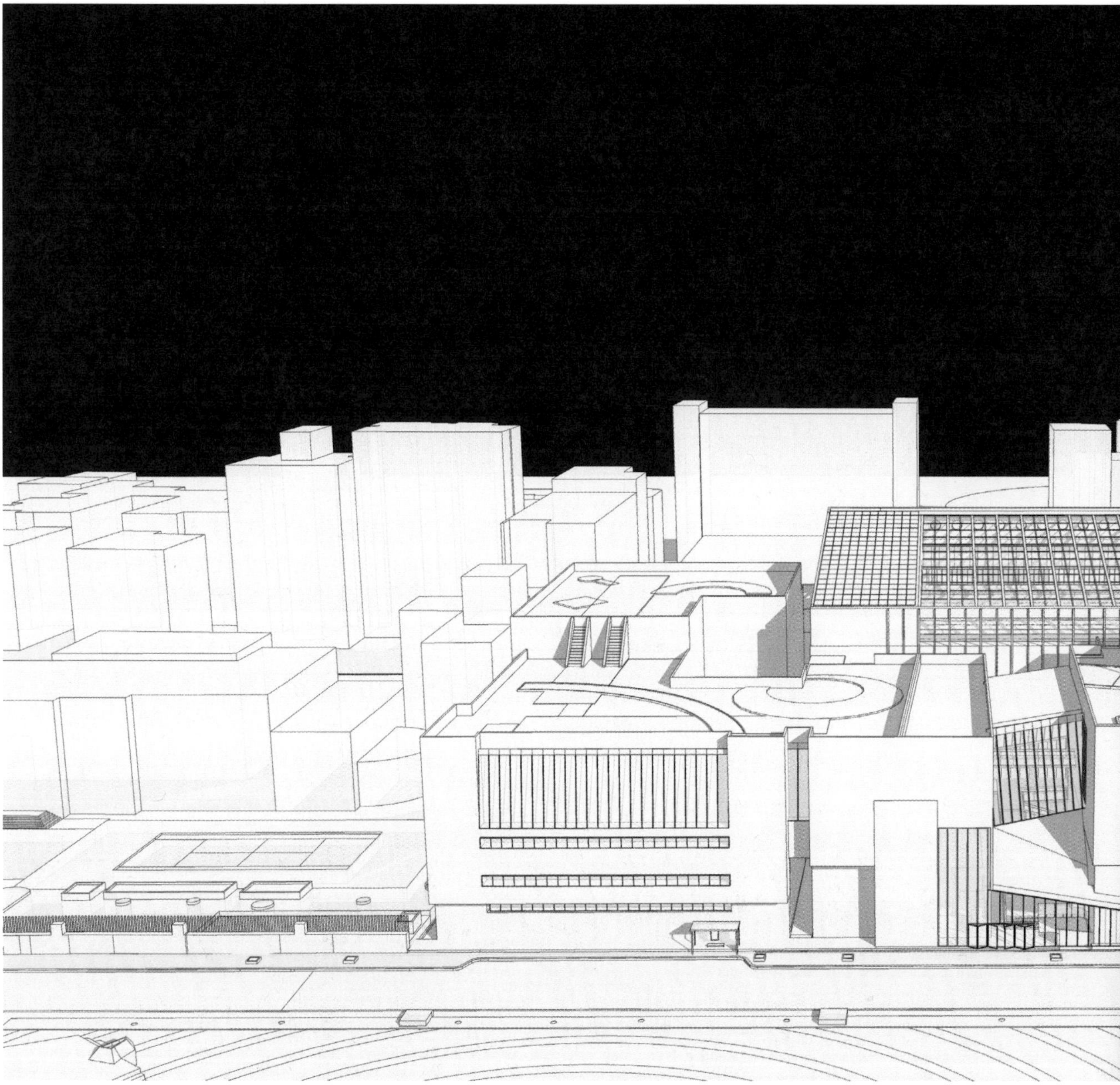

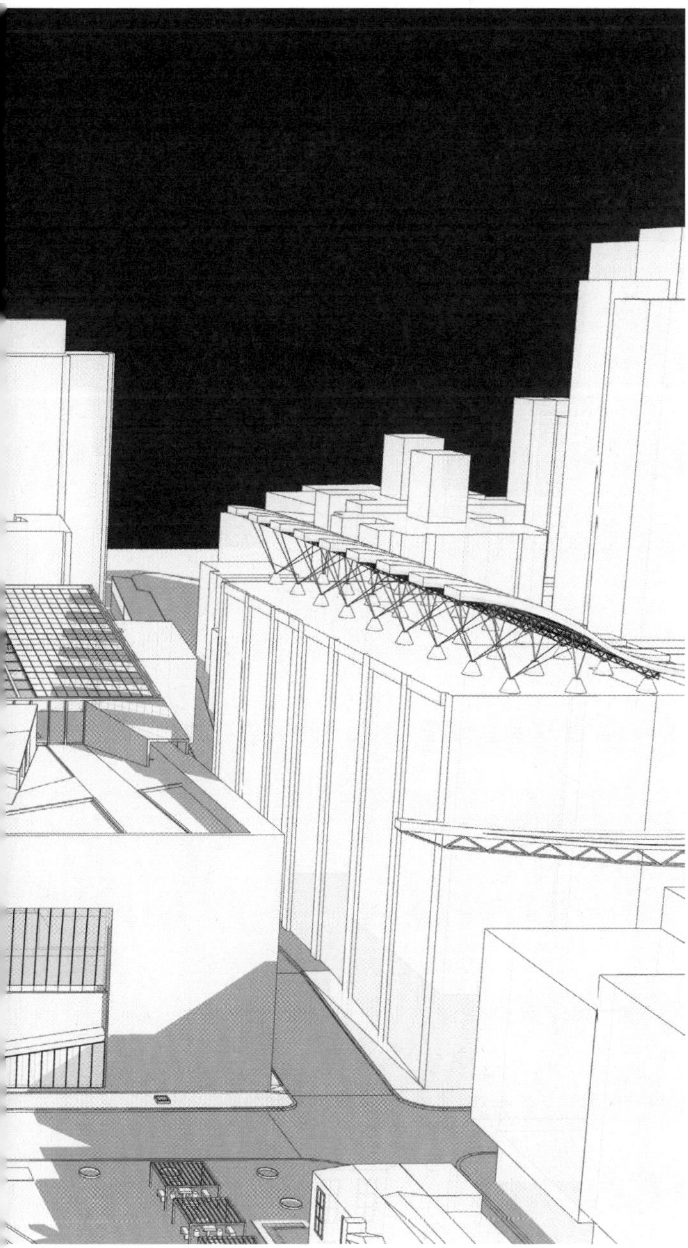

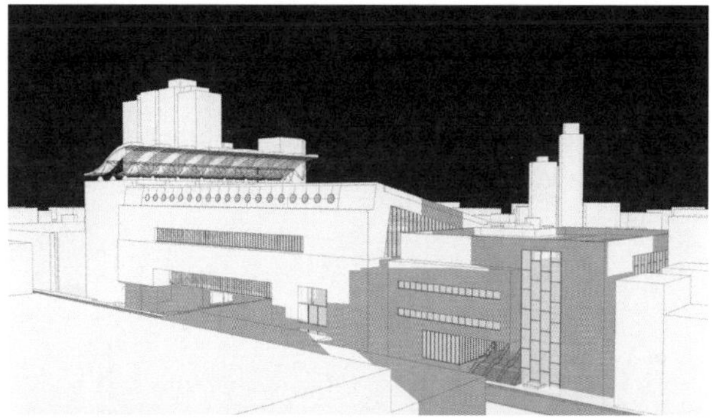

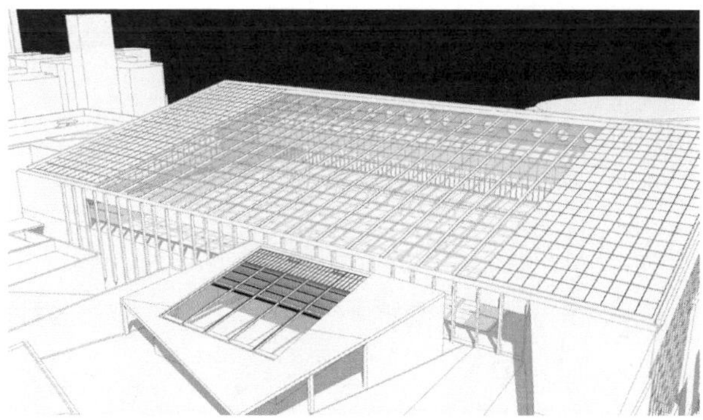

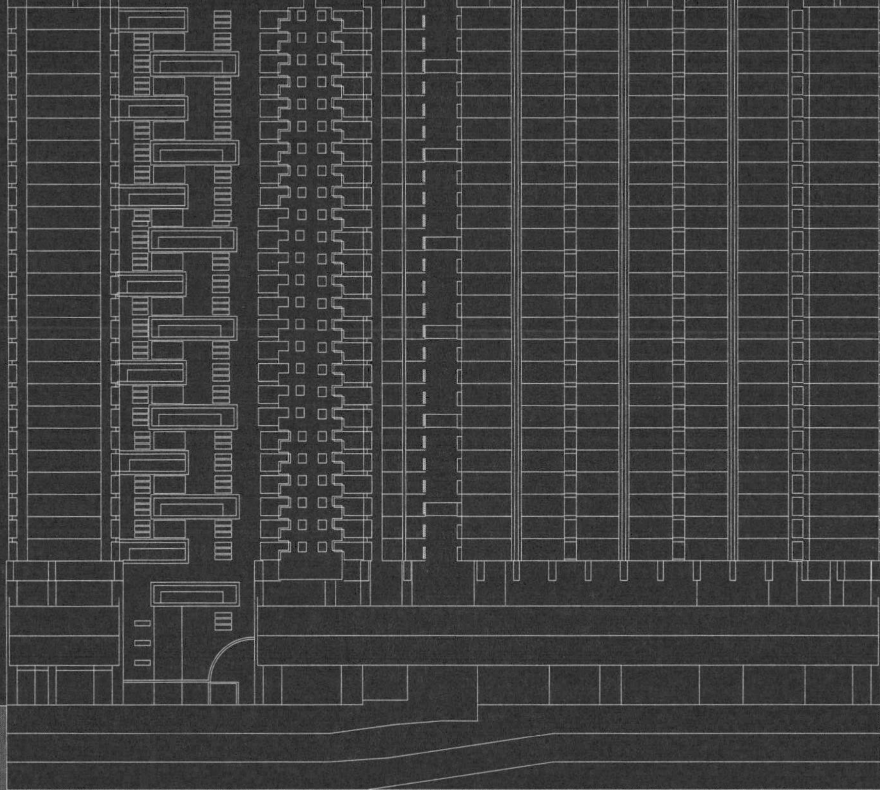

5.6. FAI CHI KEI SOCIAL HOUSING

DESIGN DATE
2010

GROSS FLOOR AREA
69,995m²

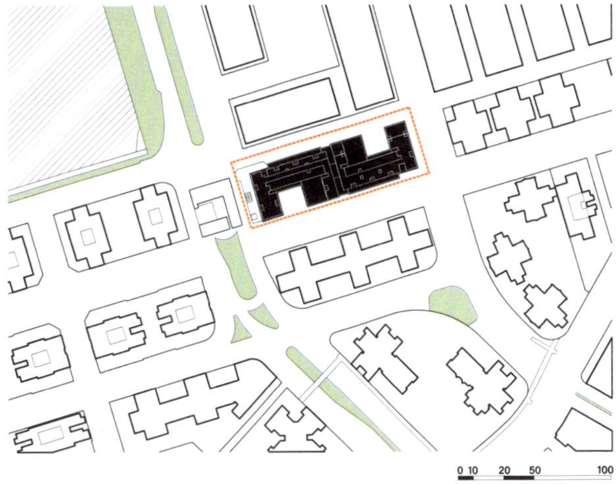

In 2009, we received the commission to design a social housing scheme to replace the previous resettlement project on the Fai Chi Kei Peninsula. The plot size was small compared with those of the surrounding constructions. The trend in the most recent land reclamations had been to increase the plot size and to develop these larger areas with the podium-and-tower typology, whereby a two-to-three-story building platform occupies the entire plot and a series of tall towers grows from the roof of this building base.

The first considerations were on the urban insertion of the building and the role it could play in a wider city context, the role of the public space within the plot, and the role of the common areas in the overall economy of the project. We started by creating an urban hierarchy of spaces through the simple act of positioning volumes. We used the street as a corridor and attached our patios to it as a widening of the sidewalk. Two open courtyards were set out as public spaces integrated into the urban plot, with a specific spatial configuration of being built up on three sides, and in direct dialogue with the surroundings. These spaces become an "accident" of space and light in an otherwise compact city continuum, purposefully free of program and function. It was our intention that they be appropriated at will.

Through the design we first defined the informal, the empty, and its relationship with the context. To this effect, we analyzed the surrounding context to understand where our design contribution could be more effective: we selected the walkway as the most important area for our urban contribution.

Fai Chi Kei Social Housing is both autonomous typological research into building a social housing block in a high-density environment and an act of negotiation between the maximum usage of the plot and the livability of the neighborhood. This translates into a negotiation between the building mass and the voids of the open areas.

What could have eventuated as a typical podium-and-tower building was transformed into a new scheme. We retained the podium-and-tower typology in its functionality (commercial areas at ground floor, social facilities at first and second floor, a garden area at third floor, housing above) in accordance with the client's expectation, but subverted its premise, which is that the plot would be used in full for three floors and that the ground-floor area would be moved to a restricted exterior area on the podium roof.

The strategies required to achieve this new hybrid typology were twofold: the first one was to explore a residential tower typology, one based not on a central plan with the lift and stairs at its core but on a corridor-and-hall plan. The second strategy was to design a base for the towers in such a way that it would not occupy the whole plot. We pursued the dematerialization of the podium volume by carving patios and opening corridors and connections. We designed a series of public spaces that create urban situations and varied typologies of common areas that are able to enrich not only the building but the entire surrounding urban area.

As a result, the project successfully uses private land to provide public spaces without compromising the total gross floor area requested by the client. We had pushed the regulations to an extreme level of efficiency that completely overruled the podium-and-tower typology by cleverly designing mass and void simultaneously.

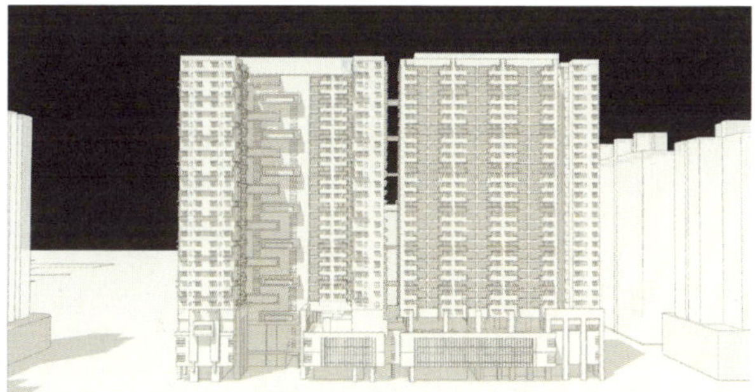

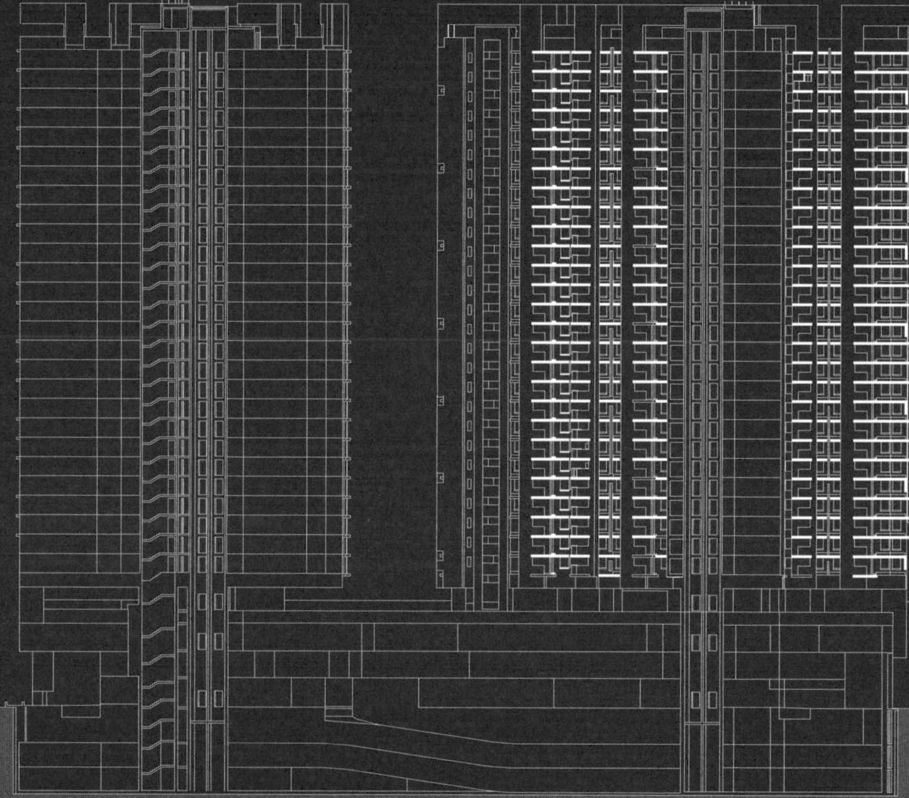

5.7. ZONE A B10 PLOT SOCIAL HOUSING

DESIGN DATE
2020

GROSS FLOOR AREA
90,872m²

B10 Social Housing is located on a mono-functional, new, reclaimed island to the east of Macau Peninsula. The site is in the middle of a cluster of social housing blocks that take up the whole of the north sector of the new reclamation. It is a long lot flanked to the west side by a green corridor that runs longitudinally along the whole island from north to south, and on its east side by the main road.

The overall planning for the area shows almost no public space for pedestrians beyond the green corridor, leaving most of the public gathering areas to the sidewalk. The project comprises a low podium with two towers on top, in a typical podium-and-tower typology.

As part of our effort to create some variety on the ground floor and to increase public space, we chose to set back the podium volume strategically so that a series of common areas can be designed that are connected to the two main pedestrian systems, the green corridor, and the main road, where the entrances to the two residential blocks and podium facilities are located.

We planned two small squares on the extremities of the site to mediate between the scale of the main road and the green corridor with the smaller spaces along the sidewalk: the northern one facing the street to be used as a common rest area, and the southern square facing the green corridor to be used as an exterior area for the ground-floor shops as well as a way of widening the green corridor. This would also reduce the perception of the podium's volume from the street and make it more consistent with the towers above it.

The majority of the podium is set back along the urban green corridor to create a leisure area that can be combined with the main public area. On this side, the set-back volume of the podium fractures and twists the block alignment so that the main public space penetrates the plot and finds connections to the main road on its east side, which ensures a high level of permeability for the plot. Design techniques such as this encourage the creation of extra common spaces to promote public use, in such a way that they are not occupied or annexed for private use.

One of the planning requirements was to set out a continuous portico around the building; we developed this constraint into varied elevations using several types of porticoes that would transition between each other according to their location. Social housing programs are systematically insensitive to the needs of the lower classes that dwell in economical housing estates, often adopting exiguous apartment areas and maximizing units per access lift while minimizing horizontal circulation that just responds to cost reduction. LBA's first ambition was the dignified and qualified definition of the housing complex, offering a rich spatial structure through the design of the condominium garden and the floor circulation areas, duly ventilated and illuminated.

This was achieved by transforming the traditional circulation spaces, like corridors and hallways, into alternative communal spaces by discreetly widening their boundaries so that extra spaces and uses can be added, breaking up their monotony with the apparent random insertion of sky gardens and open views towards the river. This project exceeded its brief by finding an appropriate typology for high-density living through the design of the communal areas.

A series of sky gardens is distributed on different levels by subtracting blocks of apartments randomly across the plan, resulting in a network of small intimate gardens arranged along the main elevation, which sets up a vertical map of external places easily accessible from the main vertical circulation.

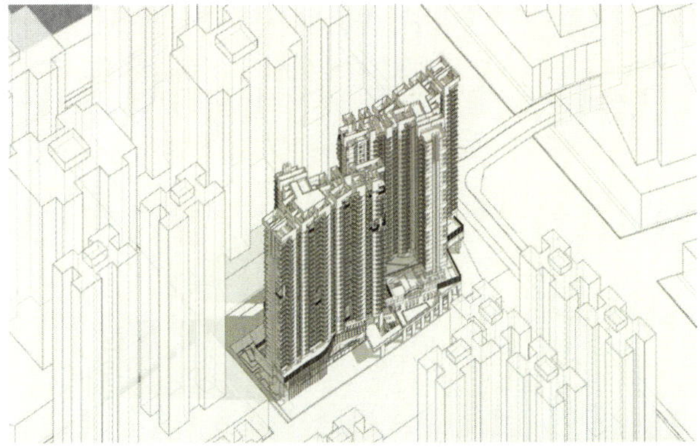

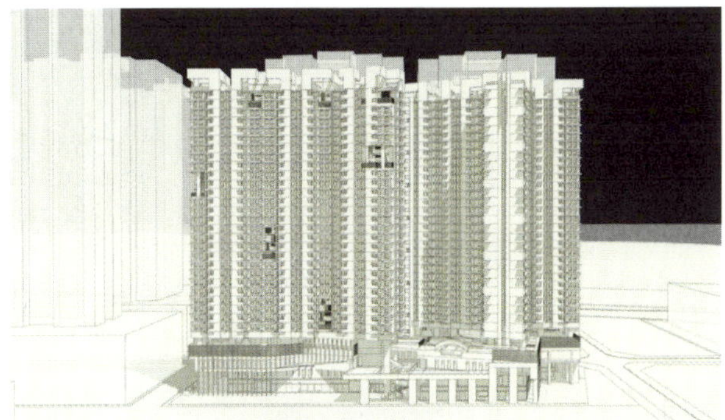

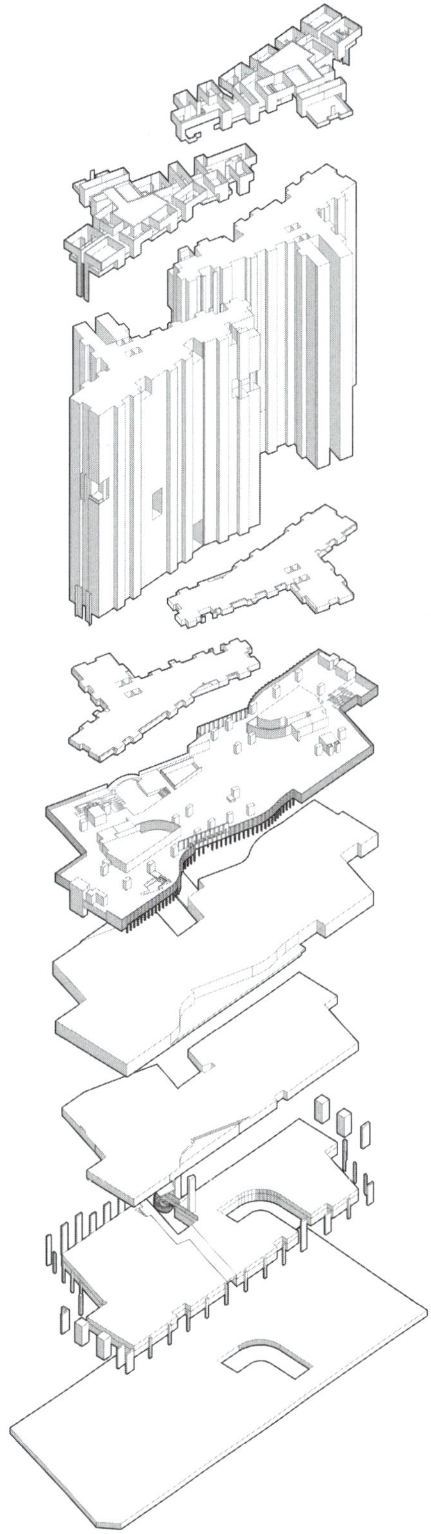

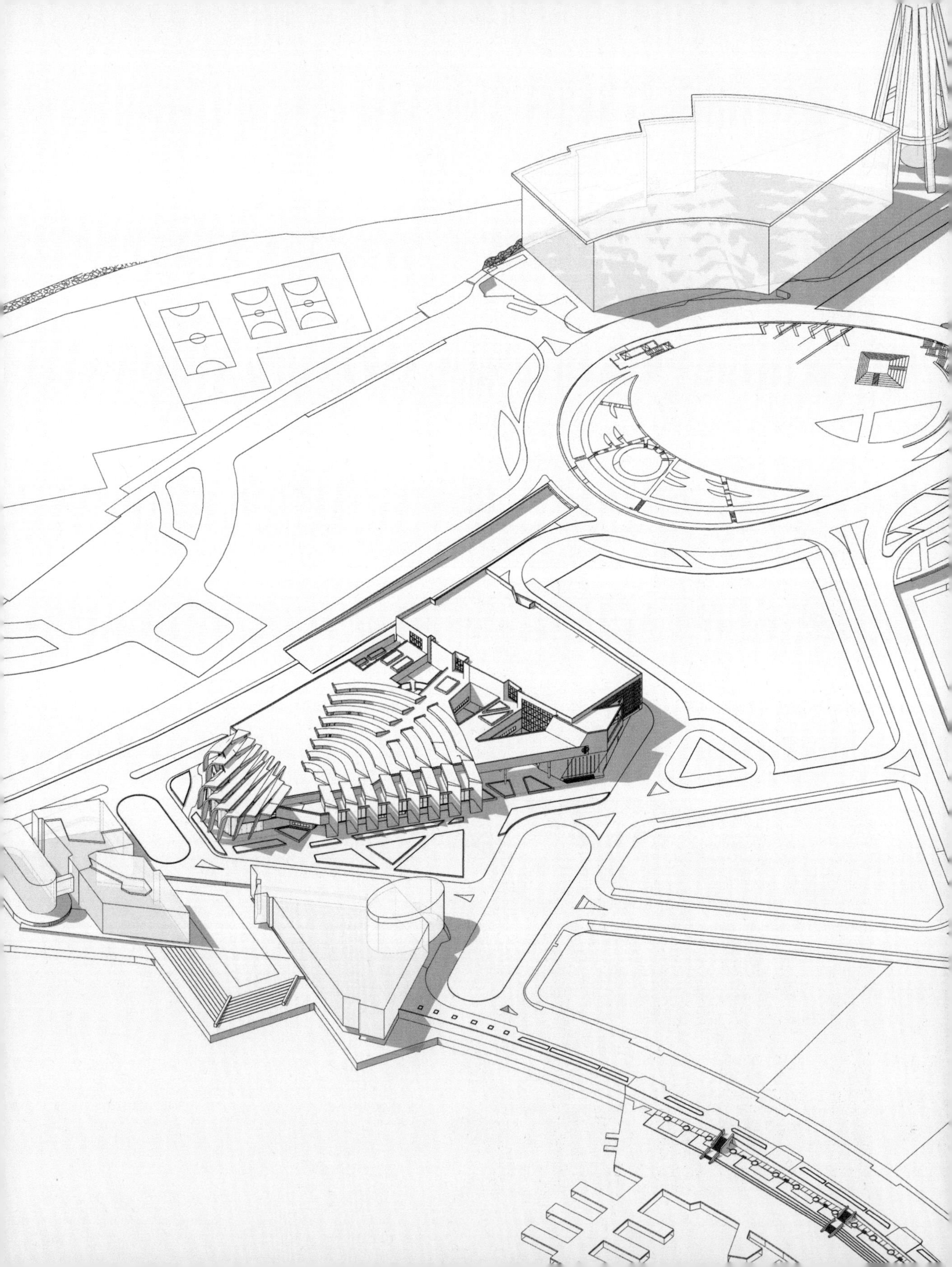

5.8. CHINA-LUSOPHONE COOPERATION BUILDING

DESIGN DATE	GROSS FLOOR AREA
2017	**58,970m²**

The program for this building embodies the application of the People's Republic of China Central Government's "Belt and Road" initiative to the political realm of Macau and the wider network of Portuguese-speaking countries. The Cooperation Building plot is at the center of the Nam Van reclamation masterplan; an area designed to be developed as the new administrative and civic center of the Special Administrative Region, in the manner of as Greek acropolis.

The site is wedged in between a high-speed thoroughfare, the Macau outer ring road, and a public square shared by other institutional buildings; the rest of the district's plots remain undeveloped.

The site being newly built, without much built context around it, the main concern in the design has been to give an architectural response to the important mainland political agenda and visualize the political relevance that the building offers to the city.

The architectural project is a testament to the region's commitment to progress, innovation, and collaboration on both a local and international scale. Positioned in close proximity to key institutional landmarks such as the Macau SAR legislative council and the high court, the building's strategic location within the envisioned administrative and civic center underscores its pivotal role in shaping the socio-political landscape of the Special Administrative Region.

The design of the structure reflects a convergence of architectural vision and urban planning objectives. Organized around a very large congress room for the Forum of Cooperation between Macau and the other Portuguese-speaking countries, the building serves as a physical embodiment of the region's aspirations for global engagement and diplomatic relations.

The design strategy has been to separate the permanent forum office areas from the congress center with an open-air patio that crosses the lot transversally, allowing for the main entrances to be located in a wide, quiet area set back from the street. Four bridges connect at high level the two volumes crossing over the entrance patio.

Central to the design approach is the notion of architectural storytelling, where the formal composition of the building serves as a medium for expressing the interconnectedness of the thematic elements embedded within the brief. Through a careful orchestration of spatial sequences, material choices, and structural dynamics, the architecture unfolds as a narrative of unity, progress, and shared purpose—mirroring the ethos of cooperation and dialogue that underpins the Forum of Cooperation.

The architecture of this design values the relationship between the formal units that build up its narrative, enforcing the concept of a collective dynamic. The communication of this architectural message, both monumental and dynamic, is fundamental in embedding the role of this complex in the economy and the communities of the SAR.

The building's design language—characterized by fluidity, movement, and interaction—transcends mere aesthetics to convey a deeper message of inclusivity, diversity, and mutual understanding. By creating an environment that fosters social engagement, cultural exchange, and economic collaboration, the project aspires to be more than a physical edifice; it aims to be a living symbol of community empowerment, innovation, and sustainable development.

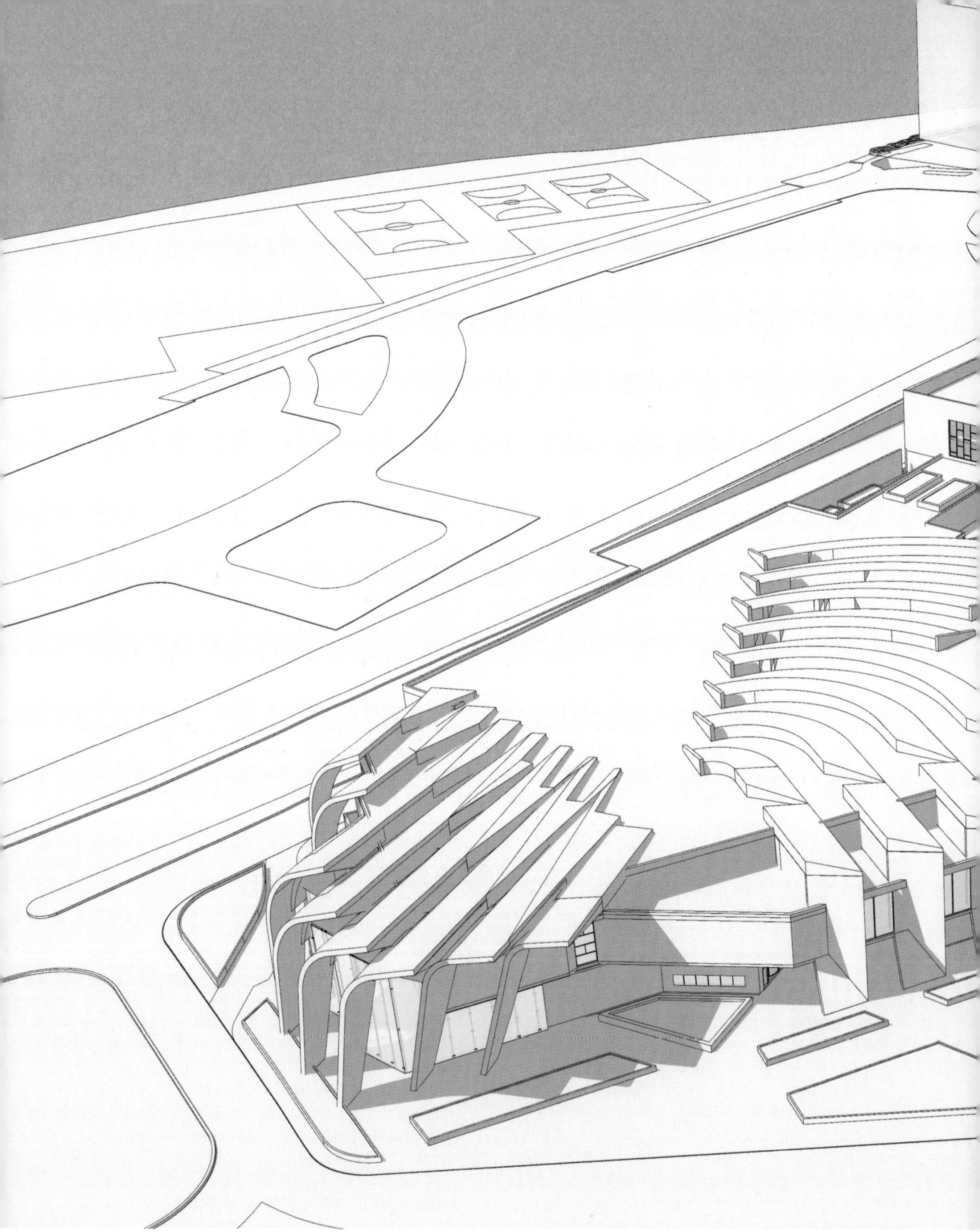

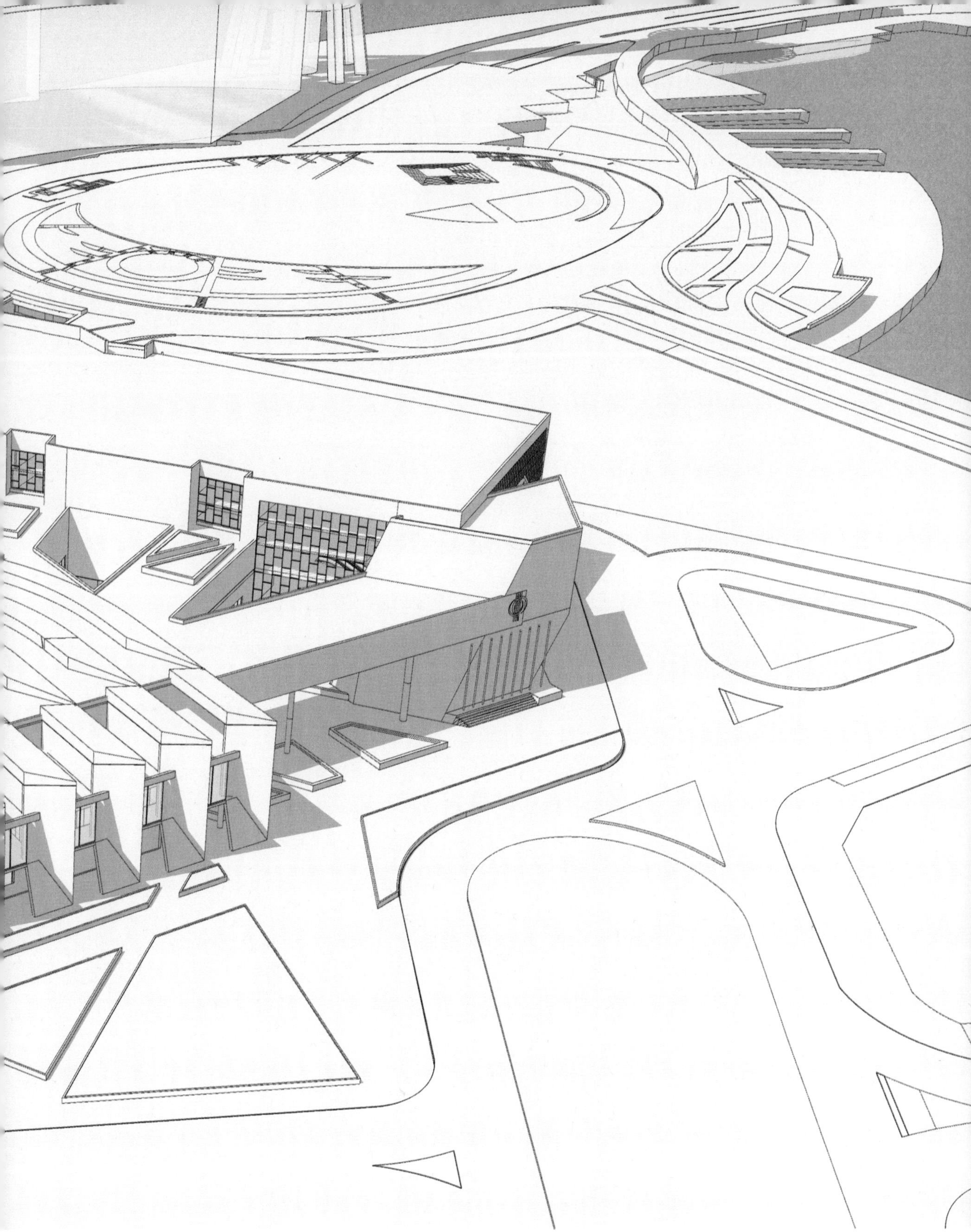

6. Post-casino Macau in the perspective of China's historical process and strategic planning

Jiang Jun and Xu Wenkai

Jun Jiang is an architect, researcher, curator, editor, and critic. He was the founding editor-in-chief of *Urban China* magazine (2005—2010) and has taught at the Strelka School of Architecture, Design, and Media in Moscow. Jiang has curated numerous events, including the China Pavilion at the 14th Venice Architecture Biennale (2014). He is currently the Dean of the School of Communication and Design and a professor at the China Academy of Art (CAA).

HISTORY AND CHOICES

Historically, Macau, which had been under Portuguese administration since the 16th century and was located at the heart of maritime trade in the Western Pacific, gradually became the focal point of the Far East trade routes which passed through this discreet outpost on the periphery of the Chinese Empire. The reason for this can be attributed not entirely to the Ming dynasty's negligence regarding maritime trade but also to the fact that, as well as facing the silver import crisis[1] and attacks by Japanese pirates, it had long since ceased to take into account the "eclectic policy" of the Guangdong authorities. After the Zhelin Mutiny,[2] a coup in 1564, in order to stop the "barbarians"— the Portuguese—in Macau, Wu Guifang[3] ordered foreign trade to be moved out of the provincial capital. At the same time, with the aim of stabilizing the political situation, he regarded the "tacit consent for the Portuguese to do business in Macau" as a solution to the then unfavourable financial situation.[4] As Portuguese tributes to the imperial court were never subject to strict regulations, the Ming and Qing dynasties also needed to take advantage of the "arrogant" Portuguese living in Macau as a window to the outside world. Thus, after entering the era of global trade, the Portuguese were offered a glimpse into the isolated empire on the one hand, and transformed Macau into an important trade route between mainland China and the rest of the world on the other. The profits generated due to this state of affairs accrued for hundreds of years. Macau, as a "small piece of land," relied on the "advantages of being the gateway" between China and Portugal and became a "place outside the law," with "free trade" and "the status of a special region" (see Figure 1).

1 Maritime Map of Macau

However, by the eve of the Opium War, Macau's status as an international trading port had already been weakened,[5] and, after the outbreak of the war and the signing of the Treaty of Nanking,[6] trade between China and the outside world could be carried out through the new "five ports"—Guangzhou, Xiamen, Fuzhou, Ningbo, and Shanghai—without passing through Macau. At the same time, the rise of Hong Kong drew away the powerful foreigners living in Macau. The implementation of the free port policy meant that the number of foreign commercial ships entering and leaving Macau fell dramatically. This series of drastic changes almost had a fatal impact on Macau at the time. "Just as Bombay destroyed Goa, Hong Kong is now destroying Macau".[7] However, as times changed, the ambition of Ferreira do Amaral,[8] who tried to break the legal authority of the Qing dynasty; the effects of the Taiping Rebellion[9] and the Second Opium War; and the total ban on gambling by the Hong Kong Colonial Government further inflamed the already intense enthusiasm for gambling in Guangdong and Macau, helping the Portuguese Government in Macau to adopt the gambling industry as a shortcut[10] to profit. It is easy to see how the astounding wealth generated from the 1840s onwards by this policy not only improved Macau's economic outlook but also became a core issue in Macau's long-term development, which touched upon geographical, social, political, and cultural dimensions (Figure 2).

2 Macau's South Bay in the mid-19th century (Source: Macau - Wikipedia, the free encyclopedia [wikipedia.org]

As the 21st century dawned, Macau's gaming industry, under the impact of the "gateway economy" and the policies of the Special Administrative Region, saw its "phased transition solution" evolve into the "predominance of a single industry." But this industry, nestled on the fringes of the socialist system, didn't just run counter to the Communist Party of China's (CCP)[11] ideology of governance; its "institutional inertia" also swallowed up Macau's true potential: the "make money fast" goals of the past, which relied on "post-colonial resources" to develop the economy, were not sustainable. As well as eroding the morale of the people, Macau also provided a place for laundering money from dubious origins in mainland China. After the Central Government and the Macau SAR Government realized this, and the great risk of over-dependence on Macau's gambling industry[12], they immediately laid out a long-term goal to develop a proper diversification of Macau's economy. Macau, after all, was not just a key point in China's global strategy but also an important platform for the full opening up of the country and the construction of its modernized economic system. Simultaneously with transforming and upgrading the local tourism and gaming industry, it became necessary to overcome the "well-trodden dependency" on traditional industries and look for the driving force of innovation and the way to economic growth. In short, as a paragon of the One Country, Two Systems principle, Macau urgently needs to create a platform for cultural exchange between China and Portuguese-speaking countries in the current international political and economic climate, and to explore its new internationalization model based on the vast resources of traditional Chinese culture and China's current national strategy. In addition, doing so creates a cultural and open space that is integrated into the national development plan, which showcases the characteristics of the world's civilisations, while taking into account Macau's economic recovery and recognition of its own cultural identity.

CONTEXT AND POSITIONING

If we take a macro view of Macau from a historical and geographical perspective, it can be regarded as a miniaturized history of China's special administrative regions—and even as a model for Hong Kong and Taiwan. Conversely, its small scale can also be used to study China's planning pattern and development trends. The so-called planning conjuncture refers to a decision of Chinese characteristics that covers all dimensions: geography, economy, society, politics, and culture. Its central mechanism is the "five-year plan[13]", which began in the 1950s with the "teachings from the Soviet Union." This "superstructure," which corresponded to the "economic base" represented by "156 industrial projects,"[14] went through the "great impulse" of the "First Five-Year Plan" and the "Great Leap Forward" of the "Second Five-Year Plan" and, after the "planning failure"[15] at the end of the 1970s and the "market failure"[16] at the end of the 1980s, the central authority decision-makers ended up giving some autonomy to local governments in the 1990s. At the same time, in order to avoid the "vassals' economy" caused by the "financial division," the Central Government implemented the "fiscal division reform" to redefine the financial powers and rights and duties of affairs between the central and local authorities, and to channel the increased revenues into the coordination of the country's major infrastructures, transfers, and payments, among other strategic expenses. However, this only took place after the "planned economy" before the period of the "Eleventh Five-Year Plan" was adjusted to "economy following planning," and the initially over-quantified "indicator plan" was replaced by the "dynamic planning" of macro control and strategic planning.

This is the context in which academics such as Hu Angang[17] have summarized China's model for drawing up five-year plans as a "brainstorming[18]" model, which is a form of decision-making based on democratic centralism, reflected in the institutional configuration. On the one hand, local autonomy is emphasized and, on the other, the concentration of power in the Central Government is safeguarded, avoiding—to a certain extent—the phenomenon of "death upon imposing control and chaos upon releasing control" that occurred during the period of the planned economy. As an independent cycle, the Five-Year Plan has the same duration as the mandate of the National Congress of the CCP and the local governments, but maintains a "time difference"[19] or lag of two to three years. This means that the objectives defined in the Five-Year Plan are, on the one hand, the mission of the current mandate[20] and, on the other, the working basis of the following mandate. This "misaligned gearing" between the five-year plans and the mandates ensures institutional stability and the continuation of policy in macroeconomic planning. However, the contradictions of "economics following planning" are reflected in the limitations that local authorities face in adapting to national development—i.e., local governments must to some extent concede partial and short-term interests to broader long-term interests, and gradually integrate regional resources into a plan achieved by local authorities through local negotiations and a system of democratic centralization.[21] Although Macau, as the representative of China's "regions", enjoys greater administrative autonomy than governments in other parts of the country, its diversified industrial structure—which it sorely needs—must be defined under the overall planning of the state's transition to the "new normal".[22]

Previously, after Macau's return to the motherland, the preferential policy of granting gaming licences reflected the Central Government's view of Macau's future, making Macau part of China's phased "dependent modernisation". With China's transition to autonomous modernization and the corresponding change in the main internal and external conflicts, Macau, as a "temporary strategy" of "predominance of the gaming sector", will gradually move to a "plan of the century" of prosperity for all sectors. It should be noted that the changes observed in the conversion from the "planned economy" to the "economy following planning" in the 11th Five-Year Plan reflect a profound change from the "planned economy" to the "socialist market economy" in China—essentially a process of incubation and innovation of the dynamics of private initiative through a public platform. This "platform" refers to the sum of infrastructure and public services led by the state, while kinetic energy refers to new industries, new business models, and new sectors, which have society as their backbone and are strongly related to the modernization of the platform. The platform is the ecosystem in which the dynamic develops and unfolds, and the platform upgrade is the process by which the old dynamic coalesces into the platform's public services via the innovations brought about by the new dynamic. By sedimenting the old dynamic's capital and technology to "increase density," the platform allows a competitive dynamic on asset-light public platforms, thus reflecting more "close-to-content" and more refined characteristics in the new urban context. The business configuration of the private dynamic and the dynamic control of the state platform together build an extremely resilient system of resource management and economic operation. From this "structural perspective", we can perceive, in the midst of the complex international situation, the logic with which Chinese decision-makers face crises.

The "US-China Strategic Rivalry" has been played for decades since the two countries established diplomatic ties in 1979. After the transformation of the economic system forced by the policy of reform and opening up, and the strategy of "keep in a low profile and hide one's strength"[23] during the disintegration of the Soviet Union, China joined the World Trade Organization (WTO) under the increasing severity of international competition. However, as a "peripheral countries",[24] China could only supply raw materials and primary products within the framework of globalization dominated by Western industrialized countries, and its industrialization relied heavily on developed industrial countries. In addition, when implementing an import substitution strategy, it encountered difficulties due to tariff barriers from developed countries, along with obstruction from domestic conservative forces,[25] politically and economically dominated by others. This period can be described as a "platform of dependence."

At the same time, following "China's accession to the WTO, Macau's gaming industry began the mercantile reform of "gaming liberalization" in 2002. This historic measure complemented the new industrial policy "spearheaded by the tourism and gaming sectors" launched by Edmund Ho Hau Wah[26] in 2001, and the policy of "individual visas for Hong Kong and Macau" implemented by the Central Government since 2003, and has led to extraordinary and miraculous growth in Macau's gaming industry.[27] As a result, the exclusive right to operate gambling enterprises, which had endured for many years in the history of the industry in Macau, was split into three. In the end, it became "three concessions and three sub-concessions" and "one licence shared by two companies"[28] (see Figure). On the other hand, the capital generated from Macau's games of chance, which had previously circulated on the Hong Kong and Macau capital markets, inevitably led to the phenomenon of "gambling capital flight" after the influx of foreign capital[29].

This also means that, during Macau's period under Portuguese administration, the control over gambling, firmly in the hands of the Chinese, was quickly swayed by other countries just a few years after the establishment of the MSAR. In addition, during this period, as well as seeing gambling capital flow abroad, Macau also served as a transit point for corrupt officials from mainland China, providing a means for them to launder and transfer "grey revenue";[30] and the illegal money changers located in Zhuhai-Macau and Shenzhen-Hong Kong, as the main escape points for gambling capital in the "Guangdong-Hong Kong-Macau" region, have a reach (impact) that covers almost the entire Pearl River Delta area. All of this was little more than a hopeless measure for Macau, and a "temporary measure" as well, after the Central Government had assessed the situation and weighed up the pros and cons. Under the halo of Macau as the special model closest to mainland China under the One Country, Two Systems principle (compared with Hong Kong and Taiwan) there lay the "grey door" of "capital flight between China and the West", concealed by gambling.

3 *Hotel Lisboa Macau owned by SJM Holdings (STDM) (Source: Wikipedia, the free encyclopedia [wikipedia.org])*

In 2015, during the period of "liquidation of the reserve" of the Chinese property market, Macau's market once again served as a reservoir of capital to contain domestic inflation and prevent capital flight abroad by retaining funds that were leaving the stock market. Together with the "Exchange Reform of 2015", in which the yuan was de-linked from the US dollar, they marked the end of 2016 with the policy of "houses are for living in, not for speculation"[31] and the "de-financialization of the real estate sector," which also pointed to a new urbanization model and the "wealth from industries" model of the "Xiong'an 2017"[32] project. With the autonomous monetary sovereignty policy, the relationship between finance and industry from "de-realization to virtualization" will be reconstructed as "from virtual to real," and will transition to the economic model of "financial support for industry" implicit in the Xiong'an 2017 project. This means that local governments will move from the "old normal" of "one-off financial income from land" to a "new normal of wealth from industries," of obtaining "constant capital flows." The disconnection between China and the US, the de-funding of the real estate sector, and the simultaneous "anti-corruption campaign in the financial sector"—along with the implementation of technologies for tracking and tracing capital flows, such as the digital yuan—had already "devastated" Macau's gambling industry even before the Covid-19 outbreak. The 2020 pandemic has significantly worsened Macau's gambling-reliant economy. However, the root of the problem lies in China's historic transition from a "dependent platform" to an "autonomous platform", and the ensuring growth pains inherent in the structural transformation of Macau's industry.

Crisis always brings new opportunities. With mainland China's transition from the "old normal" of land revenue and dependent monetary issuance to the "new normal" of industrial finance and monetary autonomy, Macau, with its gambling sector and capital-intensive investment model, will also be driven by crisis to adopt an asset-light, content-intensive operating model. In other words: previously, in the phase of accelerated economic growth, the relationship between "platform and dynamism" in urban planning manifested extensive pro-capital characteristics; however, with the transition to high-quality development initiated with the 'Xiong'an 2017' project, it now reflects refined and pro-content characteristics. Macau will also follow a development path of industrial diversification because of this: In the 14th Five-Year Plan, with the aim of "bolstering strategic strengths in science and technology," the state intends to use state capital to transform the "Guangdong-Hong Kong-Macau Greater Bay Area"[33] into a "major scientific and technological innovation platform" and to "expand the service platform for economic and trade co-operation between China and Portuguese-speaking countries."[34] In addition, it is necessary to transform Macau into a "base for exchange and co-operation which promotes the co-existence of diverse cultures",[35]— with the Chinese culture as predominant—as well as supporting the development of "refined" industries, such as the research and manufacture of traditional Chinese medicines, the financial sector with its own characteristics, high technology, conventions and exhibitions, and trade—thus fostering the appropriate diversification of its economy. Macau's gambling industry will move to ultimately achieve the eradication of "grey finance",[36] and must position itself in the future under the guidelines set out by the transformation of the national "new normal."

4 *Xiong'an New Area's Commercial Service and Exhibition Center (Source: wikipedia.org)*

POTENTIAL AND KINETIC ENERGY

There are three so-called major premises:
The first one is the economic resilience of the complete industrial chain and the complete supply chain. In order to maximize the global benefits of the world economy, the modern economy presents a phenomenon of interdependence between global industrial chains. Since China's industrial chain system is increasingly complete, it can provide developing countries with an industrial chain that Europe and America cannot provide. It is also able to use its overwhelming market share and large price advantage in the international industrial chain to guarantee the "basic survival" of Western developed countries, thereby becoming a key country in the global industrial chain. Many small countries must depend on China's entire industrial chain to complete their production, and China's industrial position in the world has formed an industrial force that has thwarted attempts by Western countries to expel China from the global industrial chain.[37] Today, China needs to actively deal with the reconstruction of the global industrial chain and changes in the supply chain at a time when the "great transformations of the century" and the "pandemic of the century" are intertwined. Only by securing the absolute advantages of mainland China's industrial supply chain can Macau really emphasize its advantages in industrial distribution.

The second one is unifying the wider market. President Xi Jinping said, "Today, the scarcest resource is the market".[38] The "wider national unified market" proposed by China is compatible with the above-mentioned approach of ensuring a smooth industrial supply chain. It is centred on "great domestic demand", the "great cycle" and the "great power economy."[39] In other words, fundamental and autonomous technology, autonomous brands, and channels can only be cultivated and developed on the basis of the country's large unified market, the continuous expansion of consumption, and the continuous liberation of needs—thereby creating a domestic value chain or an international value chain that is not subject to the restrictions of other countries in order to profoundly expand domestic demand. At the same time, it can attract a concentration of world-class resources within the country, promote the dual internal and external cycle through a large internal cycle,[40] with a view to achieving a high level of openness to the outside world. This is the notion at the heart of the "Hong Kong-Zhuhai-Macau Economic Circle,"[41] the "Guangdong-Hong Kong-Macau Greater Bay Area," the "South China Sea,"[42] and other regional cooperation markets such as "ASEAN 10 + 1."[43] Its position will be raised to the level of the national strategy of articulation with the new international system of "One Belt, One Road" initiative [44] (see Figure 5).

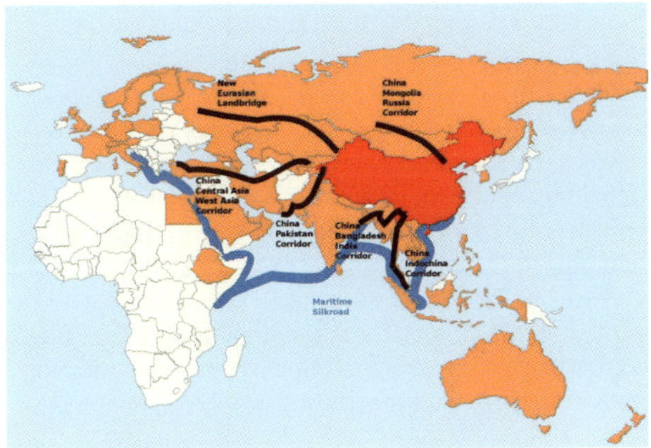

5 *Map of the "One Belt, One Road" initiative (Source: Wikipedia)*

The premise is the build-up of national defences in the South China Sea. As the South China Sea is China's "iron eye" in the global strategic arrangement, completing its construction not only guarantees that the above-mentioned "preconditions" are fulfilled, it can also ensure the security of the One Belt, One Road initiative. In the worst-case scenario, even with a trade blockade between East and West on the "Middle East-Indian Ocean-Malacca" front line, free cross-border trade and the settlement of local currency in the "South China Sea Circle", involving the countries of Southeast Asia and China, will fulfill the "Regional Cross-Border Cycle". Its profound meaning lies in the fact that One Belt, One Road, as the "international route of the proletarian class",[45] in the "north-south direction" (including the countries of southern Europe, within the economic circle of the Portuguese language), does not have the strategic objective of being a G2-type hegemony. Rather, it is meant to bring together the countries of the South, which are solidified on the periphery of global capitalism, by achieving the "rural encircling the city"[46] for the vast number of southern countries locked in the periphery of global capitalism.

In other words, a counterbalance of the majority of "exploitee" to a minority of " exploiter". The strategic objective is no longer to "export of the revolution" or the so-called Chinese model, but the "joint construction of a community with a shared future for humanity", so that the majority of human beings can "reap what they sow".

In order to help Macau better integrate into national development and open up new spaces for its long-term planning, it is necessary to integrate it into the cooperative development regions of "Hengqin, Guangdong-Macau," the "Pan-Pearl River Delta," and even the "South China Sea." This is a necessary step in order to bring Macau into national development strategies such as "Made in China 2025",[47] and "Outline of Long-Range Objectives Through 2035",[48] to fully develop the institutional advantages of the One Country, Two Systems principle and the role of scientific and technological innovation platforms, to finally strengthen Macau's function as a new gateway between the domestic cycle and the international double cycle. To that effect, as one of the regional and global strategies within the framework of the country's transformation, Macau's transformation will involve three major planning areas:

The first is at zonal level—i.e., the "Guangdong-Macau Deepened Cooperation Zone in Hengqin." Hengqin Island is located at the southern end of Zhuhai and is separated from Macau by a river; it is linked to Macau by a bridge, and boosts intrinsic advantages for cooperation between Guangdong and Macau.[49] On the one hand, the "Intensive Cooperation Zone" integrates the conditions of Macau's autonomous customs zone, free port status for international trade, and network of connections with the outside world with the advantageous space and resources of Hengqin, in order to promote the appropriate diversification of Macau's economy. On the other hand, it provides Macau residents with an "urban space" that connects with cross-border public services on both sides. The new high-level opening system of the "Hengqin-Macau integration" built on this foundation, has also become the basis for promoting the construction of the "Guangdong-Hong Kong-Macau Greater Bay" in Macau.[50]

Secondly, comes the regional level, i.e. the "Guangdong-Hong Kong-Macau Greater Bay Area". Its driving force is the "Hong Kong-Macau-Guangdong-Shenzhen" area, with the aim of becoming the "world's fourth great bay" alongside New York, San Francisco, and Tokyo, and a world-class metropolitan region. It occupies an important strategic position at the national development level: by combining the advantages of the scientific research resources of Hong Kong and Macau, the high and new technology infrastructures of Guangzhou-Shenzhen, and the advantages of the Zhuhai-Foshan industrial chain, it will strive to optimize the layout of the advanced manufacturing industry and strengthen the high-end manufacturing industry. At the same time, a strategic cluster of emerging industries will be created, and the development of the modern services sector will be accelerated. Within this framework, Macau can deepen its cooperation with Zhuhai by building a regional economic development axis, forming a networked spatial structure supported by a polar axis. Which will radiate out to boost the level of development of the west bank of the Pearl River, thereby leading the Guangdong-Hong Kong-Macau Greater Bay Area to participate deeply in international cooperation and promote integration and complementarity between the two banks of the East and the West, in order to provide strong support for the construction of the One Belt, One Road initiative.

Finally comes the global level—i.e., the "South China Sea" strategy. The autonomy of the South China Sea route will help China gain a geo-active position in the political game between East and West, while promoting the "economic unification of East Asia"—with China as its driving force—in order to realize its vision of peaceful development. China has proposed the "joint exploitation of the South China Sea" to emphasize strategic value over economic interests, by "relinquishing" part of the oil and natural gas resources to distribute their revenues to neighboring countries. This is to prevent cooperation within the framework of the dispute over geopolitical values in the South China Sea from being shaken by external forces and, consequently, to protect the new One Belt, One Road international system put forward by China. In this context, Macau can continue to play its role as a "gateway" between the economic circles of mainland China and the Portuguese-speaking countries, promoting the construction of the "Service Platform for Commercial Cooperation between China and the Portuguese-speaking Countries"—namely Brazil, Mozambique, Portugal and Goa in India— through the cultural One Belt, One Road initiative, thus establishing Macau's discursive weight in the globalized circle mediated by the Portuguese language.[51]

TRANSFORMATION AND STRATEGY

There is no doubt that, in light of the serious impact that the Covid-19 pandemic has had on Macau's economy and the fragility of its economic structure, characterized by a high degree of monolithism, the 2nd Five-Year Plan of Macau—launched in 2021—will adopt the "1 + 4" diversified and appropriate development strategy, in accordance with the requirements of the 14th National

Five-Year Plan. The 2nd Five-Year Plan fostered the development of key industries—namely, the research and manufacture of traditional Chinese medicines, the financial sector with its own characteristics, high technology, the convention and exhibition industry, and trade, among others—by organising them in a reasonable manner. At the same time, regarding the consolidation and uplifting of traditional industries not associated with gambling, the operative idea is to gradually replace the capital-intensive asset operation model with a content-intensive light asset operation model through mixed-mode and detailed configuration, and the creation of public and private fields. Gambling and shopping will thus transform this "gambling city" with a single destination into a "post-gambling gambling city" characterized by immersive, non-specific spots and destinations—thus enriching its contents as a "World Tourism and Leisure Centre".[52]

In this sense, Macau's global or cross-border tourism can take advantage of its geographical advantages in the "Greater Guangdong-Hong Kong-Macau Bay" and the central position of Hong Kong's international maritime transport to enrich tourist itineraries and a system of related products. The creation of a coastal tourism development axis linking Hong Kong and Macau will be fostered by building a leisure bay and a coastal town.[53] Similarly, through the effective implementation of "Guangdong-Hong Kong-Macau" individual pleasure boat tourism, the development of international pleasure boat tourism in Macau and neighboring cities, and the optimization of the "144-hour transit visa waiver" policy in the Pearl River Delta Region, the Guangdong-Hong Kong-Macau Greater Bay can also facilitate visits for domestic and foreign tourists over a longer period of time.

Secondly, the world heritage of Macau's historic center,[54] as a regional space, not only encompasses the traditions and customs of the industrial and commercial sectors, food, clothing, and transport of southern China, but also foreign cultures from Southeast Asia and Portuguese-speaking countries. Throughout history, Macau has been the "commercial transit port" of the maritime silk route. In the future, Macau could, through this tradition, become a cultural transit port between the cultural minorities of the "Mainland-Macau" (the Macanese are the 57th largest informal ethnic group in China) and "Macau-Lusophony". The combination of Macau's world cultural heritage with mainland China's intangible cultural heritage gives rise to an image of a small urban space with tradition, different from the dominant culture, built from ethnic minorities. Macau, with an area of just a few dozen square kilometers, could become a "small immersive quarter"—the intangible cultural heritage of China's rural areas and a reflection of the communities in southern China, which make up a part of the civilization of the Portuguese-speaking countries in Macau's territory, combined with the urban renewal of Macau's landscapes, commercial areas, communities, and public spaces as well as the revitalisation of the "Macau World Heritage Site", transforming it into a great, vibrant area (see Figure 6).
In 2022, UNESCO awarded the Prize for Innovation in Architecture[55] to the President of the International Union of Portuguese-Speaking Architects, Rui Leão, and to his partner, Macau architect Carlotta Bruni, in recognition of the construction of a public services building near the ruins of São Paulo, in Macau's old town (see Figure 7). Leão defines the site as a typical meeting point between Portuguese urbanism and Chinese urbanism, "with completely different urban styles that clash with each other in different areas of the city." For that reason, the choice of this buffer zone in the historic center of the Macau World Heritage Site to create interaction with the surrounding housing and public spaces makes this small community a microcosm and a living fossil of "mutual learning between civilizations" and "cultural transposition."

6 *Historic center of Macau (Source: Wikipedia)*

In addition, the overall content planning project for "Macau 123,"[56] led by the author, further emphasizes the integration of Macau's regional culture into the vision of the international dissemination of Chinese culture, as well as the cultural imprints of different countries and regions of the world in Macau. With content production at its core, the comprehensive strategy for the industrial and urban modernization of Macau is explored in five aspects: geographical space, industries, society and the life of the population, organizational management, and the cultural cause. Together with the cases of micro-renewal mentioned above, it reflects the structural thinking of "platform and dynamism". Under the strategy of "global immersion" to promote the "integration of the entire chain", not only can a series of brands and dynamics related to the transformation of Macau's industries be developed through the "coordination of the state of business" but also, in the integration between the "state of business" and the "field of operation," Macau's public spaces are brought to current standards in a detail-oriented fashion, akin to the case of the Courtyard of Eternal Happiness.

7 *Public services building in Macau (Source: Utility building in Historic Centre of Macau awarded by UNESCO (macaonews.org))*

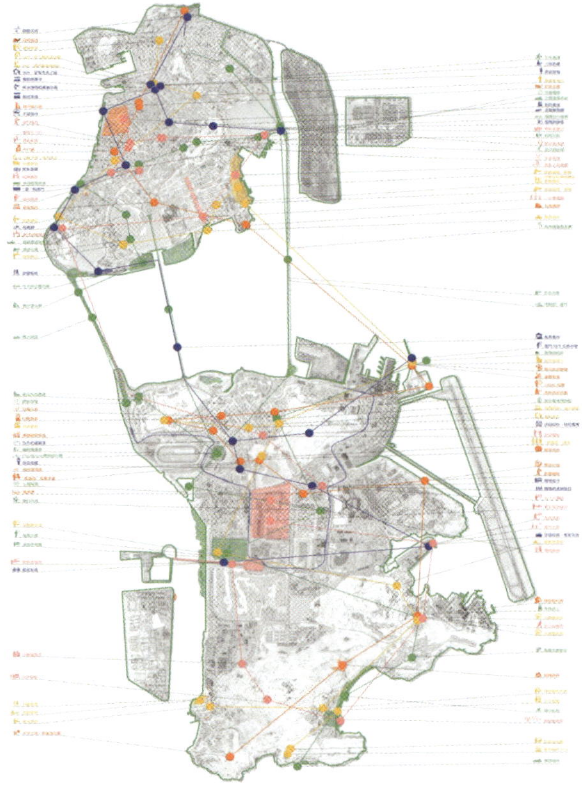

8 *Planning project of the overall content of Macau 123*

It should be noted that Macau's gaming sector, which once served as a gateway for grey capital, will complete its transformation with the modernization of modern service sectors, such as the financial sector and conventions and exhibitions. In the past, due to its 'nature as an exchange house', Macau's gaming sector was able to settle informally in offshore renminbi (RMB). Starting in 2020, China launched the 'Cross-Border Financial Management' pilot project in the Guangdong-Hong Kong-Macau Greater Bay Area, taking advantage of Macau's highly open financial system to explore the creation of a RMB-denominated securities market and an offshore digital financial center. This means that the formalization of Macau's financial function and the decomposition of the weight of Hong Kong's financial centre in relation to Macau—i.e., Hong Kong's functions in offshore RMB settlement, will create a multi-center scenario with Macau. It is clear that this transformation of Macau's role is subordinate to the national currency strategy. Macau's convention and exhibition centers and clubs related to the gaming industry will also be transformed into hotels, shopping centres, etc. Instead of putting an end to all gambling at once and for all, Macau's "gambling city" is moving towards the abolition of gambling and the diversification of industry, and probably towards "Changing the cage by changing the birds." In the end, in a "post-gambling city," the gambling sector will come to be regarded as a part of Macau's historical legacy of "post-casino Macau" in the form of a small and micro entertainment industry.

CONCLUSION

Macau, the "gambling city" that served as a gateway for grey capital, is trying to transform itself into a "post-gambling city", with the support of a wider national strategy. China is almost the most restrictive country in the world when it comes to gambling, yet it potentially has the largest group of gamblers globally, which means that there is almost a "gambling circle" around it. Macau can play a special role in this process, meaning that—theoretically—the existing "cash pooling" effect can be "solved in-house". With the strengthening of China's power in the world and its international influence, financial supervision and repeated efforts have intensified internally, while abroad, capital flight has been prevented through reinforced international cooperation. Macau's historical role as a "temporary solution" is being diluted in this process, and it is instead becoming a "plan of the century" in line with national strategies such as regional integration and the new model of globalization. Understanding Macau and its process of transformation must be based on China's underlying historical process and its vision of strategic planning—so that Macau does not become an "isolated point" of a small territory, but a "turning point" or hinge that participates and breaks into the global environment.

1 Silver, the main hard currency of the Ming dynasty, continued to flow in through exports of fabrics, ceramics, tea, and other products. The result was inflation. When the inflow of silver decreased in the late Ming dynasty, inflation would turn to deflation and the rush of capital groups to stockpile silver coincided with the large-scale contraction of small businesses, which became a vicious circle.

2 In the 43rd year of Jiajing, the sailors guarding Zhelin Ao in Raoping County, Chaozhou, Guangdong mutinied because of lack of pay and then sailed to attack the provincial capital of Guangzhou with their ships. This major incident, which shook the government and the public, was not settled until several months later. See: Chen Xianbo, "The Zhelin Mutiny and the Coastal Defense System of Guangdong in the Middle and Late Ming Dynasty," *National Navigation* 3 (2014), pp.1–2.

3 Wu Guifang (1521—1578) was appointed commander and governor of the Guangdong military affairs in the 42nd year of Jiajing, in order to quell the Japanese War in Guangdong.

4 For practical reasons (Guangdong's financial difficulties), local officials developed Macau as a place of trade and commerce that could not only alleviate the financial difficulties but also effectively control the Portuguese and other foreigners, as well as give protection against pirates. For more details, see: Wu Zhiliang, *Political History of Macau* (Shanghai: Shanghai Academy of Social Sciences Press, 1999), pp.36-43.

5 Around the second year of the Yongzheng reign (1724), Chinese merchant ships regained their freedom of navigation with Southeast Asian countries and launched fierce competition against Portuguese merchants. In view of the financial difficulties of the coastal regions, the Qing court had to lift the bans in the provinces of Guangdong, Fujian and Zhejiang. In contrast, after losing the shipping monopoly, the economic situation of Portugal reached a low ebb (the Qing court imposed restrictions on Portuguese shipping, while Portugal also terminated its rights to sail to the Portuguese mainland and Portuguese Brazil). For more details, see: Chen Yan, "Macau's special status and influence on the Modern Maritime Silk Road," *Journal of Culture* (Portugal) 13, 14 (1993), pp.44.

6 The Treaty of Nanking was the first treaty signed by the Qing dynasty as a result of its defeat by the United States and Europe. The main terms were the cession of Hong Kong Island and the opening of five ports (Guangzhou, Xiamen, Fuzhou, Ningbo, and Shanghai) to trade.

7 See: C. A. McOntalo de Jesus, *Macau in History*, trans. Huang Hongzhao and LI Baoping (Macau: Macau Foundation, 2001), p.233.

8 Ferreira do Amaral served as the 79th Governor of Macau from 1846. Immediately, he carried out the colonial expansion policy in Macau and announced the imposition of land rent on Chinese residents, extending the ruling power originally imposed on Portuguese to Chinese residents. However, he also aroused the indignation of Chinese residents and was assassinated.

9 The Taiping Rebellion was a peasant uprising war launched by Hong Xiuquan and others from the first year of Xianfeng to the three years of Tongzhi (1851—1864) against the feudal rule of the Qing dynasty and foreign capitalist aggression, and it was also the largest large-scale anti-Qing movement in China in the middle of the 19th century.

10 See: Gen, Modern History of *Gambling Industry in Macau* (Guangzhou: Guangdong People's Publishing House, 2009), pp.85–102.

11 Under China's overall plan, it is necessary to implement a more equitable economic system in accordance with its "original aspiration and mission", so as to realize the equity of socialism (fairness and justice, comprehensive development, social enrichment, etc.). In this process, with the change of major contradictions, some relatively "unfair" measures may be allowed at certain periods to take into account the overall situation.

12 For the full year 2020, Macau's gross gaming revenue was 60,441 billion patacas (MOP$, same below), down 79.3% from 292,455 billion patacas for the full year 2019. More details, see: China News: ***https://www.chinanews.com.cn/ga/2021/01-01/9376766.shtml***

13 In 1953, China began to formulate the first "Five-Year Plan", the full name of which is the "Outline of the Five-Year Plan for National Economic and Social Development of the People's Republic of China". It is an important part of national economic plan and is a long-term plan.

14 During the "First Five Year Plan" period, the Soviet Union assisted the construction of about 150 to 160 industrial projects in China; because some of the projects were cancelled, merged, or delayed, the tally was generally collectively referred to as 156.

15 The economic crisis and depression of 1979—1981 occurred successively, mainly due to the huge fiscal deficit pressure formed by the Chinese Government in the late 1970s.

16 At that time, China was in the transitional stage of economic system reform, and commodity prices implemented the "dual-track price system." In order to get rid of the invisible system cost of the dual-track price system, the government launched the radical "price invasion", which actually triggered the system cost covered by the internalized mechanism of the dual-track system.

17 Hu Angang, born in 1953, is currently the Dean of the Institute for National Studies of Tsinghua University, a senior professor of liberal arts, a professor of the School of Public Administration, and a doctoral supervisor of Tsinghua University. He is one of the pioneers and leaders of National Studies (Contemporary China Studies) which enjoys a high reputation at home and abroad.

18 The process is fully democratic by involving all stakeholders in decision-making (including central government departments, think tanks and experts, NGOs, international agencies and academics, the general public, etc.), and is designed to help decision-makers process "democracy before centralization" and "both diffusion and consensus." The aim is to help decision-makers process the vast amount of information and to take into account the interests of all parties. For more details, see: Hu Angang, "China's Unique Five-Year Plan Transformation," *Open Times* 6 (2013), pp.32–35.

19 See: Zhao Xuejun, "Some Basic Relations between the Formulation and Implementation of the Five-Year Plan – Historical Experience of the 13th Five-Year Plan," *CPC History Studies* 5 (2020), pp.127–29.

20 "The current term" and "the next term" refer to the current/next Central Committee of the Communist Party of China and National People's Congress.

21 Although it has certain limitations, its advantage lies in that it gives full play to the role of the "two hands," minimizes the governance costs, and maximizes the governance benefits. It not only gives play to local creativity but also "concentrates resources to do great things." For more details, see: Hu Angang, "China's Unique Five-Year Plan Transformation," p.36.

22 Since 2015, the highest level has positioned China's economy as having entered a "new normal," the deeper meaning of which is that after a decade-long cycle of credit easing pegged to the US dollar, broad money issuance anchored by China's real estate market has surpassed that of the US. This implies that the dependent monetary policy that began with "Made in China" has completed the "autonomy" of the currency through "Chinese city-making" and has been "internalized" in the process of further "re-anchoring" towards rural resources, and that the US and Chinese currencies have finally reached an inflection point where they can compete with each other. See also the author's article "Renewing Spontaneous China - The Resilient Transformation of Urban-Rural Relations in the New Normal".

23 The strategy of "keep in low profile and hide one's strength" was put forward by Deng Xiaoping in April 1992 when he talked about China's development, and its meaning is to "keep a firm grip on the main line of economic construction and work hard to develop ourselves."

24 Argentine economist Raul Prebisch divides the world economic system into two categories: the center and the periphery. The latter consists of the vast majority of developing countries, outside the developed countries, which are dependent on the developed countries in terms of economic and technological development and have difficulty in obtaining the benefits brought by technological progress. On the contrary, technological progress has depressed the prices of primary commodities, the main export commodities, so that they engage in unequal economic trade with the central countries.

25 See: Wen Tiejun, *Eight Crises: China's Real Experience 1949-2009* (Beijing: Oriental Press, 2013), pp.7–8.

26 Edmund Ho Hau Wah, born in 1955, has been involved in the political affairs of China and Macau since 1986, and was appointed by the State Council as the first Chief Executive of macau on May 20, 1999. He was re-elected unopposed in 2004 and served as chief executive for a total of 10 years until 2009.

27 See: Wang Wuyi, "Prosperity and contradiction: A Review of the tenth Anniversary of the opening of gambling rights in Macau," *Guangdong Social Sciences* 4 (2012), pp.108–17.

28 At present, there are six gambling licenses in Macau: "three main and three secondary." The "three main" are "SJM Holdings," founded by Macau landlord Stanley Ho; "Galaxy Entertainment," owned by Hong Kong tycoon Lui Che Woo; and "Wynn Macau," owned by the US-based Wynn Resorts. The "three vice" companies are "MGM China," owned by Pansy Ho and Sands Corp; "Sands China," which is owned by the Sands Group; and "Melco Boa," which is owned by Lawrence Ho. For more details, see: Wang Wuyi, *World Gambling Explosion and China's Economic Benefits* (Beijing: Economic Science Press, 2005), p.114.
29 See ibid., pp.117–18.
30 In China, when residents buy real estate in a city, it is equivalent to buying "shares" in the city. In other words, if city governments are treated as companies, Western cities raise money by issuing bonds while Chinese cities raise money by issuing "shares." So "land finance" refers to land income, its essence is financing (stock), rather than fiscal revenue (tax). See Zhao Yanjing, "Land finance: History, logic and choice," *Urban Development Studies* 1 (2014), p.3.
31 At the end of 2016, the Central Economic Work Conference proposed for the first time that "the house is used to live in, not to speculate," since when the real estate-related departments have introduced supporting policies, which involve the financing of housing enterprises, homebuyers' credit, and other aspects.
32 The Xiongan New Area in Hebei is of great practical and far-reaching historical significance in terms of focusing on the non-capital functions of Beijing, exploring a new model for optimizing the development of densely populated and economically populated areas, adjusting and optimizing the urban layout and spatial structure of the Beijing-Tianjin-Hebei region, and fostering a new engine of innovation-driven development.
33 The Guangdong-Hong Kong-Macau Greater Bay Area includes the Hong Kong Special Administrative Region, the Macau Special Administrative Region and the cities of Guangzhou, Shenzhen, Zhuhai, Foshan, Huizhou, Dongguan, Zhongshan, Jiangmen, and Zhaoqing in Guangdong Province. It has a long coastline, good ports and vast sea area.
34 Since Macau has linguistic and legal ties with Portuguese-speaking countries and maintains close economic and trade ties with the mainland, the state supports Macau in building a service platform for business cooperation between China and Portuguese-speaking countries, which has been included in the "Outline of the Development Plan for the Guangdong-Hong Kong-Macau Greater Bay Area."
35 China will maintain the long-term prosperity and stability of Hong Kong and Macau by supporting them to consolidate and enhance their competitive advantages, as outlined in the 14th Five-Year Plan.
36 Strictly speaking, betting games such as lotteries are not proper financial instruments, but they undoubtedly have strong "financial attributes"; when betting games are used as a financial instrument by the government, they can not only relieve the government's financial pressure but also make up for the lack of normal financial channels, and thus acquire "financial attributes." For this reason, the term "de-financialisation of the gaming industry" refers to a policy tool similar to the "de-financialization of real estate" to prevent the outflow of gambling capital.
37 For more details, see: Professor Huang Jiangnan's interpretation on the Internet: "In-depth analysis – Will China be kicked out of the world industrial chain?" https://www.bilibili.com/video/BV1LV4y1A78U/?spm_id_from=333.337.top_right_bar_window_default_collection.content.click&vd_source=9c2ec2ee3ec881036d3196c9726b56a9
38 See: Xi Jinping, "Grasping the new development stage, implementing the new development concept, and building a new development pattern," *Seeking Truth* 9 (2021).
39 See: Wang Xiaodong and Xie Lijuan's working paper "Accelerating the Construction of a Large Unified National Market: Theoretical Basis and Practice in China," to be published in *Teaching and Research*.
40 In 2020, a new development pattern was proposed and accelerated to build "a new development pattern with the domestic circulation as the main body and the domestic and international circulation promoting each other"—i.e., a new pattern built mainly by unblocking the national economic circulation, aiming to solve the obstruction problem in China's economic development. At the same time, a high level of opening up to the outside world is needed to create new advantages in international cooperation and competition.
41 After the completion of the Hong Kong-Zhuhai-Macau Bridge, the free flow of internal elements and the optimization and integration of resources in the Greater Bay Area will make new attempts in the Hong Kong-Zhuhai-Macau Greater Bay Area with the help of blockchain technology, and thus form the Hong Kong-Zhuhai-Macau "one-hour economic circle."
42 The South China Sea is located off the southern part of the Chinese mainland and in the western part of the Pacific Ocean. It is the traffic artery connecting the Pacific and the Indian oceans. With an area of 3.5 million square kilometers, it is the third largest sea in the world. The countries within its scope include China, the Philippines, Malaysia, Indonesia, Brunei, Singapore, Cambodia, Vietnam, and Thailand.
43 The China–ASEAN "10+1" mechanism is a cooperation mechanism established by China and the Association of Southeast Asian Nations (ASEAN). Since its establishment in 1997, cooperation between the two sides has been continuously expanded and deepened, and has now developed into a close political and economic organization and become one of the main mechanisms for regional cooperation in East Asia.
44 The Belt and Road initiative, short for the "Silk Road Economic Belt and the 21st Century Maritime Silk Road," is an open and inclusive economic cooperation initiative provided by China to the world as a platform for international cooperation and a public good.
45 The "mass line" is the fundamental attitude, working method, and ideological line of the Communist Party of China and the organs of state power in dealing with the relationship with the people. It takes the approach of "from the masses, to the masses" and tests the validity of these opinions in mass action.

46 Originally, this meant that in rural areas where the enemy's ruling power was relatively weak, it took the lead in launching an armed uprising of peasants and establishing revolutionary base areas, combining armed struggle, agrarian revolution, and the establishment of political power; making them strategic bases for supporting a long-term revolutionary war; and relying on the base areas to accumulate and develop revolutionary forces—gradually creating a strategic situation in which the countryside surrounded the cities, and finally winning the revolution.

47 "Made in China 2025" is the action program of the first decade of China's implementation of the strategy of manufacturing power.

48 By 2035, China will have basically realized socialist modernization, and its economic strength, scientific and technological strength, and comprehensive national strength will have greatly improved.

49 See: Chapter 1 "General Requirements" of the "Overall Plan for the Construction of Hengqin Guangdong-Macau In-Depth Cooperation Zone issued by the Central Committee of the Communist Party of China and the State Council."

50 See: Chapter 19 of the "Second Five-Year Plan for the Economic and Social Development of the Macau Special Administrative Region (2021-2025)", prepared by the Macau Government, "Accelerating the Construction of the Hengqin Guangdong-Macau In-Depth Cooperation Zone."

51 In line with the One Belt, One Road initiative, the TDC co-organizes the International Infrastructure Investment and Construction Summit in Macau with the China Chamber of Commerce for Foreign Contracted Projects, with 56 government officials at ministerial level or above from nearly 40 countries and regions attending the 2018 forum. In addition, to complement the construction of the Sino-Portuguese Platform, with the support of the relevant Central Government ministries and commissions, the Macau SAR Government and the state-owned Assets Supervision and Administration Commission of the State-Council co-hosted the Summit on Central Enterprises' Support for the construction of the Sino-Portuguese Platform in Macau in 2017 and 2019 respectively, inviting representatives from about 30 central enterprises, as well as a number of Portuguese-speaking countries and local enterprises, among others, to participate.

52 See Chapter 61 "Maintaining the long-term prosperity and stability of Hong Kong and Macau" of the "Outline of the 14th Five-Year Plan and Vision 2035 of the National Economic and Social Development of the People's Republic of China"; please also refer to Chapter 2 "Basic Principles, Development Goals and Major Tasks" of the "Second Five-Year Plan for the Economic and Social Development of the Macau Special Administrative Region (2021-2025)".

53 See Chapter 8, Section 3 "Constructing a Leisure Bay Area" of the "Outline of the Outline Development Plan for the Guangdong-Hong Kong-Macau Greater Bay Area issued by the Central Committee of the Communist Party of China and the State Council".

54 The historic center of Macau is the oldest, largest, best-preserved, and most concentrated coexistence of Eastern and Western styles in China, including the oldest church ruins and monasteries in China, the oldest Christian cemetery, the oldest Western-style fortress complex, the first modern lighthouse, and the first Western-style university.

55 Since 2000, the UNESCO Asia-Pacific Awards for Cultural Heritage Conservation program has been recognizing the efforts of individuals and private organizations in the restoration, conservation, and renovation of buildings and structures of heritage value in the region. To date, the winning projects have demonstrated various conservation criteria such as expression of the spirit of the site, technical achievement, appropriate use or adaptation, involvement of the project with the local community, and contribution to improving the sustainability of the site's surroundings and other environments.

56 The RISS (Research Institute of Society & Strategy) of the China Academy of Art aims to rebuild the design humanities and integrate cross-border teaching, and seeks to cultivate talents that cover the overall knowledge structure of "intelligent science and technology" required for innovative design education.

6.1. M30 POWER SUPPLY INTEGRATED INFRASTRUCTURE

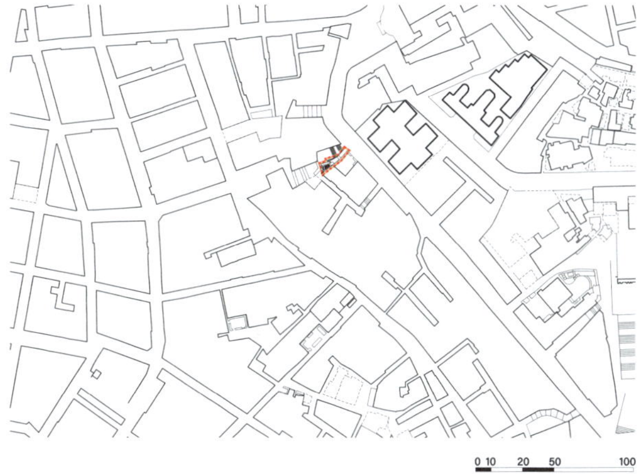

DESIGN DATE	GROSS FLOOR AREA
2016	**42m²**

The project is an integrated infrastructure building for power supply and waste collection located in the old district of Inner Harbor, Macau, with the code M30. Faced with the challenge in upgrading the electrical supply and waste collection in the old town, in 2016, CEM, the Macau Electrical Company, and IAM, the Municipal Affairs Bureau of Macau, decided collectively to commission these two types of infrastructure by assigning a single plot of land to both and having them stacked up in multiple levels.

The plot is situated along a pedestrian stepped lane, characterized by an uneven alley with flights of steps that connect the main road at the high level (Rua de Santo António at +12.00 mean sea level) with the old main street on the lower lying Inner Harbor district (Rua da Tercena in the West at +2.2 mean sea level). The plot doesn't have vehicular access and is used by many pedestrians moving from the northern district of the peninsula towards the Inner Harbor.

The plot of land designated for M30— the Integrated Infrastructure for Power Supply and Waste Collection Room—is located at an intermediate "landing" off this stepped lane (at +9.05 mean sea level), a space that works as the main social gathering space, apart from being a pedestrian thoroughfare, with a secondary access via a narrow ramp which connects to the main road at the higher level.

The project, with a total built area of 30 square meters, although small, was complex to solve: we had the engineering and pragmatic requirements of two different clients to satisfy on a tight site as well as the dilemma of how to insert a new industrial building in a historical residential district. The building needed to be considered at multiple scales. We therefore adopted several design tactics in order to resolve the contradictions of the brief and its integration into the urban fabric—namely on massing, working with section, reconciling circulation and use of materials.

We expanded the brief and the goals of the project to go beyond satisfying the programmatic requirements of the infrastructure brief, and to capitalize on the site's unique position at this junction of patios and historic laneways which define the contemporary and historic city. Our objective for the building was that it would bridge these conditions, and enhance the historic site with the potential to generate a vibrant heritage-based district to benefit Macau's status as a heritage destination.

The transformer room is located at the lower level (+9.05 msl) and supplies electricity to a wide area of the historical center. The waste collection room is stacked over it at level +12.85 msl and serves the neighborhood with differentiated waste disposal, with a capacity for three large waste containers. The external space between this storage area and the sidewalk was also integrated into the scope of the project.

The relationship between the program of modern infrastructure and a site of historical significance is an uneasy one, because heritage awareness was never reflected in the brief. The project was resolved through a very delicate manipulation of the site levels to integrate the new infrastructure, through the design of the two infrastructure programmes as a vertical object set against the historical houses of the lanes adjacent; and by making the new access work like a public circuit. The ramp is designed as a large-scale horizontal element that connects and reconciles the public stairways and the pre-existing walls with the new volume of the integrated infrastructure.

The new infrastructure is a sculpted mass, shrunk and stacked to relate to the mass of buildings in this historic area, making its insertion perfectly scaled. It is a mass that turns corners to allow for views across the site, and places a cantilevered walkway where the ramp overlooks the main public patio below. Its flank wall both cleaves and connects to the adjacent historic structure. The height of the building was carefully defined to coincide with the adjacent volume. In the corner of the building and against the adjacent historic building, we used corten steel as a cleaver, making the new construction touch and simultaneously set itself apart from the adjacent brick building. The contrast of the two adopted materials was important for the new building to critically play, detach, frame, and relate to the historic context of the old buildings of the patio, the pre-existent retaining walls, and the public space.

The choice and disposition of materials for this project was essential to the integration of the old houses in Chinese typology and typical *Lingnan* architectural features (i.e., green brick) with the needs of the contemporary infrastructure program (i.e., cantilevered steel walkways, metal handrails, and stainless steel gutters). The building does not intend to mimic its context but rather to frame, enhance, and rejuvenate its urban context.

The stacking of the program gives the new building the necessary scale for it to work as an urban pivot, a focal point at the edge of the two urban typologies, indicating the way up the hill for pedestrians walking across the district and announcing the location of the old Chinese patios halfway along the hillside. With its long corten tail, rising over the old stairway wall towards the vertical massing of the new building, the M30 project embraces the main landing of the stepped lane, giving it a civic dimension through the rise of the brick walls and the cantilevered passage over the main landing of the lane.

The project also becomes a hinge between the vehicular and non-vehicular circulation as its volume becomes associated with the residents' walking path towards the waste recycling facility and an iconic background for the stepped rise towards the main street, where the cars become part of street life.

The new building acts as urban gateway, framing the view of pedestrians entering the stepped lane from both the high level and the lower district, and clearly defining two different patios at different levels—below it and beyond it. The massing and layout of the corten element animates the space and creates a sense of direction, by pointing towards the two directions of circulation.

Inserting an infrastructure into a historic residential area was a difficult thing to do, and we embraced it unapologetically through design, making it work like a gateway into the district—not only to provide a service amenity but also to add social and cultural value to the life of the district.

The project works like a built reference, announcing itself to the main circulation axis of the stepped lane and the easily overlooked heritage cluster of the Chinese patios adjacent to it, and successfully designing the corner element of the heritage cluster—which, typically, is a blank wall along the plot's edge.

The project thus takes advantage of its critical site location, at the intersection between *the stepped lane*, a Portuguese-type of street modulated on different leveled platforms, and *the Chinese traditional patios*, of Patio da Eterna Felicidade. The volume of the project sets up a contemporary cubistic mass all covered by traditional green brickwork, which is the constructive "workhorse" of the entire Chinese heritage cluster beyond the site.

By using traditional Chinese brickwork, the project pulls out this iconic image of Chinese traditional culture onto the main public space of *the stepped lane*, where there is a constant flow of people moving from the northern districts towards the Inner Harbor, raising the curiosity of passersby, who may then slow down to look at the façades or divert towards the hidden lane of *the Chinese patios.*

In principle, the proposed program for the site would be highly undesirable, due to the almost inevitable visual impact of the new infrastructure on the delicate scale and the heritage value of the old Chinese patios. Looking back at this commission, we think it was a rare opportunity to take a big constraint as implied in the brief, and use the project to demonstrate how to avert a bad intervention with a sophisticated response to the site—in addition to the brief, strictly speaking.

The program gave us the opportunity to make an urban move, to resolve and reconcile the layers of pedestrian and vehicular access and to make a hinge on the site, where the different urban components of the district are announced and reflected through the complex definition of the new architectural insertion.

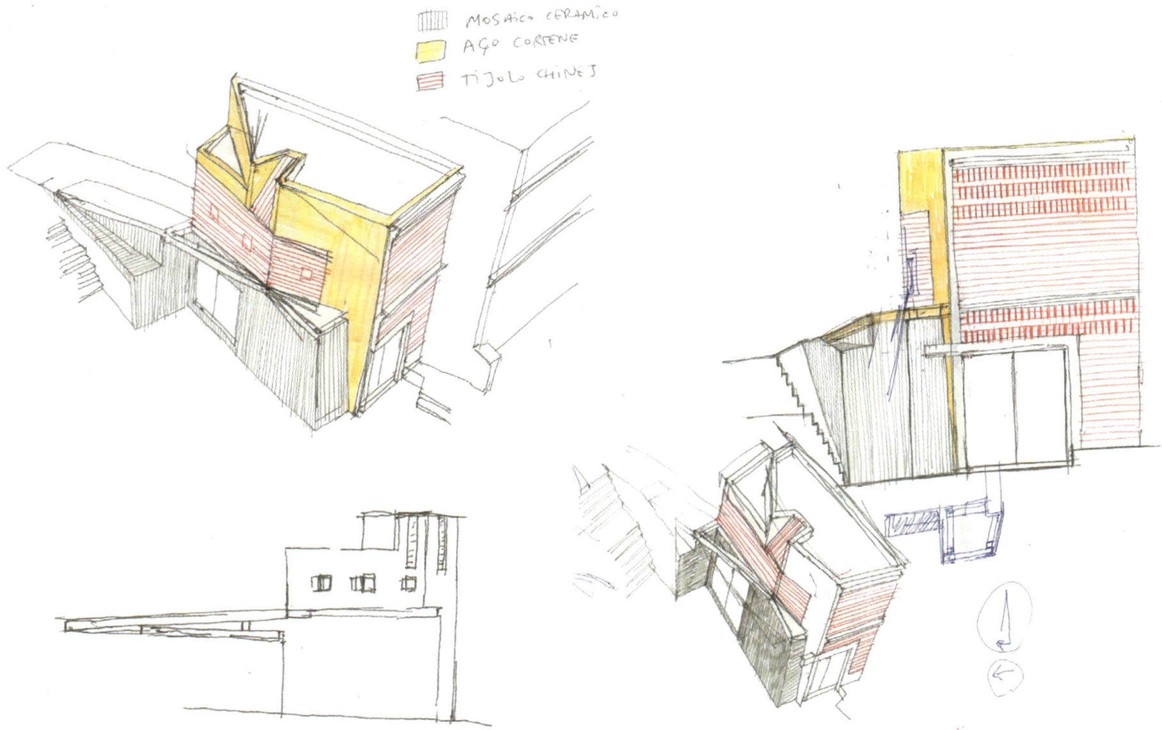

Upon looking at the built project, we have understood that there are at least three issues that it deals with and responds to successfully. Firstly, this project demonstrates that it is possible to add modern infrastructure to historic sites with a sensible design strategy for that; secondly, the project for the new infrastructure and new buildings can be integrated with a site without mimicking its heritage language; and thirdly, that we can improve the quality of the urban fabric through the insertion of a new project in a heritage context. In spite of its being small, the scale of the project worked as an advantage.

↑ M30 Integrated Infrastructure for Power Supply and Waste collection: General views of the building, conceptual evolution

PT 2126
Neighbourhood

WASTE ROOM
TRANSFORMER ROOM

±280

電池收集點
垃圾站
DEPÓSITO
DE LIXO
M30
CSR
66581221

DAISO

DEPOSITO
DE LIXO
N30

7. Layering the city

Rui Leão
F. Carlotta Bruni

With our practice, we have kept a critical position of resistance during the post-handover context of Macau, as the city made efforts to rethink its political order and deal with the new challenges of praxis—since the inherited colonial system of governance was both too informal in its processes and too formalized in its language.

We understand our practice of resistance to enforcing the basic values of the profession as both an act of generosity and an effort to accommodate and respond to the particular "loose", political conditions of this place.

Due to the circumstances of the urban context where our projects are located, we have been working on sites with challenging briefs—like making a square in traffic interchange or designing a park between a highway and below a bridge. These challenges developed in our practice a type of intent that inserted into the projects additional layers which allow us to respond laterally to the brief and to offer more to the city than just the commissioned design. Our systematic resilience in this process of designing has developed into an opportunistic urbanism where the designers play various roles to enact a scenario of discussion with all stakeholders, thus creating opportunities through new social and urban agendas to "feed" the projects. The outcome of our methodology of working through this critical discussion of the design programs results in a formative process involving all stakeholders in finding solutions through an agile political urbanism which allows us to navigate in the current political system and shift policy through practice.

We engage in resilient, infrastructural, civic urbanism as an alternative form of urban practice using the design of infrastructure to generate the design of the site context at various scales, demonstrating that designing infrastructure for a single purpose is a strategic mistake. Instead, the large investments to which our commissioned work corresponds can be made to serve a variety of different agendas—to include not only transportation but also real estate, ecological diversity, and public space. Furthermore, a sound infrastructural design permits utility in a variety of completely different circumstances. This is not a call to make infrastructural investments more complex and expensive, but to make them more versatile and open-ended. Our work reflects the relevance of infrastructure for urban design and exemplifies how infrastructural urbanism complements conventional architectural urbanism.

Macau being a small and compact city where everything is adjacent to everything else, it is unusual to receive an uncompromised site or a simple design brief. The "adjacency" factor has become an opportunity for our practice to study atypical solutions that most of the time combine functionalities and speak to new ways of designing compactness.

There is also a persistence in our projects, responding to the lack of planning and over-densification of the city by investigating the relationship between the building and its surrounding space, which has allowed for the discovery of a collateral of un-purposed space inserted into the commissioned projects. These are public or common spaces within residential buildings, public spaces intertwined with traffic infrastructure, and connective circulation spaces in the urban context.

Un-purposed space is the designer's addition to the building program. It is intended to allow for any type of foreseen or unforeseen use without impacting the overall functionality of the project. It adds new layers of community interaction and cultural use to the overall design. Un-purposed space can be found in interior designs where the functional areas mix with the circulation space through the design of space pockets and widening of circulations, corners, or large entrances. It can also be found in building projects where the shape of the city block, its porosity, and its expanded thresholds allow for a non-prescriptive use that relates the project to the urban experience of its surrounding context.

We have been developing strategies to make programmatic, public, common, open spaces within private ownership, with the aim of replicating the quality of the small clusters within the built continuum, and allowing for appropriation of public space according to the way people use it locally. These spaces add value to the design program and to the barely planned city.

Indetermination in the use of common space has been one of the strategies that we have used to allow for its free cultural appropriation by the local population. We have let ourselves be "contaminated" by the local usage of common areas and we have been considerate in providing spaces for this usage to continue. Through observation, we have found strategies to control the full appropriation of common space by a single party, by allowing for the overlapping of functions.

One of our main concerns is to fulfill the economical expectations of the client while also interpreting local regulations to allow for public spaces within private plots. This is an unprecedented strategy in the context of Macau. Due to the local political circumstances, we have shifted the responsibility of planning for an urban quality of life from the local administration to the designer, and the burden of actually providing the space for this from the government to the private client. We have developed strategies that blur the line between the public and privately owned through the overuse of the plot, the incremental growth of public areas (public areas are not accounted for in the local allowed gross floor area index), and translated both into the new urban typologies of vertical village and three-dimensional public space.

As a result of our mode of resistance, we have built public buildings that are examples of an a-typological way of increasing the public space of the city and that stand as legacy for the local government to use and apply as policies.

OPPORTUNISTIC URBANISM

In the field of urbanism in Macau, LBA is setting precedent in innovative and creative interpretations of the sites—bridging urban gaps and creating new physical connections by occupying the edge and the underneath leftover spaces, creating and discovering opportunities in the urban context, and by designing additional uses onto the infrastructure of our commissioned projects for activities which aren't being addressed with current architecture procurements. We are using these projects to add a walking scale across the sites, allowing the surrounding city to relate to the new context of our projects. We are also adding urban agendas to new infrastructure with the intent of integrating them with the logic of the historic city, demonstrating that the new scale of the infrastructure is compatible with the historic context.

In the particular political context of Macau, our contribution in raising certain aspects that are not foreseen in the policy and that are marginal to the discussion in the public debate are critical to validate a system which has very few means to map the social realm. This leads us to take many roles in advocating for certain agendas in a constructive way, to create checks and balances for a city that has to deal with very disparate scales of issues and design.

Our practice can be seen as having a certain political agility, underpinned by our desire to improve the civic, public spaces of Macau, but also motivated to evolve a model of practice that can accommodate and respond to the particular "loose", political conditions of this place. This is evidenced through our ability and practice of "adding value" to commissions, expanding the scope of the brief to projects such that they address and respond realistically to the complex urban implications of the brief as well as the wider political context.

We have changed the fate of the south of the peninsula of Macau, an area earmarked for major road infrastructure in the reclamation masterplans for NAPE and Praia Grande Bay Closure—neither of which defined any civic intent beyond the strict perimeter of their urban grids. Our design interventions upgraded the length of the southern shore of the city into a rich environment of qualified public and green space which has become purposeful urban land with a civic role, inverting the process of urbanization, which will see the development of the majority of plots materialize into a functioning, qualified, rich, urban space integrated into the public image and realm of the city.

We believe that the scale of the commissions and the subsequent complexity that is inserted into the briefs has led us towards a process of incrementally planning the realm of the lake, bringing together the spheres of architecture and agency. By this, we don't mean to say that the projects are incomplete or awaiting additions, but rather that the project-structure is made up of different components that interplay with different realms of the project such as site context, agendas brought in by us and by other stakeholders. We have come to understand the project as a platform of acceptance of all justified agendas, where the task of the designer is to operate and calibrate the different and conflicting intent into a designed solution.

Our intervention in the city through the projects is proof that through a process of collaboration with the government and decision-making stakeholders, designers have the opportunity to experiment and innovate at an urban scale. By sometimes becoming agents of change, sometimes negotiators and policymakers, architects have an important role to play in changing both the culture of commissioning projects and the actual design solutions and spatial propositions for the future city of Macau, which faces constant challenges of new scales of user and new types of urban culture, arising from the tourism industry and the ultra-dense context of this territory.

INFRASTRUCTURAL URBANISM

In a context where there are few built examples of successful urban design, the innovations of our practice have resulted in design work that also lays the foundations for future works, as well as strategies developed to make that possible. As evidenced in the design for the Nam Van Square, Sai Van Park, the LRT stations for the Macau line and the Barra PTI project, our practice builds design knowledge through example and precedent. Our experiment with these projects, all related to the infrastructure typology—working with leftover spaces above infrastructure, underneath flyovers, next to the water's edge, or within large public housing schemes, on a territory always lacking spaces between buildings—has allowed us to find a civic dimension within the building function and to envision the non-typological public spaces that consequently led to better commissioning of projects by Macau's administration.

Following on from Manuel Vicente, our built work has set precedents and led to changes in policy based on the outcome of the work as an example for viable change, laying the foundations for future practices. Through our projects, we started to advocate for reclamations to be dealt with creatively to avoid passive offsets of the coastline and infrastructure destined for a single use. In the first projects for the lagoons which we developed with Manuel Vicente, Nam Van Square, we made the project a manifesto of our advocacy for a new agenda for custom-made reclamation, articulating public space, landscaping, and infrastructure on the waterfront.

We use every project to test and relate our thoughts around the design work with our urban visions, aiming to expand the framework of architecture. This allows us to negotiate and curate the projects from a set of points of view which contribute to making significant shifts on the briefs, the impact, and the scope of the projects—expanding the briefs, the intervention sites and the wider discussion on the urban approach to infrastructure, leading to an expanded role for the architect.

Some projects were opportunities to test innovative procurement strategies for architecture and planning: here, we added large-scale infrastructure to the building program and came up with complex architectural solutions, working with section and making opportunities in every part of the project to respond to different government agendas. Through this process of negotiation, and through our design response to it, we were leading by example to set our projects as benchmarks for the possibilities that architecture can achieve for Macau.

UN-PURPOSED SPACE

While asserting our commitment to the urban practice of connecting "pieces of the city" and creating new centralities with the design of public spaces within large infrastructure projects, we noticed that the special condition of Macau as an extremely dense city has inspired a second type of reaction in our practice: within the design of single buildings, our practice of resistance has focused on designing what we now call un-purposed spaces.

Un-purposed space derives from a generosity of the designer in allocating space beyond the commissioned agendas, in offering "spatial gifts" that surround and connect the building program. The idea is not new. Historical architecture is full of un-purposed spaces and architecture's main typologies were developed under these principles. But when architecture is enslaved to economics or function, the un-purposed space disappears because it is not a function and cannot be named.

The quest for un-purposed space in our projects is related to Macau as a context, where the local mentality of profit-driven urbanism that permeates both the private and public sectors enslaves the production of architecture, restricting design to be exercised only in the areas-for-profit of the buildings. Decisions are made according to quantities—square meters—and not according to the quality of the design. In this context, the un-purposed space is not a given; it has to be championed by the designer.

Our personal understanding of un-purposed space is echoed in Giancarlo De Carlo's idea of participation in architecture and in Yvonne Farrell and Shelley Mc Namara's curatorship of the 2018 Venice Biennale.

In the paper "An Architecture of Participation", De Carlo rhetorically reverses some of the axioms of the modernist movement, and the results are surprisingly contemporary. He shifts the focus of architecture from the ideal man towards the real human being, and from function towards usage. He advocates that the architect has to be contaminated with the context, inclusive of space and users. These considerations lie at the foundation of our interaction with the context of Macau, where we have observed a striking contrast between the scarcity of civic spaces and the excessiveness with which the local population uses and appropriates every single area of the city.

We can find a trace of De Carlo's ideas in the "Freespace Manifesto" by Farrell and McNamara: "FREESPACE celebrates architecture's capacity to find additional and unexpected generosity in each project—even within the most private, defensive, exclusive or commercially restricted conditions... FREESPACE can be a space for opportunity, a democratic space, un-programmed and free for uses yet to be defined. There is an exchange between people and buildings that happens, even if not intended or designed, so buildings themselves find ways of sharing and engaging with people over time, long after the architect has left the scene. Architecture has an active as well as a passive life".

The un-purposed space in an urban context is a public space that lies in between the formal and functional and the informal and flexible.

We wish to outline our position towards designing un-purposed spaces. The first is that the un-purposed space shall be indeterminate in its function to allow for any type of use according to eventual needs. The second is that its design shall promote a dialogue between people and architecture, while the third is that the design of the un-purposed space has to permit disorder and appropriation with the local informality without the loss of the architectural characteristics of the design.

INDETERMINACY

For a space to be un-purposed, it must first relinquish a sense of function. This is a challenge when practicing in a dense and profit-oriented context. Our personal approach regarding this issue is either to add indeterminate spaces alongside functional ones or to stack them above or below the main building program. Our ambition is to fit these spaces into the overall design in such a way that they cannot be erased or blocked out later on. Inverting the modernist axiom of "form follows function", De Carlo proposes that new forms will generate new functions or purposes for the space: the un-purposed-ness is a technique to allow different uses for the spaces. In our projects, we have tried to layer the connective tissue of the design with several functions and possibilities. We have always looked to offer extra spaces in association with space connectors so that these areas will continue to be interdependent with the other, functional spaces of the project and not end up being transformed into another enclosed space. The extra space is configured as a new form, expectant of any additional function but averse to being appropriated by a single function or closed off from the shared space.

At an urban scale, we have achieved the design of indeterminacy through the overlapping of public spaces; the increase in the quantity of public areas has given the possibility to spare part of it for indeterminate use.

We have pursued a new typology of public spaces for Macau: generally multileveled, vertical, and topographical. We have never managed to produce a single project that could be described in a word or a single phrase; we avoid diagrammatic architecture. Somehow, designing the empty space has given us freedom to not have to pursue a volumetric intention that enslaves the whole design. The phenomenological method that we pursue in our practice—one of joining together pieces around an empty space—allows a new dialogue as a possible alternative to the city-making process.

DIALOGUE BETWEEN PEOPLE AND ARCHITECTURE

The dialogue between people and architecture is another condition of the un-purposed space. Given that the surrounding context participates in the project through special areas left for articulation, this exchange happens at thresholds where the exchange between design and context takes place. This dialogue is interpretative of the context and the users, sensitive to the surroundings of the building, and should promote openness in the design.

The dialogue between people and architecture can be designed through sectional or vertical thresholds that are an efficient strategy in bringing public space into the building design without losing the full plot area. In line with our idea of overlapping public spaces, these are a way of increasing the density of the common areas.

The civic spaces that we see as appropriate for citizens, in the context of this city, are structured spaces whose usage is intended to remain indeterminate by design. This perception is also important when designing for a cultural other. It has been our experience that the local collective use of the space is continuously changing, with food festivals, parades, and fairs being held. The personal usage of the public areas is very varied, ranging from exercise to meditation. Thus a non-functionalized space can be an architectural proposition to allow this cultural freedom.

INFORMALITY

Informality is a cultural characteristic of Macau's context. We have been refining our design strategies to achieve contextualized public spaces. One characteristic of this strategy is their capacity to frame appropriation and disorder.

The informal cannot be designed, but informality and disorder can be admitted through a surplus of space (un-purposed spaces) and rigorous architectural design. Working in East Asia, we are not worried about designing to invite appropriation, or concerned about making a sociological study on the culture of how the spaces that we design are occupied. We feel satisfied in our role of having allowed for extra, undetermined space and feel confident that the local culture will find a way to put it to use.

Our understanding is that it is possible to frame rather than curb appropriation by creating a hierarchy of spaces. Somehow, we find ourselves conflicted in our assessment of the informality of use of public space in Macau. We are, on the one hand, fascinated by the creativity of the designs and strategies associated with it, but cautious, however, about how much freedom should be allowed for the private appropriation of common areas. We follow two main lines of thought regarding informality: The first is that we want to understand the way in which the local population could be expected to use the spaces that we provide. The second line of thought is our desire for these spaces to be available to everyone and not just to whoever might have privileged access to them. These two observations are the common threads that run through all our design agendas.

8. Appendix

Interviews

Ana Vaz Milheiro

Ana Vaz Milheiro is a full researcher at Dinâmia, Iscte-IUL (University Institute of Lisbon) and a former Associate Professor, Faculty of Architecture (University of Lisbon). ERC Advanced Grantee "Architecture, Colonialism and Labour. The role and legacy of mass labour in the design, planning and construction of Public Works in former African territories under Portuguese colonial rule" (ArchLabour) (2024—28). She has also been an associate researcher at DINÂMIA'CET-Iscte and a researcher at African Studies Center (University of Porto). As a former IIAS Fellow (Hebrew University of Jerusalem), she wrote "Re-Theorizing Housing" (2019—20). She has a PhD in Architecture from the University of São Paulo. Since 2010, she has coordinated research projects in architecture and urbanism related to Portuguese colonial history and its influence in Africa and Asia, including the ongoing "ArchLabMacao-Mass labour impact on Public Works in Macau under Portuguese administration (1849—1999)," which addresses the contribution to design of the anonymous workforce that worked on public infrastructure and buildings in Macau. She has been an invited researcher at Ghent University (2015-16); fellow researcher at São Paulo University (2018); and former chair of the Cost Ac-on CA18137 "European Middle-Class Mass Housing." Architectural critic for the newspaper *Publico* since 1995, she has also been deputy director of the *JA-Jornal dos Arquitectos* of the Portuguese Architects' Association.

Ana Vaz Milheiro (AVM) My first question for both of you, I would like to know the difference between your architectural researches which you have developed in your PhD. You chose different topics, but the object of your research, your work, and your relation with Macau are the same and maybe your motivation is also similar. So could you explain the difference between your approaches, and how each of you accomplished a different theoretical point of view?

Carlotta Bruni (CB) I think, the separation was quite easy, because it was a separation that stemmed naturally from the way we divide the work between ourselves. We have a very intense collaboration while working, but each one of us approaches different ideas during the design phase. Sometimes Rui's ideas will prevail in the work, some other time my ideas will imprint the final layout. We try to be fair to each other, while acknowledging which ideas are best suited for the design. I found out that I was focusing more on the compositional aspect of architecture: how objects sit in space, how they organize space within the context and between themselves. On the other hand, Rui has been doing a lot of work in the field of activism in Macau, like lobbying for urban policy and heritage awareness. To a certain extent, I think he has gained a better overall view on what is the political, social, and urban context of Macau and how to approach this subject. So that's how we divided our dissertations, whilst using the same projects as a basis.

Rui Leão (RL) Our individual relationships with Macau are different. As I grew up here, I feel very close to this reality, where there are always many points of view—i.e., the institutional, the informal, the Chinese, the Portuguese. I try to understand these different points of view opportunistically, because I think Macau has been for a long time a land of opportunities; but these opportunities sometimes can't come to fruition because there is not enough dialogue among the players.

For me, besides the work we do at the studio, the projects are also about the observation of possibilities and trying to understand what else the project can deal with, things that are not probably referred to in the brief or are typically ignored. So there are little areas of innovation and expansion that each project can tackle, and I am very engaged with pulling out those strings, so my contribution to the projects is different in that sense.

AVM I'd ask how many years have you worked together in the same office?

CB 25 years.

AVM What I find quite interesting in what Carlotta said, is the way that she defines herself as an office architect, where she stays in the office dealing with the bulk of the design production, whereas Rui has more public life and a more political approach to the work, dealing with the Architects Association in Macau, and then CIALP (International Council of Portuguese-Speaking Architects)[1] and Docomomo Macau. For Carlotta when she arrived in Macau, in a way, she was a foreigner. She's an Italian architect. So she has a European cultural point of view. And Rui of course comes from Portugal but mostly from Macau as he grew up there, and he speaks Cantonese. Given these contrasting cultural points of view, how do you position yourselves in the public realm of Macau? Within all the debates revolving around the city and its urban planning, how does that contrast with the architectural culture in Macau? And how do your different backgrounds influence the way you talk and work together.

Before you elaborate on the above question Carlotta, I'd like us to go back to the question of how you present yourselves in the public eye. How an architect and their firm deals with a reality like Macau, because it's a Chinese reality, but I suppose it's different from other Chinese realities, because of its history and its current political status. To summarize, what's your own interpretation and position in the public sphere of Macau? Moreover, I think all the work that Rui developed as a public figure is important, but equally important, is the work that you have done in the office: how has that developed in all these 25 years?

CB What I think happens is that we don't get the very fancy projects. Lately, to even manage to get big commissions has been difficult; most of the commissions that we get are through tenders. So we have to put ourselves out, produce most of the work in Chinese and tender out our work to the Macau SAR Government. We quite exclusively do government work. We have very few commissions in the private sector.

When you ask "what is our way of setting into the Macau frame of work," I think that at the beginning we try to make changes that can be significant for the government. The government can understand that these changes bring something useful to them. I'll use the Fai Chi Kei as an example: we designed this social housing in 2010, and it was finished around 2013. After that, we received international prizes, but then we also received a lot of praise from the local community. And most recently, we have been commissioned to design more social housing where we pushed further a concept similar to the Fai Chi Kei scheme: integrating public spaces at ground floor, and each floor of the social housing. And strangely enough, we didn't get any resistance from the government; they were quite open to addressing this different design for public housing, which says a lot about how we can implement change in a place like Macau. It is by setting out examples and small changes at a time.

RL I think that the first years of Macau after the handover represented a window of opportunity. There were not a lot of rules in terms of what the policy was for architecture and urban planning. The fact is that in the year 2000, there was an opportunity to discuss ideas, in the strict sense. These ideas contained certain qualities in terms of policy, and what was interesting was to build and reach a sort of consensus. In the early stages of our practice, for example, we realized that there was no action being taken on the future of urban planning—thus we started to develop speculative masterplans that focused on reclamation and a vision of an extended territory. These ideas were implemented in our projects, bringing up the issues of public space, issues of common space, condominium space, and so on, and a lot of these designs were built. The experience that the stakeholders, the government, and the community had was so positive that some of the implemented ideas became the policy for future projects in Macau. Some of these ideas become easily accepted. For example, there was a period just after the handover where all the gardens and parks were designed by the city council. They were all enclosed spaces with fences, and they would lock up at 7:00 pm. Then we started to design the Nam Van Square and the Sai Van Park, which were public spaces along roads and along the lakes which could not be enclosed. So this presented a situation that the government and the city council had to deal with, and they had to face the fact that there was no real crime if parks were kept open 24/7, and people were happy they could go out at night and stay out in these spaces. So the projects somehow destroyed this myth that the population was in a state of unbalance, which was an urban myth from the 1980s, back when there were a lot of boat people arriving from Vietnam and illegal immigration from China; people had this unsteady feeling because there was a lot of petty crime back then.

AVM So, in a way, you still believe that architecture can change the community, the laws, and the rules, by example. You think that with your work and your proposals and with what you were able to accomplish as architects, you are not only changing the frame of the city, and the public space, but also changing the way the community feels and identifies. Do you think that in communities like Macau, the architect still can have this kind of relevance?

CB I think the problem is that communities like Macau are much unregulated. Macau is a city that is built for profit, which means that it doesn't have a socially reflective masterplan or a policy to build public space. So as architects, I believe we have this added responsibility. I think, in other places like Lisbon, Milan you don't have these type of constraints and you'd be able to focus on other aspects of the profession, like new materials, new type of construction methods, forms or typologies, etc. which is not exactly the condition we are in. We still don't have this luxury here. We are laying the groundwork for something that is still very basic in the architectural profession.

AVM Do you think that the absence of those kinds of rules you've mentioned gives you a social responsibility as architects and makes the architectural context of Macau different from other places?

Do you think that the fact that you are not able to use all the tools that architects in other places have at their disposal, in Europe, for instance, more focused on the technological approach of design, as you have mentioned, that this has led you to become more focused on the public realm or the public significance of your own projects? Could we say that it's still important in places like Macau: this very high social commitment in terms of how the architect can design?

RL To focus on issues of technology and sustainability in Macau would be a lost cause, from the point of view of the designer. I say this because you won't be able to find the necessary people and organizations to generate a dialogue. For example, Macau is next to the place where most of the

construction materials are produced, which is the Pearl River Delta in Guangdong Province; the political and cultural barriers that Macau still has with the rest of the province of Guangdong make it very difficult for us to engage with the industry and with the construction sector. We have colleagues across the border, in Guangdong, and we see them doing incredible work in terms of using their projects to innovate in technology, all the while working with the factories and products directly. What they do is incredible, but we wouldn't be able to do that from here because we don't have the scale or a shared language to engage—plus, across the border, the industry is working at a global market scale and, in Macau, our policymakers only understand the here and now. There are lots of barriers.
The same thing happens with environmental issues: many people say Macau could be a wonderful place to start a very functional environmentally conscious city, but that is not true because you have to have very well educated people, all across the spectrum, to make a shift in the paradigm in the mentality. You need people with whom you can initiate a conversation! In Macau, because we are a city of gambling and that's the only strong pillar of the economy, we find ourselves with a community that is very passive, because we're all indirectly receiving our pay from the gambling industry. So the gambling industry is at the forefront, and it doesn't pertain to push a discussion or dialogue on these issues.

AVM I think it's quite interesting to think on the history of these two territories, Macau and Hong Kong, the Portuguese Government decided in the 1960s to award the gambling monopoly to STDM. Do you think that the colonial decision of turning Macau into a gambling city, even if it wasn't what it is today, geared the territory to revolve their logic around profit and gambling? Do you think that the course of Macau started with that?

CB I think that is true. And I think if you look at our architectural designs over the years, there has been a lot of invention with the aid of the gambling industry. We have the Morpheus Hotel, a great building by Zaha Hadid, we have the Venetian, the biggest casino on earth... and the best industry techniques in Macau are all related to the architecture and construction of casinos. And most certainly, it has to do with the power of investment. That is the Finance sector in Hong Kong and in the case of Macau, the Gambling sector.

AVM Even with such high gambling revenues? Even when there is such a lot of money rolling into the territory?

CB The territory expenditure on public works is always around 10 percent of the revenue. So we don't spend on building more than 10 percent of what we get each year from the gambling industry.

So you can see... if you find somebody who is a little bit more enlightened and wants to spend 20, 30, 40 percent, you can have a green city, green buses, green cars, beautiful buildings, state of the art architecture, state of the art urban planning, and so on. But the reality is that the expenditure is always fixed at 10 percent.

AVM Considering all the constraints that Carlotta is stating, with all the difference in practice from your European, American, or even Hong Kong colleagues, do you think that you could define yourselves as Macanese architects?

RL If it's about identifying with the local culture and whatever heritage is still left here in the city, then definitely, I'm a Macanese architect. My memory as a child growing up in Macau was that it was a marvelous enchanted place: every second street was beautiful and was filled with the architecture of palaces. Even though when you looked in, those buildings that look like palaces were just, in fact, social housing with normal people living there, there was still this huge charge of architecture being used to build this beautiful urban fabric. I'm always thinking about how we can create beautiful moments for people, not beautiful objects, but beautiful moments and places where people can discover something marvelous. I think that this is very meaningful for an ultra-packed city where people are always so constrained by a lack of public space, by the lack of places for civic encounter. We think about that a lot when designing the projects and how the projects can somehow be innovative by changing that packed-up notion of the public realm.

AVM The charming Macau of the past...you're talking about a kind of nostalgia? For architects, memories are strong when designing. So what do you think it means to combine these memories that you two share together? If we were talking about challenges, what are the challenges that you've faced in Macau? You've mentioned social housing because we know that there is a shortage of housing in Macau. You've also talked about the lack of public space or, more specifically, the quality of public spaces. Do you find these challenges when you have a new commission? Do you think that the people who commission you share the same eagerness to improve on the issue of public space or do you feel you're alone, dealing with this matter?

CB I think that we have been building on that. In the beginning, I don't think we were consciously thinking on that in our projects. You could say that it was an organic approach to the projects, those projects were successful in mastering these complex issues, thus, eventually, our commissioners came to us specifically to tackle the aforementioned issues. So I think we have made a small hole in the wall, and we are managing to make it a little bit bigger project by project.

RL There were different experiences along the years with different projects. In the case of the addition of the reading room to the Portuguese School, which was a project for a small room on the patio, this project came out in a very special way because we were very concerned that the building was at risk of demolition during the period in which we were designing it. This project was completely inserted on the patio of that building, and we wanted to experiment with different points of view so that you could look from the new project, back into the building and vice-versa. We used the project to make a space from which you could look into the modernist pre-existence in a new way. I think this is what brought attention to the project: the fact that it was a place where you could see the old school from a new point of view and I think we weren't really conscious of what the project was until it got built. Because it was such a small commission, it had seemed impossible to use the project to make a statement or a manifesto with it. However, it was a success because the project was what prevented the school from being demolished.

AVM I think it's very nice when Carlotta says that you were able to change some rules through your projects, by designing, by proving that it was possible to change, and also how you were able to change the minds of the people that invited you to design, by showing that it was possible to design in another way. You are thinking that we as architects, can produce change by design.

This fear of demolition is so prevalent in the Asian context, and yet, these small interventions, like the reading room in the Portuguese School, show that renovation brings new life to these old buildings. Because the idea of "new" is so important in the Asian context, then it's through these small works that you're able to spark in them the ideas of expanding the lifetime of the old buildings. How it is for European-trained architects, to deal with the idea that your buildings can easily disappear in the span of a couple of decades after being built?

CB We have had already two demolitions of our buildings during our time in Macau. It's not good, it's not fun. It's a negation of what we are purposed and programmed to do as architects.

AVM Now during 25 years, it's not so bad having only two works demolished. I think it's a good score, but I was also interested in understanding how this affected your work? It feels quite precarious, even after the effort and time that you've put into designing the building.

RL I think it's a very complicated issue here, because the line between what has merit to be preserved, maintained and what doesn't becomes sort of like a stock exchange of values. The reason why I set up the Docomomo Macau chapter was because of the Portuguese School being at risk of demolition and that we felt I couldn't fight this battle alone. We've had maybe four or five big battles since 2004, against the demolition of this single building; we have managed to win the battles until now, but the building can disappear at any time, because it doesn't have any legal protection. Then, there are buildings that have little relevance in terms of their architectural significance, like for example, the Hotel Estoril which will be demolished soon, but which raised huge battles for its preservation in the civic society.

One of our projects, the Nam Van Square, for example, was under risk of being destroyed by the government; there was a plan to reduce it to some kind of theme park, It was a very interesting example of how the community and public opinion completely destroyed an insensible and absurd plan.

CB They wanted to convert a successful public space into a recreational facility.

AVM Do you have other examples of the community being consulted? Another example of when the government had decided to demolish a public space?

CB Recently, that has become policy.

AVM That is quite interesting, because the reason an architect desires to preserve a site or a building is not the same as the reason that makes a population or community want to do the same. So it's quite interesting that in the case of the community, they found that place important and decided to preserve it. Because we know that the project won several important awards, it was in international exhibitions, it was published just after being built. But as an architect, after undergoing that process, what did you learn from it and what did you find out?

CB What we do now, systematically, is we submit all our projects for international awards. We understood that the authorship law defends the rights of buildings that are internationally awarded. So we fight vigorously, me and Rui, to prevent our projects from being demolished. So we tend to have huge discussions with the government on that.

RL Looking back at the Nam Van Square and the Sai Van Park projects, what I have learned is that these public space projects were not about how to furnish a specific functional use for the people. It was all about creating spaces for people to interpret and to make use of them in different ways. The projects allow people to engage creatively along the years with the space. For example, in the Nam Van Square project, there is an open hand in the center of the space, something between a sculpture and an auditorium. Along the years, people have interpreted the space: initially, it was used for tai chi classes; then we found some kids sliding through the "fingers"; and so it was used as a playground; and later, there were some skaters that found the hand sculpture to be a good, daring skating exercise, so it became heavily used by skaters.

AVM The best buildings are the ones which have functional flexibility; they stand the test of time because of their openness to what happens inside, and they can become landmarks because they welcome all kinds of generations by giving them freedom to choose what to make of them. Lastly for today, I want to bring up the practical issue of language. I realize that the community here doesn't speak your language; they speak Cantonese, so how do you communicate your ideas? Moreover, you differ as well culturally, so how do you overcome that different mindset?

RL The official languages are Portuguese and Cantonese, but more and more people are speaking Mandarin. We still have a common language, which is English, which allows us to bridge the communication at a reasonable level. However, language is only a barrier when people feel there is an insurmountable barrier in the communication, which in Macau, over the past 500 years, we have collectively overcome that.

CB I also think that we don't actively aim to convey the philosophy of the design to our clients. The conversations we have are, generally, about square meters, about building heights, regulations, compliance. There is little discussion about what it will mean for the city and community; sometimes we do have an official who's interested and enlightened and asks questions regarding that, but generally it doesn't happen. Our clients tend to be surprised with how the projects look in real life, and I suspect that most of the time, they are not 100 percent sure of what we are creating.

RL For example, we were doing a very small intervention: a compound wall for a police headquarters. Initially, there was another architect that was designing it, whom the police had commissioned. It was right next to our project, so we said if you have an architect working on it, we'll be hands off. However, they expressed their discontent with the commissioned architect and they asked us to design the wall. I had never thought of designing a wall, a very high wall, which somehow creates an imprisoning environment. Moreover, these notions of police barracks and prisons feel quite perverse from my point of view. We wanted to design something that experimented with the light and the shadow on the wall, and wanted to use color: the blue and white colors created the illusion that there was sky around them, like a painted sky next to the real sky. When it was complete, the police boss sent me a message through our client to say that they were very satisfied, that they liked the wall, that it was a beautiful wall. I was really proud because the police are a client that usually doesn't make such a compliment. It's not in their genealogy.

AVM I was thinking on how a discussion would develop if you'd share with your clients some of the ideas and concepts that you imbed in your work? As Carlotta said, back then these weren't conscious decisions; however, now they are clearer. And while you were describing how you were happy with the design of the wall at the police headquarters, I was trying to understand the border of an architect's discipline. Because you live in the real world, you bring into your work the worries of the day-to-day (i.e., the wall in the police headquarters: the desire to bring light into a project that would otherwise be seen as gray). How do you make it all work?

CB Generally, in Chinese culture, when you explain a project, people get fixed on an idea that is very abstract and also very literal, something like a metaphor. Like you'd say: I'm doing this building to look like a phoenix, or I do this building to look like a palm tree...it becomes very difficult for us to play this game. We have not been successful with many projects, because we still have not cracked the communication issue. I think when we try and communicate what's within our soul and what we are wishing for the building to be, but often, on the other side of the dialogue there is no reciprocity. That's my personal feeling.

RL We have not cracked it because, in many cases, there is no wish for architecture. There is no desire for architecture to represent something; because what they call the "Sô-Fá," in Mandarin, meaning the theme of the project, this theme is how you can explain it to a 5-year-old: I think that is just a will that the project be universally communicated. It's not a will that it stands for something or represents something to people. As architecture is not a socially shared code in China, you are not really able to explain a project until it is built. More recently, we're doing a project for a new government office, comprising two towers on the waterfront. And the people who are commissioning the building have clearly asked that they want these towers to be an upgrade from office spaces in Macau. So there is a wish to use architecture, to position the government institutions as something with more quality and sophistication than the typical office buildings of the whole district. I felt very excited with this simple prerequisite, because I felt that, finally, there is somebody asking us for something that is more than just summing square meters or offering piled up programs.

AVM Do you feel that that lack of architectural desire to be changing now? You feel that maybe that can change?

RL I feel here it's changing very quickly. I think, in China, because of the huge scale of cities and competitiveness, the desire for architecture has escalated in the past 20 to 30 years. Today, even for private housing, the developers are very demanding because they know that the buyers will make a choice not just based on the economy but on the quality of the materials, the quality of space, and the type of design as well. So people have become very conscious in China. In Macau, it's different because people become conscious through the casino architecture—for being iconic, flashy, and tacky. Locally, there isn't a cultural connect to understand architecture as part of the culture. Maybe because it was an essential component in the colonial period, because architecture is an essential form of expression for the Portuguese and that was misinterpreted as a colonial ideological barrier? I think that here it is only going to happen very slowly because you cannot expect people to change from one moment to the other.

AVM Now, related to the other Chinese architects who work in Macau, do you think they bring a different perspective to the city from the old generation of architects who were already in Macau?

RL The architects that became significant right after the handover, I don't think they had another alternative, and they were not very interested; those who had influence did not make the effort to create or to establish that alternative culture in Macau. I have some hope in the younger Chinese architects who are starting to create interesting projects; they are working with very current programs of housing and interior design and, moreover, they are really bringing something new from their experiences, having studied in Europe or Australia. More specifically, unlike the older generation, they aren't just service providers assisting developers to make business. I see a difference now in this younger generation of architects, 40 and below.

AVM You've been trying to promote architecture culture in the Macanese context, through exhibitions, books, conferences. Do you think all this effort you've been putting in for three decades has paid off in changing the policies?

RL I think it has been fruitful; however, not as much as I envisioned. But after 1999, I was the first person to organize and invite international people to talk here; then, of course, the Architects' Association made significant work in organizing some other international conferences after the handover. Somehow now, everything has slowed down, The association has not kept up its role to inspire the industry. Nowadays, I don't see universities organizing these international connections and making an impact. And I think we are still a little bit isolated, especially if we compare ourselves with Hong Kong universities, and the Hong Kong Institute of Architects. I think there are a lot of good designers in Hong Kong, because the schools and the architects' institute are always developing this culture of communication, and not just internationally but also reaching across the Pearl River Delta, but here we are very provincial: we are usually happy with our bowl of rice.

CB But I think it's also a matter of size, Hong Kong Has almost 8 million people. So we are comparing a city of 8 million with the city of 620,000, there is no comparison; they have five schools of architecture. The clever thing to do in Macau would be to link up with the programs that they have in Hong Kong and bring them over, and that doesn't happen for some reason and it's difficult to understand.

AVM But it is so near!

CB That's what I mean, we have local young architects that are teaching in Hong Kong universities; we have the Hong Kong architects that sometimes come and teach in our universities, but the connection is not very strong and it could be much stronger to the benefit of Macau for sure, but Hong Kong probably has other priorities.

AVM So what is your intention with launching this book? All of this reflection on you work for these 25 years written in this book, was it to create some challenge, to create a point of conversation about Macau? Not just what's happening internally but also externally? Or is this about what it can bring to the future of the city and the territory?

CB For me, the point of balance, like you say, was the PhD research. It was a wonderful experience; I think both of us managed to find many things about our work that we were not even aware of. It has enabled us to talk about it, which I think is a difficult task—especially for architects, because we can only do that if we dedicate plenty of time to think on how and why we undertake the projects. Also because the PhD doesn't have wide dissemination, the book is a way to say: "I think we found something, I think that what we found in Macau can be applied elsewhere". Maybe not in the same way that it happens here, because the circumstances are different, but I think many of the things that we do are creative and substantially different and they are worth sharing. Launching this book will also enable us to follow this next step: our willingness to move into other programs, to find other types of commission; I think we are gathering the balance to make that jump.

RL For me, the book presents an opportunity to make a statement on what is the role of the architect, not just in the context in Macau but also in a generic sense. Moreover, to dialogue about what architectural culture is, because I think there are a lot of misconceptions: we are in Macau, as architects, we can intervene a lot and we can contribute a lot. I feel that there are a lot of lost opportunities because people keep looking into Singapore, Spain, the UK and looking at what others are doing. There is no sin in that but I feel that in many cases that is silly, because whatever others in other countries were doing makes sense as a response to our own context and culture. There is a loss in authenticity and auto-determination in the exercise.

AVM I was thinking that when we started this discussion, Carlotta said that you work with another kind of specificity, because you have to deal with a more reality—for instance, when compared with Europe—in terms of public policies and our housing policies and so on. But at the same time, you have a different spectrum of action. I don't know if you follow me, but this idea that you have a different commitment so you have a different spectrum of action and that can be a way of leading to other solutions, to other ways of doing it. Do you feel that somehow you are being challenged in a different way that puts you on a different path: not necessarily worse, but a different path?

CB I think the specificity that we were discussing has to do with the density of Macau, and the way that we find different strategies to overcome this condition. Density is a theme that is very dear to the architectural community, because you wish that you didn't use so much land. I think we do this experiment of density in Macau every day because we don't have any more land to use. At a certain point when we say that the book can be inspirational or can be a sharing moment of strategies, it would also be like this because you've been to Hong Kong and you know what it is to walk on those pedestrian flyovers where you never touch the ground where the cars flow, and what a wonderful idea would be if that would transform itself into architecture—and not just as an equation of efficiency to move people within the city or how beautiful it would be if architecture could connect metro stations with buildings and public spaces in a beautiful way. I think that what we try to do with our practice is enact these scenarios, and try to find a way that the scenario can work in an architectural framework and not just a utilitarian one. I think that's one of the ideas for the book: for it to grow from a small place like Macau and try to become a little more universal for cities that don't want to sprawl so much, that want to concentrate while expanding and so on.

AVM Cities that need to be compact... This idea is very beautiful; it's a vision of turning all these utilitarian devices into architecture, right? And this idea of density and how to deal with it because, as you said, you don't have enough land, so you have to think in a different way. So I find it quite interesting: it is not only an exercise but also as a cultural path, this idea of turning everything into architecture in the way you were describing it, Carlotta.

RL It was beautifully said by Carlotta, because extreme conditions don't necessarily get an architectural expression until one day for some reason it happens, and there are many different conditions that happen in this context of Macau, Hong Kong, and China. Sometimes it's such a simple thing, like we discovered in the project for Barra's Station 12: that the station had a huge amount of technical areas, a huge volume and there was nothing we can do about that—half of it is ventilation; it would be occupying this beautiful, historic waterfront—to then realizing that if we use all the roof area as a park, we have a huge park parallel to the old waterfront. It's not about what is inside the building, it's about transforming the roof into a landscaped form. It become a really marvelous place, independent of the fact that it is a train station.

AVM On the major works of Foster and I. M. Pei in Hong Kong, what makes them so relevant, and why have they survived in the international culture? Was it because they were able to make this kind of transformation? It seems that they were able to turn these financial programs, these bright headquarters into architecture and something that means something to the city, and the way people use it. I think it's the same when we were talking about the Nam Van Square, it's the same process when you transform the opportunity of making that square in the middle of nowhere only with that circulation and roads and the tower; and you make it a into an architectural device, and I think that it's quite impressive. Then we have the second level when people understand that and they use it, and they claim it for themselves and don't want to give it up anymore. So I think the book can be something about working, as you said, in a very radical condition, but at the same time that architecture is quite a reversal in the way it changes the territories, changes peoples' lives, something like that, and how we able to share the process with others.

1 Since 2023, Rui Leão is UIA Secretary General

INTERVIEW, MARCH 13, 2022

Ana Vaz Milheiro (AVM) In this interview, we should start by analyzing the works that you think were important for your career, and also important for the city you are working upon. I think there are some key works that are important to underline in our conversation. we can end our conversation talking about the future and the path which you are currently on.

What is the importance that Macau has in terms of its geostrategic position in the Chinese context, and can it play an important role for the greater China region?

Rui Leão (RL) The first large-scale projects we did were already in the around the handover period, but right in the beginning and still in partnership with Manuel Vicente: Nam Van Square in 2001 and Sai Van Park in 2003. At that moment, we were going through the change of administration from colonial to local, which occurred with a lot of difficulty as there was very little transfer of know-how.

I think that in Macau, as a Portuguese colony, most of the policy was not so much written on paper, but was managed efficiently by people who were very experienced. The fact that all of these people moved away at the same time left a big void after the handover. It was a big challenge to design and coordinate large projects at the time, especially the Nan Van Square, articulating large infrastructure, roads, and flyovers. We were interfering with the traffic (at a city-wide scale). All the interfaces with the water and structural issues related to that, and doing a large-scale public space in the middle of a roundabout was a very big challenge, but equally important: it was only possible because there were not a lot of rules on the ground.

I think that nowadays, probably most projects like those (Nam Van Square and Sai Van Park)would be impossible to happen, because no one really had any idea of all the challenges they posed and how impossible it was to do a park in the middle of a highway and under a bridge and do a public square in the middle of a roundabout. I think we took those as opportunities which we managed at that time because it was easy to go dialogue with government officials to set up new types of solutions. It all happened in conversations around a table. Our role as designers was really instrumental in the realization of those projects, pushing those projects to where they ended up.

Both of you learned to operate in the void that was left with the transition between systems, because then it seemed like it was possible to try everything. new-found freedom was a clear new framework for architecture in the post-handover period. It was an opportunity to experiment with a new approach to design?

Carlotta Bruni (CB) I think there was this historical new benchmark upon the handover for the people in public office. I also think that there was a special enthusiasm on our side, for the fact that these were the very first projects that we were doing. I think that we didn't know exactly what we were looking for. So we were experimenting much more with the freedom we were given compared with the present situation. That window is closed.

And from a certain point of view, I think that the two projects are a little bit strange in the sense that they exist in a city that doesn't have a periphery, but they look a little bit peripheral. It looks like they bring things that are of a dimension of leisure and the countryside to the heart of the city.

I feel that's the beauty of it. And there is also the beauty of being young architects without many restrictions or a scripted system of rules and precedence.

AVM I remember that, when I visit the Nam Van Lake square for the first time, it seemed like that. There was nowhere around a trace of an urban context, but at the same time it already had a very strong identity. What kind of message do you think that this project gave at the time? A vision of the new identity of Macau, for Macau after the Portuguese had left, embracing the People's Republic of China, but at the same time, also being an autonomous region? Do you think that, at the time, that square came to symbolize or represent the possibility for a new direction and hope for the city, in its new chapter of political history?

RL I think it was. Starting from the official point of view, the new government had commissioned three new public squares, the first three large commissions of the post-colonial period, and the notion of "square" is clearly an European typology. The location for the Nam Van Lake square was associated more with the landscape of the river and with the Macau Tower, an iconic tower which had just been inaugurated on the coastline, so it was really a place of representation for the new government. Our proposal had that desire to reconfigure the relationship between the parts: the landscaping, the infrastructure, the water space, the scale of the collective space. We were challenged by a daring political commission!

The new scale of the square, and as Carlotta was saying before, this sense of being in an imagined periphery, it was probably the only place in the whole of this territory where you could be out in the outdoors and people were distanced from you, you couldn't recognize them in the space. I felt a freedom with this idea that people also could become part of the landscape.

AVM You are saying that the square surpassed its condition of being a representative place of political power and official events, when people start to using the place in different ways.

I remember you describing that people start using the square for tai chi training and collective gymnastics, for instance, so they occupied the spaces to change the initial static purpose of the design of the square, they change it by using it in a different ways. Why did that surprise you? Was that was not supposed to happen?

CB As I was saying, for a certain amount of time the square was a peripheral space in the city. Mainly because of that, the government didn't use it. Later on, people started using it for jogging and for strolling and then, more recently, it started to be used it for parades, big parades crossing the city and arriving at the square; usually, they then set up a big stage on the square where these parades ended in festivities. It's also used as a spot to look at firework shows and for food festivals with open-air with stalls and so on. Currently, the government is using it fully, which is interesting because nowadays you always have events in the square, and starting from around four in the afternoon there are lots of people using it for all sorts of things: jogging, tai chi, gymnastics, bringing the kids. So it's actually become a very important place for Macau people. I think it is recognizable in its shape and it offers different ways of use, which is really important for the city.

RL We have used the two projects (Nam Van Square and Sai Van Park) to create continuity for people walking along the lake shore. It offers a new type of connectivity: you can start somewhere and arrive on the other side of the city. It's a new typology of use to have this long, linked stretch. I think because of its contribution for new connectivity, the square and the park have built up their current many users.

AVM Can you talk on how the park project (Sai Van Urban Park) was integrated with the square a few years later, two years later?

RL It was an awkward commission. The new Sai Van Bridge was under construction and just six months before its inauguration, there were some Beijing government officials coming to inaugurate it. It was the biggest infrastructure project developed after handover, and the government realized that there was a lot of reclaimed land built below the bridge which was bare land and hadn't been landscaped. So the local government called us and asked us just to beautify it in a fast track. We had six months to design and build the project.

When we started looking at the site, we thought that in a place like Macau, where there is such a chronic lack of public space and where people have little opportunity to experience the natural environment, that it would be a crime not to design a public space for the people, the site being along the river and the lake. So we gave ourselves that challenge and it was a big challenge because we had isolated pieces of land surrounded by high speed roads.

Connecting the site to the water space required several moves, like working with section to lift the site up, so that people would walk away from the roads and face the two water landscapes. We could somehow resolve all these issues without having to do walls, or having to further confine the spaces. That all worked out in the end: we managed to prove that with creativity, designers can add public space in almost any given circumstances.

AVM This is interesting, and can take us to the subject of your more recent works. When you talk about working in Macau, about the restraints that you face and the context, it sounds like something different from working in other geographies. One of the challenges seems to be the scarcity of public space.

Can you tell us how you address the issue of generating Public space when working with urban infrastructure or large housing schemes? How do you approach this issue of public space? Is it a Western influence or is it something consensual within Chinese culture?

RL Regarding the second part of your question, there are a lot of great recent projects on public space in China, but culturally, the idea of raising up the issue of the public domain as a means to expand and improve a project's brief is something which is rarely seen in this cultural context. And I think this in fact comes from the sense of importance that the collective has in our European upbringing. Our late partner Manuel Vicente used to say that one big difference between the Europeans and Chinese is that we consider the sidewalk the place which doesn't belong to the individual, because it belongs to all, whereas the local Chinese act as if the sidewalk is the place that doesn't belong to anyone. As if it doesn't concern us.

Until recently, public space was never addressed in briefs, and even though there are some public space commissions, there still isn't any policy to address it, as a social right or benefit.

CB I want to add that, even though people may not have a social consciousness of public space, doesn't mean that they don't use it. In fact, we can observe that local people overuse all the common spaces, bringing their own chairs to the sidewalk and leaving them there so that they can every morning go there to sit. They do funny things that we wouldn't do in a public space, like gym classes or dancing classes, or play the violin—they just do it. They don't have the extra space in their home.

I agree with what Rui says but, to contextualize our practice on Macau, I think that the first thing we did was to address all common space as public space, which is something that in Europe, you don't do because, when you have your stairs and then you have the entrance of your house which is a shared space between neighbors, you feel the right of ownership of the shared space, and you expect your neighbors to have the same understanding of it. I think that Europeans strongly defend this middle space, and that local Chinese people don't. They don't see it as a communal ground. So they are little bit more free in this respect. So I guess that for us, the revolution in our architecture is to reclaim those common areas as proper common property for everybody, and make them of a size and of a shape that can be freely used. You cannot leave your daughter's stroller on your landing, because there is not enough space to do that. Designin these thresholds make these boundaries of ownership and belonging become visible in the space.

AVM What you are describing, is a new typology of space. You say that for us Europeans, being more aware of the transition spaces, we have strategies to define the transitional spaces, and we are very aware about the borders and the edges.

Could you use some of your works to illustrate how you interpret that through design, these more Chinese sorts of behaviors relating to the awareness of ownership?

CB We tend to claim ownership. We put the doormat outside to state our co-opted ownership of the share space.

I will give you some examples. In the Fai Chi Kei project, these hanging patios that define a collective space beyond the threshold of the corridors. How? Firstly, they don't have any door to a private apartment on their perimeter, and secondly, they are impossible to to seal off because on every side there is a constraint that doesn't allow blocking the space off from public use. So it is a very different space from anything that the residents can identify with; thus, they have to interpret it—and when they do that collectively, they end up claiming it as a communal area.

The spaces at street level in the Fai Chi Kei project have the same quality at an urban scale. The small squares connect to all sides of the plot, so you can never occupy or seal them away from the public. These spaces can either be perceived as an widening of the sidewalk, as a housing block foyer, or as a public square—and in each of its ambiguous roles, the space allows for different appropriations.

RL The notion of claiming and assuming our ownership, and the fact that we share the concept, comes from the fact that space is theorized in Europe. What becomes different in the context of China and Macau is that, because there isn't a consensus, the typology is not sedimented, which results in a lot more freedom in the type of solutions. Whatever you propose, people will not feel constrained to use it: they will give it a new meaning, and that makes designing public space in this context very interesting because everything you do is then tested and it ends up working.

AVM But for instance, when you do did the new public housing block at Fai Chi Kei, I remember that you were very preoccupied in designing the common areas , the housing units were very small because it's the allowed typology for public housing schemes, and you were trying to widen the corridors and the entrances, to make space for people to get a sense of community. And we know how private the Chinese are. So they don't really all share and they, share their houses with others. So they are very private persons and very formal in that way. But at the same time, I remember that you were very preoccupied with all these small details that could give some significance to those common spaces? Could you please talk a little about these kind of moments and spaces? They are where the architect can really make a difference.

CB I think in places like Macau and Hong Kong, the tower typology creates a big disconnect, because suddenly you are on the 30th floor of a tower that has twenty apartments per floor, and in the scale of this apparatus you feel dehumanized, you lose your human scale. If you plan a social scheme where the smallest house is less than 20 square meters, and then you place 800 units in one small city block and you don't give residents anything else, all these people can do is to walk down and go to the sidewalk. There is nothing more dehumanizing than that: that in order to have any sort of human interaction, they must eject themselves from their housing block.

Ours was an act of restitution. We understood that the local regulation only accounted for usable areas, which is the actual area of the apartment itself. All the areas that are corridor circulation, lift lobby, stairs, and so on are not counted in the area that you can build into a city block, so what we did is we just designed the common areas to the maximum that we could get in terms of maximum land use.

RL In the Fai Chi Kei project, our strategy of slotting in common areas and public spaces across the housing program was quite important because it was a way to navigate through the common understanding of public housing schemes, which in Macau and Hong Kong are understood in a very top-down manner. We wanted to demonstrate that it is still possible to respond with a humanistic result for the residents.

In Hong Kong, most of the housing schemes are designed by the Housing Authority themselves. As public workers, the architects will just follow the regulations; they will not add anything to the design inside or outside the buildings. People find themselves with no way to occupy the space, so these neighborhoods become divisive. This creates a lot of social problems, not only crimes but somehow people feel excluded from the actual realm of society, because in their neighborhood it is not possible to meet and interact with others.

So what we did was first to cut out some spaces at the street level to create small patios And then started to pull out passages that punch across the blocks, so that residents can cross the urban block in all directions going from one patio to the other patio. The patios are open to the street. All of this was achieved by reducing the occupation of the building at street level. Public housing buildings don't need to generate revenue from tenants, right?

Another strategy was to create multiple sidewalks. So we have a sidewalk, which is by the road; a second sidewalk that is a little bit higher; and then a third sidewalk, which is covered by the gallery. This solution creates richness on the sidewalk space because some people are just hanging around, the kids can play on the sidewalk and take the bicycle down, etc.
In the towers, we packed the apartments tightly so we could free up a whole column of space in each block, and there we designed the vertical patios all through the building, which becomes a vertical village, with all these stacked patios connecting every two floors. These spaces are connected to the corridors and the lift lobbies, which creates a very interesting interface on every floor with grand views of the city. The residents really use it because it's safe and it's theirs. Somehow it's a substitute of the street: a way for them to recreate the street on various levels.

CB We were concerned to leave these spaces as open spaces, both in terms of circulation and of natural ventilation. They are generally open to fresh air, so there is this vertical and horizontal stack of naturally ventilated spaces, which makes the common areas a sustainable passive energy system.

AVM You describe a set of strategies that you set up for this project which could be reproduced in other projects. Are these strategies successfully understood by the stakeholders? Do you think that the building is being used in the way you envisioned it? And most importantly, do you think that your approach has changed the way people understand and relate to these kinds of residential programs?

RL The people who run the building management told us that when the first residents started to move into the first block, all the residents from other buildings around started calling the Housing Bureau saying that they wanted to move to the Fai Chi Kei block because it was much better then theirs, and that it wasn't fair that they couldn't opt to move to the Fai Chi Kei.

CB For the past what three years, we have been working on another social housing block, where we perfected these concepts. In this new scheme, we have unevenly distributed sky patios scattered along the building's section.

RL In this new housing scheme, these sky patios create a kind of geography of common spaces in section, so that residents can discover through time this hidden order of places within the block, which have all different scales and sections. If they look at the building from the outside, they will keep on finding new spaces in this embedded geography of sky gardens. These patios are going to be amazing because they will have incredible views to the Pearl River in all directions.

CB And in this case, the hanging patios are 100 percent exterior spaces. The patios in the Fai Chi Kei project raised some issues because Macau is a typhoon-affected area, and when there are heavy rains and typhoons the fact that the patios are partly interior and partly exterior raised some problems when rain pours in. So these patios in the B10 project are totally exterior and they are landscaped. In the Fai Chi Kei project, we had assumed that people would find freedom to use these spaces, so we didn't consider the role of condominium management, and the management actually curbs the appropriation of the spaces. So the poor residents had a hard time to make use of these spaces.

RL In the Fai Chi Kei project, we didn't design any seating in the patios, thinking that something might happen organically with the users. When we went back, after the residents had moved in, we learned that they had to bring their chairs from home every time they used the patio, because the building management controlled them.

AVM So you are improving the typology. You are creating a new typology. I think that is really great because it's with small gestures like that you can change people's lives.

CB If you are sensible and observe what is going on, you will see what works and what doesn't. In this case, we also had a very good client who loved the first building and is 100 percent on our side on the innovations we proposed for the second project.

AVM Can you talk on how you are involved with the housing issue with public policies, and how you build up ideas that respond to the public realm on housing?

RL Access to housing became a real crisis with the process of mega-inflation which kicked-off in 2008. With the new gambling contract of 2002, Macau became an attractive destination for the Chinese population, which used Macau's real estate as a means to store their surplus liquidity, to keep their savings out of China's mainland banks that don't give them any interest. That grew to a scale at which local people couldn't move out of their family houses or get married, because they couldn't afford any apartment rents, which was a real drama. The government had up to then maintained a laisser-faire approach towards emerging social issues, always avoiding implementing preventive policies, and this was the issue that forced the government to grow into a more responsive policy-driver. From 1999 to 2010, there was zero public housing policy update.

The housing projects initiated in 2010 represent the first trial of implementing housing policy in the post-colonial context.

AVM I want to go over to the issue of the urban context, specifically on adapting the project to its context in face of the mechanical repetition of the typical plan, which in housing projects is an inevitable thing to address. I have two considerations which I would like you to address, for different reasons: firstly, on something which you have taught me, which is that Chinese people, they really appreciate new things, so they really appreciate new houses and not so fond of old buildings. Why it is so important in the Chinese culture? Secondly, how does this affect your work?

To work in a city that changes so quickly. This is culturally a very different context than what we are dealing with in Europe, where the retention of the built fabric is a common ground. How is it to think, as architects, that your built works maybe won't last in this constant process of urban renewal?

CB Going back to the beginning of our conversation, on the meaning of public space and the meaning of ownership, most buildings don't have a condominium, as a result, nobody takes care of the public areas of buildings and there is a rapid pace of degradation. That's simply the reason why people want new buildings, because old buildings are decrepit and they are not renewed continuously as is common practice in Europe. Then there is the question of the city being small and very dense. So there is a systemic need to demolish some blocks in order to make space for new, larger developments to increase the square meter ratio per person.

These are the reasons why things are demolished and substituted frequently.

Regarding the second part of your question, we have had some sad occasions, seeing part of our work being demolished, which is never nice to witness. For me, the saddest moment was to see the children's playground at Sai Van Park being demolished. The park was a very creative way to interpret a gated area for children and I felt that that it was unjustified to demolish it and do nothing else with it.

We have been talking about the Fai Chi Kei project, and that was another painful experience for us. Because in the place where our Fai Chi Kei block came up, there was another scheme, which was a very beautiful building which was pushed for demolition for these same reasons, of decay and the rise of density. The question is, what do we do?

We were part of the fight to try and keep the old Fai Chi Kei. The first instinct is stop the demolition. Try to make sense and balance the reasons to fight for what we think is meaningful. Not only our buildings, but for all important heritage and significant modern buildings.

AVM I'd like you to share with us your experience on infrastructure, on how to deal with designing for a place and designing a city that is always changing at high speed. That is difficult to understand for us Europeans. We are not used to the speed...

RL The problem with doing things at high speed, resides mainly in having policymakers, the people in the government, and the public throwing overboard the complexity of the issues which the project has to address, transforming the debate into a one-layered resolution: we needed housing, so we build these blocks and put the people in, forgetting that there were visual impacts on the surrounding neighborhood, that a thousand more people in an urban block have a measured impact on the infrastructure and the life of the neighborhood, meaning more pedestrians, more cars, and more consumers. You cannot just keep on adding up. This has been a hard learning process for Macau. The government departments have been learning that public satisfaction is equally important, especially when you are spending so much money.

It's not only about delivering a functional response. It's about the beauty, the comfort, and creating conditions to address the social layer.

CB The situation in Macau is always a bit inverted. There is a different approach to planning: we are always running after the changes. As Rui was hinting at, the urban analysis doesn't instruct the planning guidelines. It usually doesn't matter. You can add a thousand people to a scheme, on a site surrounded with narrow lanes. The project gets built and only in the aftermath will someone deal with the consequences of the excessive density.

AVM In Macau, you have been experimenting for several years with a very different modality of designing, where the planning doesn't precede the design of the buildings and the infrastructure, and where instead these two activities happen simultaneously as a continuous cause—effect dialectic. Do you think that the kind of opportunities that arise from this inversion, this way in which Macau has been operating, is something that places you as architects on a different trajectory?

I'm sure that if you were operating in another part of the world, you would be having different outcomes: the same people, with the same backgrounds, but playing a different role under different rules. To what extent has this context led you to prioritize differently? Can we assume this as a paradigm change in architecture?

CB I never thought about what you are saying: that this could be assumed as an alternate strategy rather than a sequence of hiccups. I always felt that we lacked the framework to do another type of work, more oriented to architectural detailing or about researching to discover new materials. I guess that the reason why we don't have those luxuries lies in the fact that we are constantly trying to sort out other types of things. Our energy is spent in organizing urban frameworks for our projects. It has to do with resilience of reasoning on the main issues, like people's well-being and public space, etc., in a process that takes us constantly from the concept phase to the working drawings during the whole design process.

RL Letting things happen, to then map and reframe is also interesting, because the city creates certain conditions of proximity and competition among people, making very special kinds of environments of concentration. There are some places in Macau that are really interesting because of the over-accumulation of things, not only in terms of image, but in terms of use, in terms of experience, and so on. That is very, very interesting. And it also creates situations that we become very fascinated with, and we want to reproduce them in the projects. Not visually, but in terms of putting as many layers into the project as possible.

AVM What I have always found very interesting in your work was exactly that, which I think really works well in your designs. It's that idea that we are always on an edge, while working in the edge: that we can at any given moment have the freedom to move towards one side or the other, because there isn't an order of a single path.

RL In that respect, I am very fascinated with the Indian ragas. This has a simultaneous fascination with the rhythm of order and disorder. It's a fascination of having order in the disorder and having disorder in the order.

I think that is what makes architecture in my vision; architecture becomes something that is alive, because it is dealing with the impossibility of fitting everything into order, and the improbability of recognizing disorder. It's a complexity that the projects can accumulate.

AVM Nowadays we are having all these huge debates about how Europeans shaped the world and how we can change that, giving voice to other cultures at a the global scale, and what we are describing is something that is really different from our way of understanding and doing things as Westerners, and can represent a different path for the discipline of architecture.

I find it very interesting.

So being in Macau has led you to explore things that don't relate to the Western vision of architecture. And your work doesn't need the same principles that you would need to promote it in a Western context, because you are living and working to transform a whole different set of challenges and also on a different chronology.

I find it quite impressive!

CB We are not doing colonial work here, for sure.

We are not bringing European models to China, and we should not be mistaken in thinking that we are doing what Chinese architects would be doing, because we are not!

When we talked about resilience regarding our work, I think that what we are really trying to say is dissenting, which is surely not the common practice in Macau: it's not something that a local architect will do. The local architect would not resist the system nor would they find ways to persevere around the system in order to change the briefs to redefine the plan. They work to fulfill theur client's dreams and will only divert with that in mind.

That's the reason why our experience is unique: because of this resistenace and restitution purpose, because we don't we feel that we have to exclusively serve our client. We feel that we are always providing a service to the city. There are many aspects of it which are quite unique in our practice.

AVM The notion that Macau is this place of overlap seems to be part of the equation and the unfolding of the work. For you, Macau should continue to be this kind of a mixed place, some place which is difficult to describe from just one perspective. A place where we could find a comprehensive way of understanding a little more the Chinese or a comprehensive way of understanding a little more of the European? As something in between?

CB Yes, that is true but it's not identitarian yet.

I think that Macau as a place doesn't yet operate as a defined identity. It's being reclaimed by China year after year. So even regarding masterplans, we are starting to see planning, but the planning comes from the mainland into Macau. It's not ours to do, to question, to enact.

I guess that our next challenge is going to be to try and undo the current planning of Macau, or try to question it through the architectural sphere. Looking to *dissent* on what is imposed upon us. That's what I think of the future.

AVM I think that makes sense.

Can you learn something with your neighbors, who are much stronger than Macau—from Hong Kong, for example?

RL Hong Kong is critical in a defiant manner. Being critical in a Chinese context requires that we define the exact tone of the dialectic position of the stakeholders. To dissent is to differ in sentiment and not necessarily to challenge the starting point per se.

CB It's a very different concept.

AVM I would say so; it changes all the discourse. In the case of the Hong Kong protests, they really defied the system.

RL It's just walking a very thin line, that there is space for another point of view and which is more able to address the nature of your concerns. We are trying to influence the other, but we are also open to the other and to redefine the narrative.

BACKGROUND

LBA, Arquitectura e Planeamento is a shared partnership between Carlotta Bruni, an expatriate Italian architect and Rui Leão, an architect with an upbringing in the Portuguese colonial territories. His family is originally from Goa (India) but he was born in São Tomé and Principe, a former Portuguese colony off the west coast of Africa. He lived in Lisbon and in the Azores islands for a brief period before finally settling in Macau with his family of origin in 1977. Rui commenced his studies at the University of Porto in 1987 and moved back to Macau in 1996. As a result of being of Indian origin and brought up in the Portuguese colonial system in Africa, Portugal and Asia, Rui is the paradigm of the cross-cultural Third Space.[1]

Carlotta lived and studied in Milan until 1992, when she moved first to Lisbon and later to Porto to complete her university studies through the Erasmus program.

Both moved to Macau in 1996 to practice.

Their joint practice is the result of several business arrangements that have changed over time. In 1998, Rui and Carlotta opened a small firm called LEAO, Atelier de Arquitectura. At the time, Carlotta was still collaborating at Manuel Vincente's office on masterplans and large social housing schemes. The first shared practice did small jobs on the side and tendered out for some public competitions, which came to be discontinued due to the impending change in administration. After the handover, Vicente's office had to close for lack of business. Later in 2001, Vicente was commissioned to design Nam Van Square, while LEAO, Atelier de Arquitectura was commissioned to renovate the Moorish Barracks. Working in partnership with Vicente and also having their own commissions, the partners suddenly had enough work to open their own office. Starting in that year, they launched a dual-mode practice, based physically in the same premises. On the one hand, they were collaborating as Vicente's partners in VLB (Vicente, Leão, Bruni) Arquitectura and Planeamento, and on the other, they were developing a parallel set of design works under their collaborative practice, LEAO Atelier. Concurrently with working and learning with their mentor, they had the time to develop their own set of design ideas bridging them back and forth between partnerships. In 2008, they dissolved the partnership with Vicente and consolidated their work under one company called LBA, Arquitectura e Planeamento Ltd. Their practice, therefore, includes some projects designed in co-authorship with Vicente and others that are solely the result of their own collaboration. While the two contemporaneous practices exhibited some fundamental differences in their formal results—and there were several "cross-overs"—above all, they influenced each other.

CARLOTTA BRUNI

Carlotta is an Italian expatriate who has been living and working in Macau, a Special Administrative Region of China, for over 20 years. Practicing in Macau has enabled her to keep her architectural identity as the result of two specific conditions: the fact that Macau is historically accustomed to cultural hybridizations and the fact that she has been trained to be very respectful of the context in which she operates.

Due to its marginal location both from Portugal and from China, and its new post-colonial status, Macau has always been and continues to be everybody's land, a condition that has enabled a fruitful cross-cultural dialogue.

Carlotta's architectural studies took place between the late 1980s and early 1990s at the Milan Polytechnic, an extremely context-oriented and context-dependent architectural school. Her design strategies stem from this intellectual approach and are very much focused on the interpretation of the site. She arrived in Macau in 1996, where, over the course of 20 years, she has developed architectural strategies directed to the reality of this fast-developing Chinese city—unpacking the disconnection, the gap, between her cultural background and that of Macau to understanding the implications of these circumstances. This career trajectory stimulated her desire to reflect upon the nature of the relationship between context and design: the connection between the physical site, usually inserted into a more complex urban environment, and the transformative action of the architect who operates on a given plot with his or her personal techniques.

Carlotta's academic trajectory took her from four years of study at the Milan Polytechnic to Portugal, where she undertook one year of study at Escola Superior de Belas Artes in Lisbon, a further year at architecture school in Porto, then finally on to an internship in Manuel Vicente's office in Macau, before she was ready to do her master's thesis.

In Milan, she was taught how to dissect the built environment, to understand its components and reassemble them in a creative way without losing the original spirit of the environment. This methodology felt logical and safe, a somehow straightforward deductive process where each step forward was taken with at least three fixed points, as if one were climbing a steep mountain with two feet and one hand anchored to the ground for stability.

In Lisbon and Porto, she was able to approach a design method that let loose some of the abstract deductive process and privileged observation of the existing built space as formal inspiration for shapes and textures, light and shadows. Arriving in Macau in 1996, she worked with Manuel Vicente, one of the founding fathers of Portuguese contemporary architecture and one of the first contemporary architects to open a practice in the city. Vicente taught her how to live and operate in a context that is foreign to one's identity, what and how to observe in this new environment, and the importance of practicing in the periphery: a tool for letting go of all mainstream theoretical approaches and rethinking our typologies creatively. All three experiences have given her tools for observation and for understanding the city, which she has been doing systematically. The result of her observations and the discovery of the mechanisms applied to Macau's urbanism and architecture does not translate in her acceptance of the current condition—she doesn't work within the logic of the place. Rather, she performs a critical review of the state of affairs and use the outcome as an instrument for transformation achieved through design.

She is applying a specific point of view to this context, bringing her personal architectural identity constituted from spaces that cannot be dissociated from memories and life experiences—a sort of spatial inheritance. These spaces were experienced during childhood; we learned how to inhabit them. They are typologies that we carry within us. They are part of our vocabulary. Since we understand their meaning and value deeply, it is natural that we would try to recreate similar conditions as architects.

The relationship between context and identity, as defined above, is a matter of point of view, perspective, or bias. Of all the different Macaus that could be perceived by any one of us, she elected her Macau, the city that she has observed from her point of view, as the physical context for her practice, with one of the intentions of her research being to examine how identity reads, and operates on context.

RUI LEÃO

Rui has experienced decolonization several times during his life. Firstly in 1972, on the occasion of his family's rushed exit of São Tomé e Principe, where he was born in 1969; then in 1974, in Lisbon, with the fall of the fascist regime; lastly, and for the first time as an adult, in 1999, when Macau was handed back over to China.

He had a colonial Portuguese upbringing due to his Goan ancestry. Historically, people of Goan origin and of Indo-Portuguese descent made up many of the cadres of the administration in the Portuguese colonies. For this reason, his family upbringing was focused on being Portuguese and avoiding the realisation of his Indian-ness.

He developed a hybrid identity in Macau a diverse community made up of Chinese, Portuguese, and Macanese (those of mixed Portuguese and Asian descent), where he arrived as a child in 1977. Here, he belongs to the local community, flowing easily between the Portuguese, Macanese, and Chinese communities. The Portuguese see him as Portuguese, while the Macanese and the Chinese may see him as a local Portuguese or as a Macanese.

His situation fits within the notion of third space as defined by Homi Bhabha in his book *The Location of Culture*: the condition of each person through the role of culture iin the mind—i.e., how the mind develops by incorporating the community's shared artifacts accumulated over generations, specifically in the case of hybrid post-colonial identities.[2]

He left Macau to study architecture in Porto. The culture of the city was, especially among architects, a strong part of their commitment both to the morphology of the city, and to the city as an object of observation, from which a direct process of learning through observation could be devised.

At the Porto school, he was offered the overlay of a new identity, identifying with a community of architects that fiercely offered a consistent front of intellectual resistance to the propaganda of the regime.

His apprenticeship at the Porto school brought him to focus on issues such as the reinterpretation of traditional typologies, the genius loci and the re-visitation of modernity. The school's down-to-earth methodology meant that buildings and spaces drawn up in the projects had to ideally communicate their formulation non-intellectually to the average citizen. The project was considered as a cultural manifesto, anchored on the cultural notion of place, of which the architect is merely a reader of the social formative context. He learned in Porto that when the architect prioritizes the context of the site in the project, it leads him to produce unrepeatable crafted spaces that celebrate the place and the territory through its dwelling.

The confrontation with these two conditions of architectural dialectics—the collective struggle of the class and critical regionalism—would later become an essential source from which to draw knowledge[3] to confront the reality of Macau and deal with its post-handover condition, where Rui set out to contest the status of the praxis when he moved back there to practice. This new identity and sense of emancipation is what allowed him to return to Macau with a new perspective and a mission.

Upon his return to Macau in 1996, just before its handover to mainland China, he discovered that architecture practice there had no system of communicating and reflecting upon the contributions it made to the city and its society: it was limited to a few practices that responded efficiently to both government and private investors but were silent about the merit of their performance. Almost everything was silent in Macau.

He started working with Manuel Vicente in 1996. The conceptual openness that he discovered in Vicente and his projects taught him that architecture can be infinitely inclusive, and that our affinities are not necessarily confined to our strict cultural framework.

Rui learned with Vicente that there was an enormous freedom to what we could bring to the project, provided that we were critical, generous, poetic, transformational, prosaic, and celebratory of how we brought it into the narrative of a new architecture. He took his militancy to dialogue with the city upon himself, both on the projects and on the public sphere, and the constant exercise of being critical of the context, the pre-conditions, the rules, others, and us.

Rui worked for Manuel Vicente in Macau, from 1996 until 1999, when he and Carlotta opened their first shared practice.

THE PRACTICE

Through the continuous dialogue that Carlotta and Rui enjoy during the design process, they create the conditions for a progressive readjustment to each other's design strategies and, as a consequence, a layering of the design with different assumptions: Carlotta's neo-rationalist organization of the layouts and Rui's Portuguese phenomenological spatial design. In the end, their projects are the formalization of both their agendas and are actually sometimes left open-ended to allow for other's agendas to overlap their own.

Every practice in Macau has to deal with the city's three main physical constraints: its extreme density, the profit-driven urbanism (which exists in place of a masterplan) that drives development, and land expansion through reclamation. The main logistical constraints faced in Macau are the lack of critical mass, an outdated construction industry, and the inevitable time constraints involved in every project.

Amidst all this lies a hidden cultural issue that arise from the need to give face to the hybrid identity of the local community—a mix of permanent local residents, new immigrants from mainland China, Portuguese, and other foreign nationals—all of whom are stranded in limbo for 50 years during the transitional period that started with the handover in 1999 and will end when the proper post-colonial phase under Chinese rule commences in 2049.

LBA has been dealing with and adapting to these characteristics of their working environment for the past 18 years. While it has consistently been commissioned for public jobs from the Macau Government, this has less to do with its capability than with the character of such jobs. These jobs entail greater amounts of work, since they are not serialized or repetitive. Thus, LBA's local colleagues—who have more connections to the private sector—are not interested in bidding for such jobs.

As a consequence, LBA has come to specialize in public spaces and infrastructure, in designs that are non-specific and atypical, and that have a high level of public use. These programs usually raise urgent issues of social identity related to place, to institutional role, to heritage, or to narrative.

In their practice, Rui and Carlotta believe that a project has an influence that extends far beyond the borders of its physical plot. Thus, in the design phase, they make sure to assess the urban implications of the design, and they use the project as an opportunity to create a positive transformation on the surroundings. As such jobs are managed on limited budgets and time-frames; their architectural investigation has focused on the urban transformation subsequent to the insertion of the project into the city continuum, creating urban situations that can interpret and organize the surrounding city structure—namely through public space.

Rui Leão
F. Carlotta Bruni

1 The Third Space Theory explains the uniqueness of each person, actor or context as a "hybrid". It is attributed to Homi K. Bhabha and Edward W. Soja
2 Homi Bhabha, *The Location of Culture* (London: Routledge, 1994).
3 Sérgio Fernandez, *Percurso: Arquitectura Portuguesa 1930/1974* (Porto: Edições da FAUP, 1988).

	NAME OF THE PROJECT	TYPE	ADDRESS	DESIGN DATE
BUILT PROJECTS	**NAM VAN SQUARE (SAI VAN LAKE)**	PUBLIC SPACE - SQUARE	MACAU, PRAÇA DO LAGO SAI VAN	2001
	SAI VAN LAKE PARK	PUBLIC SPACE - PARK	MACAU, AV. PANORAMICA DO LAGO SAI VAN	2004
	FAI CHI KEI SOCIAL HOUSING	SOCIAL HOUSING	MACAU, RUA DO CMTE. JOAO BELO / RUA DO GEN. IVENS FERRAZ	2010
	BARRA PUBLIC TRANSPORT INTERCHANGE	PUBLIC TRANSPORT INFRASTRUCTURE	MACAU, AV. PANORAMICA DO LAGO SAI VAN / RUA DE S.TIAGO DA BARRA	2013
	MACAU LRT TRAIN DEPOT	INFRASTRUCTURE	TAIPA, AV. DO AEROPORTO	2016
	M30 POWER SUPPLY INTEGRATED INFRASTRUCTURE	INFRASTRUCTURE	BECO DOS FATIÕES	2016
	LRT BARRA STATION 12	PUBLIC TRANSPORT INFRASTRUCTURE	MACAU, AV. PANORAMICA DO LAGO SAI VAN	2017
PROJECTS COMPLETED/ UNDER CONSTRUCTION	**DRAGON BOAT STALLS (SAI VAN LAKE)**	PUBLIC SPACE - INFRASTRUCTURE	MACAU, AV. DR. STANLEY HO	2004
	BARRA WATERFRONT PARK	PUBLIC SPACE - PARK	MACAU, AV. PANORAMICA DO LAGO SAI VAN	2015
	ZONE A B10 PLOT SOCIAL HOUSING	SOCIAL HOUSING	MACAU, NOVOS ATERROS DA ZONA A	2020
COMPETITIONS	**CEM DISPATCH CENTER**	INFRASTRUCTURE	COLOANE, ESTR. DA BARRAGEM DE KA HO	2016
	IPM LIBRARY (POLYTECHNIC UNIVERSITY OF MACAU)	LIBRARY	MACAU, RUA DE LUIS GONZAGA GOMES	2016
	COOPERATION BUILDING	CONGRESS CENTER	MACAU, AV. DR. SUN YAT-SEN	2017
	TAP SEAC YOUTH CENTER	MULTIFUNCTION BUILDING	MACAU, AV. SIDONIO PAIS	2018
	MACAU CENTRAL LIBRARY	LIBRARY	MACAU, AV. DA PRAIA GRANDE	2018

CONSTRUCTION COMPLETION DATE	DESIGN TEAM
2003	MANUEL VICENTE, RUI LEÃO, CARLOTTA BRUNI, DIOGO ZUQUETE
2005	RUI LEÃO, CARLOTTA BRUNI, HELENA ALCOFORADO, JOSE CLAUDIO SILVA, FOK CHENG IO
2013	RUI LEÃO, CARLOTTA BRUNI, NUNO ASSIS, ROGERIO OLIVEIRA, JEANIE CHU, SUSANA LEI, HUGO COELHO, CATARINA LAMY, BENNY CHU, ARKA BISWAS
2019	RUI LEÃO, CARLOTTA BRUNI, HUGO COELHO, ARKA BISWAS, RICHARD TAM, TODD LAM, DENNIS CHUNG
2018	RUI LEÃO, CARLOTTA BRUNI, CATARINA LAMY, HUGO COELHO, RITA CERQUEIRA, AFONSO ONOFRE, ARKA BISWAS, HOUMOUS LEONG
2022	RUI LEÃO, CARLOTTA BRUNI, NELSON SILVA, BEATRIZ VELOSA, RITA CERQUEIRA
2023	RUI LEÃO, CARLOTTA BRUNI, NUNO ASSIS, TATIANA CHONG, RITA CERQUEIRA, DUARTE SANTANA, KEONG CHAN, LEONARDO LAO, ARKA BISWAS,ANA BEATRIZ VELOSA, YOLANDA AO CHAN
DETAIL DESIGN STAGE DISCONTINUED	MANUEL VICENTE, RUI LEÃO, CARLOTTA BRUNI, FERNANDO MARTINS, LEI WAI FAN
DETAIL DESIGN STAGE	RUI LEÃO, CARLOTTA BRUNI, RITA CERQUEIRA, TATIANA CHONG, JOAO SEQUEIRA, ARKA BISWAS
UNDER CONSTRUCTION	RUI LEÃO, CARLOTTA BRUNI, NELSON SILVA, MAFALDA REBELO, ANDRÉ VIANA, ANA BEATRIZ VELOSA, YOLANDA AO CHAN, LEONARDO LAO
COMPETITION STAGE	RUI LEÃO, CARLOTTA BRUNI, RITA CERQUEIRA, ARKA BISWAS, SUSANA LEI
COMPETITION STAGE	RUI LEÃO, CARLOTTA BRUNI, SERGIO SPENCER, TATIANA CHONG, ARKA BISWAS, HOUMOUS LEONG, AFONSO ONOFRE
COMPETITION STAGE	RUI LEÃO, CARLOTTA BRUNI, TATIANA CHONG, ARKA BISWAS, DUARTE SANTANA
COMPETITION STAGE	RUI LEÃO, CARLOTTA BRUNI, RITA CERQUEIRA, ANA BEATRIZ VELOSA, YOLANDA AO CHAN, ARKA BISWAS, JOANA SILVA
COMPETITION STAGE	RUI LEÃO, CARLOTTA BRUNI, RITA CERQUEIRA, ANA BEATRIZ VELOSA, ARKA BISWAS, JOANA SILVA

	NAME OF THE PROJECT	PARTNERS/CONSULTANTS	GROSS FLOOR AREA M^2
BUILT PROJECTS	**NAM VAN SQUARE (SAI VAN LAKE)**	PAL ASIACONSULT, C.K.WONG	30,600.00 m^2
	SAI VAN LAKE PARK	PAL ASIACONSULT, TECPROENG MACAU, C.K.WONG	42,450.00 m^2
	FAI CHI KEI SOCIAL HOUSING	CIVIL, TECPROENG MACAU, C.K.WONG	69,995.98 m^2
	BARRA PUBLIC TRANSPORT INTERCHANGE	PARSONS AND BINKERHOFF, C.K.WONG	38,225.10 m^2
	MACAU LRT TRAIN DEPOT	CONSULASIA MACAU, C.K.WONG	144,567.00 m^2
	M30 POWER SUPPLY INTEGRATED INFRASTRUCTURE	SIPCA, TECPROENG	42.45m^2
	LRT BARRA STATION 12	PAL ASIACONSULT, C.K.WONG	14,430.90 m^2
PROJECTS COMPLETED/ UNDER CONSTRUCTION	**DRAGON BOAT STALLS (SAI VAN LAKE)**	PAL ASIACONSULT	19932.75 m^2
	BARRA WATERFRONT PARK	URS, C.K.WONG	14,935.00 m^2
	ZONE A B10 PLOT SOCIAL HOUSING	PAL ASIACONSULT, INCHSCAPE	90,872.29 m^2
COMPETITIONS	**CEM DISPATCH CENTER**	TECPROENG MACAU, PENGEST	5.049m^2
	IPM LIBRARY (POLYTECHNIC UNIVERSITY OF MACAU)	TECPROENG MACAU, SIPCA	47,979.00 m^2
	CHINA-LUSOPHONE COOPERATION BUILDING	PAL ASIACONSULT	58,970.27 m^2
	TAP SEAC YOUTH CENTER	PAL ASIACONSULT	59,487.00 m^2
	MACAU CENTRAL LIBRARY	PAL ASIACONSULT, GONÇALO ALVIM, MANUEL CORREIA DA SILVA	18,264.79 m^2

CLIENT	CONSTRUCTION COST	AWARDS
G.D.I., GABINETE PARA O DESENVOLVIMENTO DE INFRAESTRUTURAS	MOP$ 34.868.388,00	ARCASIA GOLD MEDAL 2005—2006
G.D.I., GABINETE PARA O DESENVOLVIMENTO DE INFRAESTRUTURAS	MOP$ 45,000,000.00	ARCASIA HONOURABLE MENTION 2007-2008
G.D.I., GABINETE PARA O DESENVOLVIMENTO DE INFRAESTRUTURAS	MOP$ 495,187,905,63	100 ARCHITECTS OF THE YEAR 2017; 3RD AWARD RETHINKING THE FUTURE RTF/ACDA 2020; ARCHITECTURE & DESIGN COLLECTION AWARDS 2022; GOLD WINNER MERIT AWARD CROSS-STRAITS ARCHITECTURAL AWARDS 2024; 2018 AAM ARCHITECTURAL AWARDS GOLD MEDAL
G.I.T. GABINETE DE INFRAESTRUTURAS DE TRANSPORTES	MOP$ 1,360,364,911.00	100 ARCHITECTS OF THE YEAR 2020; 2ND AWARD RETHINKING THE FUTURE RTF/ACDA 2020 ARCHITECTURE & DESIGN COLLECTION AWARDS 2022 GOLD WINNER
G.I.T. GABINETE DE INFRAESTRUTURAS DE TRANSPORTES	MOP$ 1,106,163,000.00	UIA/KIA 100 ARCHITECTS OF THE YEAR 2019
CEM, COMPANHIA DE ELECTRICIDADE DE MACAU	MOP$ 2,960,000	ARCHITECTURE & DESIGN COLLECTION AWARDS 2022 SILVER WINNER; GOLD MEDAL MACAU ARCHITECTURE AWARDS 2024; UNESCO ASIA-PACIFIC AWARDS FOR CULTURAL HERITAGE CONSERVATION AWARD FOR NEW DESIGN IN HERITAGE CONTEXTS
G.I.T. GABINETE DE INFRAESTRUTURAS DE TRANSPORTES	MOP$ 1,178,200,000.00	HKIA CROSS-STRAIT ARCHITECTURAL DESIGN AWARDS 2024 NOMINATED AWARD TRANSPORT AND INFRASTRUCTURE FACILITIES
G.D.I., GABINETE PARA O DESENVOLVIMENTO DE INFRAESTRUTURAS	NOT AWARDED TO BE BUILT	
D.S.S.O.P.T. DIRECÇÃO DOS SERVIÇOS DE SOLOS OBRAS PUBLICAS E TRANSPORTES	MOP$ 78,043,323.20	
G.D.I., GABINETE PARA O DESENVOLVIMENTO DE INFRAESTRUTURAS	MOP$ 784,049,764.00	
C.E.M. COMPANHIA DE ELECTRICIDADE DE MACAU		
I.P.M. INSTITUTO POLITECNICO DE MACAU		
D.S.S.O.P.T. DIRECÇÃO DOS SERVIÇOS DE SOLOS OBRAS PUBLICAS E TRANSPORTES		
D.S.E.J. DIREÇÀO DOS SERVIÇOS DE EDUCAÇÃO E JOVENTUDE		
I.C. INSTITUTO CULTURAL		

8
23
11
18
14
25
12
22
7
16
21
19
3
2
24
5
6
9
1
17
4
13
15
20
10

MAP OF MACAU
WITH PROJECT LOCATIONS

Projects mentioned in the book

PHOTO CREDITS

PROJECT	PHOTOGRAPHER	PAGE
NAM VAN SQUARE (SAI VAN LAKE)	YAN FEI	42—48
	CARLOTTA BRUNI	48 (right bottom)
	LUIS ALMOSTER	49
SAI VAN LAKE PARK	YAN FEI	52, 54 (top two), 55
	LUIS ALMOSTER	53
	CARLOTTA BRUNI	54 (bottom two), 56—57
BARRA PUBLIC TRANSPORT INTERCHANGE	ARKA BISWAS	65 (middle), 66 (bottom two), 67 (bottom)
	YAN FEI	64, 65 (top and bottom), 66 (upper), 67 (upper)
	ANTONIO SANMARFUL	68—71
LRT BARRA STATION 12	YAN FEI	80—83
	ANTONIO SANMARFUL	84—87
MACAU LRT TRAIN DEPOT	PEDRO SANTOS	109, 114—115
	YAN FEI	106—107, 108, 109 (top right), 110—111, 112, 113
	CARLOTTA BRUNI	109 (bottom right), 114 (upper left)
FAI CHI KEI SOCIAL HOUSING	MIL HOMENS	130—131, 132—133
	YAN FEI	126—127, 128, 129, 132 (upper right), 133 (bottom), 135
ZONE A B10 PLOT SOCIAL HOUSING	NELSON M. S. SILVA	138—145
	ANTONIO SANMARFUL	139 (bottom left)
M30 POWER SUPPLY INTEGRATED INFRASTRUCTURE	NELSON M. S. SILVA	170—177